MCTS: WINDOWS® SERVER 2008 70-640 Q&A

Pierre Askmo, dti Publishing

Course Technology PTR
A part of Cengage Learning

COURSE TECHNOLOGY
CENGAGE Learning™

Australia, Brazil, Japan, Korea, Mexico, Singapore, Spain, United Kingdom, United States

MCTS: Windows® Server 2008 70-640 Q&A
Pierre Askmo, dti Publishing

Publisher and General Manager, Course Technology PTR:
Stacy L. Hiquet

Associate Director of Marketing:
Sarah Panella

Manager of Editorial Services:
Heather Talbot

Marketing Manager:
Mark Hughes

Acquisitions Editor:
Megan Belanger

Project/Copy Editor:
Kezia Endsley

PTR Editorial Services Coordinator:
Jen Blaney

Interior Layout Tech:
Bill Hartman

CD-ROM Producer:
Brandon Penticuff

Cover Designer:
Mike Tanamachi

Proofreader:
Sandy Doell

Library of Congress Control Number: 2009924526

ISBN-13: 978-1-59863-892-9

ISBN-10: 1-59863-892-0

Course Technology, a part of Cengage Learning
20 Channel Center Street
Boston, MA 02210
USA

Cengage Learning is a leading provider of customized learning solutions with office locations around the globe, including Singapore, the United Kingdom, Australia, Mexico, Brazil, and Japan. Locate your local office at: **international.cengage.com/region**.

Cengage Learning products are represented in Canada by Nelson Education, Ltd.

For your lifelong learning solutions, visit **courseptr.com**.

Visit our corporate Web site at **cengage.com**.

Printed in the United States of America
1 2 3 4 5 6 7 12 11 10 09

ACKNOWLEDGMENTS

I want to thank and recognize the dti Publishing team that made this book possible—Joe Celona and Joey Celona Jr. for their irreplaceable contributions to the formulation of the questions. Robert Miller should be recognized for his patient and hard work on the entirety of the texts and thanks to John Macomber and Anne-Marie Suckley for their very dedicated efforts in building and compiling the companion CertBlaster software on the CD.

ABOUT THE AUTHOR

President and founder of dti Publishing Corp., **Pierre Askmo** has extensive experience in the IT certification field. He is the designer of the dtiMetrics™ assessment system. Mr. Askmo's deep involvement in the IT industry is testified to by his early days' involvement as a Cornerstone Founding Partner of the A+ Certification program at the Computing Technology Industry Association (CompTIA). Mr. Askmo went on to sit on the A+ Executive committee that designed the A+ certification program and to participate in the Network+ and Server+ Advisory panels.

As a former member of the IT Skills Curriculum Group of the U.S. Department of Labor, Mr. Askmo contributed to define the mix of skills deemed necessary to succeed in the IT professions.

Mr. Askmo has co-authored the Thomson Course Technology book *A+ Q & A,* and in 2004 was a co-author with Robert Miller of the book *Network+ Certification* (Prentice Hall).

Mr. Askmo is also an item writer for IT certifications and has worked on CertBlaster test preparation titles for MCSE, MCSA, and now MCTS and MCITP. Mr. Askmo is also the designer of the new powerful and user-friendly dtiMetrics™ assessment system solution that helps students master essential computer concepts and prepare for IT certification.

CONTENTS

PART I: PREPARING FOR THE TEST

PART II: PRACTICE TESTS

PART III: ANSWERS TO PRACTICE TESTS

PART IV: SUPPLEMENTARY INFORMATION

INTRODUCTION

Welcome to *MCTS: Windows Server 2008 70-640 Q&A*. It is the exam preparation guide to help you pass Microsoft's exam 70-640, which is one of three core exams in the Windows Server 2008 certification program. This book is aimed strictly at test preparation and review and includes review questions covering all exam 70-640 objectives, including:

- Configuring Domain Name System (DNS) for Active Directory
- Configuring the Active Directory infrastructure
- Configuring additional Active Directory server roles
- Creating and maintaining Active Directory objects
- Maintaining the Active Directory environment
- Configuring Active Directory Certificate Services

This book also incorporates four full practice exams on the powerful CertBlaster test prep and exam simulation software on the CD (for installation instructions, see Appendix C). Before you study this text, you should start by using the CertBlaster test prep software for one exam in Assessment mode. This will yield, after the test, a "Personal Study Plan" (PSP) that will tell you which exam objectives you need to focus on. If the PSP tells you that you need to study it all, so be it; it is still not a waste of time (more on CertBlaster in Chapter 2).

Note that the chapters in this book are organized per main exam objective. Chapters 3 through 8 cover successively the main objectives seen in the previous list. Therefore, if the PSP directs you to just focus on a few objectives, you can easily zoom in on them in this book because of the way it is structured.

If this book and the CertBlaster software are your only tools for preparing for this exam, you better be quite experienced or be in a class that covers the actual foundational knowledge required for the 70-640 exam. This book will help prepare the knowledgeable. It doesn't teach the relevant content; it helps you prepare and take the exam. If you are on your own preparing for this exam and need additional material, check out *Configuring Windows Server 2008 Active Directory*, by Tony Northrup and Dan Holme (published by MS Press).

Good luck!

Part I

PREPARING FOR THE TEST

CHAPTER

1

UNDERSTANDING EXAM 70-640: THE MICROSOFT CERTIFIED PROFESSIONAL (MCP) PROGRAM

The MCP program has, over the years, seen many evolutions and today has grown into a complete, complex, and mature program. Currently the MCP includes a multitude of distinct tracks, although this book does not cover them all. Instead, it covers the certifications related to exam 70-640. Here are the MCTS and MCITP tracks:

- MCITP stands for Microsoft Certified Information Technology Professional
- MCTS stands for Microsoft Certified Technology Specialist

"Professional" ranks higher in the Microsoft certification hierarchy than "Specialist." All the newer exams are prefaced by the "TS" for Technology Specialist or "PRO," obviously for Professional, as in Information Technology Professional.

The Microsoft Certified Technology Specialist (MCTS) is someone who has completed at least one MCTS exam. The MCTS denotes an individual who has demonstrated skills and knowledge of one product and is thus product specific. The Microsoft Certified Information Technology Professional (MCITP), on the other hand, is someone who has completed a suite of MCTS exams, determined by Microsoft. The MCITP denotes an individual who has demonstrated skills and knowledge over a group of Microsoft products. These product groupings are organized by Microsoft to reflect a well-defined IT job. The MCTS has knowledge about a specific product, whereas the wider-reaching MCITP has competence in a professional area (see Figure 1.1).

You are studying this book to prepare for one or more of the following Microsoft certifications:

- MCTS: Windows Server 2008 Active Directory, Configuring
- MCITP: Server Administrator
- MCITP: Enterprise Administrator

To be an MCTS for Windows Server 2008 Active Directory, Configuring, you need to successfully sit for exam 70-640.

Using exam 70-640 to become an MCITP opens up two possibilities. You can become an MCITP: Server Administrator or an MCITP: Enterprise Administrator.

The MCITP: Server Administrator requires that you pass three exams. You will need to pass two Microsoft Certified Technology Specialist (MCTS) exams, what Microsoft refers to as *prerequisite exams,* and you will also need one Professional Series exam.

Figure 1.1
The MCITP versus
the MCTS.

The three exams are:

- Exam 70-640, which earns you MCTS: Windows Server 2008 Active Directory, Configuration
- Exam 70-642, which earns you MCTS: Windows Server 2008 Network Infrastructure, Configuration
- Exam 70-646, which earns you PRO: Windows Server 2008, Server Administrator

The MCITP: Enterprise Administrator requires that you pass five exams (the three required for the MCITP: Server Administrator, plus two others):

- MCTS Exam 70-640, which earns you Windows Server 2008 Active Directory, Configuration
- MCTS Exam 70-642, which earns you Windows Server 2008 Network Infrastructure, Configuration
- MCTS Exam 70-643, which earns you Windows Server 2008 Applications Infrastructure, Configuring
- Either Exam 70-620, MCTS: Windows Vista, Configuring or Exam 70-624, MCTS: Deploying and Maintaining Windows Vista Client and 2007 Microsoft Office System Desktops
- PRO Exam 70-647, Windows Server 2008, Enterprise Administrator

WHO IS THE 70-640 EXAM INTENDED FOR?

According to Microsoft, the MCTS for Windows Server 2008 Active Directory, Configuring exam is a credential aimed at IT professionals working in a computing environment of medium- to large-size companies. The MCTS candidate is expected to have a minimum of one year of experience implementing and managing a network operating system in an organization with the following characteristics:

- Approximately 250 to 5,000 users
- A minimum of three physical locations
- A minimum of three domain controllers

- The typical services found on this type of network, such as messaging, a database, file and print, a proxy server, a firewall, the Internet, an intranet, remote access, and client computer management
- The typical connectivity requirements found on this type of network, such as connecting branch offices and individual users in remote locations to the corporate network and corporate networks connected to the Internet

As you can see, Microsoft expects you to have experience with a fairly complex computing environment. Having experience using these technologies is a necessary but probably not sufficient requirement. In fact, in a small way, your experience can at times get in the way of exam success. This is because some of the solutions implemented in the field, even though they work well or are fast and efficient, are not always the "correct answer" on the test. Having said that, experience will be useful more often on the exam than it will be a hindrance. If you are short on experience, you will have to make it up with training, alone or in a classroom.

> **NOTE**
>
> If you are on your own preparing for this exam and need additional material, check out the book, *Configuring Windows Server 2008 Network Infrastructure* by Tony Northrup and J.C. Mackin (published by MS Press). This book covers all the exam objectives effectively and, to deepen your understanding of the subject, includes case scenarios, exercises, and best practices. For more training resources, check out Microsoft's website at http://www.microsoft.com/learning/en/us/exams/70-640.mspx.
>
> If by the time you enter this link, it has been moved or does not work anymore, just go to www.microsoft.com and type **70-640** in the Search field.

THE EXAM OBJECTIVES

Exam 70-640 is made up of the six following main objectives:

- Configuring a Domain Name System (DNS) for Active Directory
- Configuring the Active Directory infrastructure
- Configuring additional Active Directory server roles
- Creating and maintaining Active Directory objects
- Maintaining the Active Directory environment
- Configuring Active Directory Certificate Services

Each of these has between three and eight sub-objectives. Making sure you familiarize yourself with these objectives will help you in laying out your exam preparation strategy (see Chapter 2). The main point in understanding these objectives is that doing so will enable you to make your own decisions as to what is central and what is peripheral to your preparation for exam 70-640.

Main Objective 1: Configuring a Domain Name System (DNS) for Active Directory

This first main objective has been given a relative weight of 16% (out of the six main objectives) by Microsoft. The relative weight is a numerical way to represent the relative importance of the objective, which typically translates in approximate number of questions on the exam. Assuming your exam consists of a total of 55 questions, it is reasonable to expect that this objective would be reflected in about nine of those questions (.16 × 55). For a detailed description of the issues covered in this objective, see Appendix B.

Main Objective 2: Configuring the Active Directory Infrastructure

This second main objective has been given a relative weight of 25%, so if your exam consists of 55 questions, it's reasonable to expect that this objective will be represented in about 14 of those questions (.25 × 55). For a detailed description of the issues covered in this objective, see Appendix B.

Main Objective 3: Configuring Additional Active Directory Server Roles

This third main objective has been given a relative weight of 9%. If you assume your exam consists of a total of 55 questions, this objective would be represented in about five of those questions. For a detailed description of the issues covered in this objective, see Appendix B.

Main Objective 4: Creating and Maintaining Active Directory Objects

This objective has a relative weight of 24%, which means it would be represented in about 13 of 55 total questions. For a detailed description of the issues covered in this objective, see Appendix B.

Main Objective 5: Maintaining the Active Directory Environment

This fifth main objective has a relative weight of 13%. Expect it therefore to consist of about seven questions. For a detailed description of the issues covered in this objective, see Appendix B.

Main Objective 6: Configuring Active Directory Certificate Services

This main objective has a relative weight of 13%. Expect it therefore to consist of about seven questions. For a detailed description of the issues covered in this objective, see Appendix B.

SUMMARY

As you have seen here, Microsoft expects you to have experience from a fairly complex computing environment. In addition to coming to the exam with this experience, make sure to study the exam objectives until you really understand their context and you understand not only why they are selected but also how one objective relates to another. Understanding the spirit in which the exam is constructed will help you focus your studies for maximum efficiency. If you are planning to prepare on your own for this exam and need additional material, I recommend *Configuring Windows Server 2008 Network Infrastructure* by Tony Northrup and J.C. Mackin (published by MS Press). This book covers all the exam objectives effectively and, to help you deepen your understanding of the subject, it includes case scenarios, exercises, and best practices.

2

EXAM STRATEGIES AND TACTICS

Taking an exam is always a stressful experience so I have put together this chapter to help you minimize your stress and maximize your meaningful preparations. The first and best way to minimize the impact of stress is through knowledge—knowledge of the exam topic, knowledge of the exam format and finally, knowledge of the question types. The second best way to alleviate stress is through preparation. Preparation happens through careful planning and practice, practice, and then some more practice! So this chapter contains a few tidbits and some guidance on how to prepare.

SIGNING UP FOR THE TEST

To take the test, you need to buy a voucher (the cost is $125.00 at the time of this printing) and schedule your date. To do that, go to www.prometric.com and click on For Test Takers, as you can see in Figure 2.1. By the time you get there these pages may have changed but the idea should be more or less the same.

Figure 2.1
Click on For Test Takers to sign up for the test.

This takes you to the next screen, where you use the drop-down menus to select Information Technology (IT) Certification and Microsoft, as shown in Figure 2.2. Once your selection is done, click GO.

From the next screen, choose Schedule, Reschedule, Cancel, or Confirm an Exam. Next you can either Locate a Test Site or Schedule an Appointment; either one eventually gets you to the same steps of registering for the exam, selecting a time and date, and making payment (or if you have a paid voucher you will find a place to enter the voucher code). You will need a credit card to do the entire transaction online. If you do not have a credit card, you can mail in your payment but you will then have to wait for it to clear before booking your exam date.

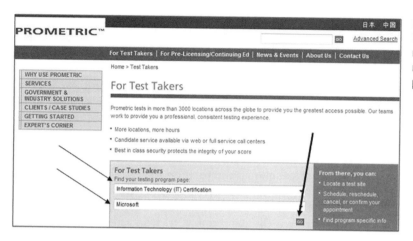

Figure 2.2
Use the drop-down menus to find the right testing program.

AT THE TESTING CENTER

When you signed up, the program suggested a testing location (or several) to you. Make sure to leave yourself more time than you think it may take you to get there. Factors such as traffic or your unfamiliarity with the testing center area can add quite some time to your trip, and the last thing you need on exam day is a bunch of extra stress!

When you arrive at your destination, you will need to sign in with the exam coordinator. He or she will ask you to show *two* forms of ID, with at least one of them being a government-issued photo ID. If you are really early and have some time to kill before your scheduled time, you can use your laptop to take the CertBlaster exams in Flash mode. This mode simulates flash cards where you press the spacebar to see the question, press it again to see the answer, and so on. Once you are signed in and your scheduled time is upon you, you will be asked to leave behind any and all books, bags, and anything else you brought (this is because all Microsoft Certification exams are completely closed book). After that you will be led into a closed examination room.

> **NOTE**
> Although rare, every so often the exam software or the machine will crash. If that happens, remain calm; you will not be penalized. Call the exam coordinator and he or she will reboot the machine and relaunch the exam software. The program will "remember" your score, where you were, and how much time you have left. Resume calmly as if nothing happened.

All Prometric exams in general and all Microsoft exams in particular are computer based. You are not allowed to bring anything of your own into the testing room, but the exam coordinator will provide you with a sheet of paper and a pen. You will be given an opportunity to take a sample exam before the actual exam. You should take it to make sure you are comfortable with all the navigation features of the exam software (your CertBlaster is pretty close to it but not identical in all respects). You can take it more than once, but it's questionable whether that would be an efficient use of your time. Once you are ready, tell the exam coordinator and you can now start your exam. It's the moment of truth!

THE EXAM

Always assume that the test will be harder and more stressful than you expect it to be; typically this is what most candidates feel once they sat for this test. This means prepare a lot, test yourself, and then prepare a lot more.

In order to pass the test and thus get certified, you need to score 700 out of 1,000. The number of questions will vary, but for this one assume you'll be given about 50–55 questions; it can be a bit less or a bit more. Say you have 50 questions on the exam, with a required score of 700 out of 1,000; you would figure that 35 correct (70% of 50) will guarantee a win. *Wrong*. Each question is individually weighted. So, one person might miss 16 questions and pass while another could arguably miss only 13 and fail. Some questions are multi-part and assigned partial credit. What this means is—never relax during the exam by assuming you got 35 correct and are home free. Since you don't have the key to the weight given to each question, you don't know what the exact cut-off is on your exam until you get the results.

For this exam you will likely be facing a "fixed length" exam although you could also see a "short-form test." At the time of printing of the book, Microsoft did not offer the adaptive testing for this exam so we are not going to elaborate on that format here.

- In the fixed-length test you will be facing 50 to 70 questions, typically 50–55. All questions in this format (as well as in the short form test) enable you to mark the questions for review (from the check box in the top-left corner of the exam software). This allows you to return to a question as many times as you need (restricted by the time left on your exam, of course). I'll discuss how to best use this feature later in this chapter.

- The short-form test has 25 to 30 questions with navigation features identical to the ones for the fixed-length format.

TEST TAKING STRATEGIES

There is no silver bullet when it comes to test taking. There are probably as many test taking strategies as there are test takers out there. In the following sections, I list a couple of strategies that have served a lot of candidates well, including this author.

Circle In

This strategy involves four major steps:

1. Go through the entire test quickly and answer all the "easy" ones.
2. Answer all the ones where you think you know the answer within a few seconds. If you are not sure, mark these for review.
3. For any questions where you draw a blank, mark these for review and do not answer them.
4. Circle back to all the questions marked for review.

Your goal here is to identify the questions you need more time with and review those over and over again until you are done. You should skip any question when you do not immediately know the answer. When you do this (that is skip in the first run through), don't mark any of the answers so as to not lead yourself down the potentially wrong path when you revisit them. Now, of course you do click answers for any and all questions you are confident about.

Next if you are not sure about the answer, mark it for review (check the box on the top-left corner of the exam software). Afterwards, go back and re-read these questions to make sure you answered them correctly. By the end of the test, you might very well have circled back to some of the questions three to four times before you answer them.

This will allow you to answer more questions with a high degree of confidence. An additional benefit of this method is that your brain doesn't stop working on a question just because you are skipping to the next. Sometimes what seems insolvable on the first look becomes easy several minutes later on a second look. Finally, on occasion you will discover that a related or unrelated question that you read later may jog your memory and make it easier to answer a question you initially had a hard time with.

The Rake

Some candidates prefer to answer every question the first time around and just mark for review (check the box in the top-left corner of the exam software) the ones they feel uncertain about. The idea is that this way you will be sure to have an answer for every question even if you run out of time. The risk with this strategy is of course that you let yourself get stuck on a couple of hard ones and still run out of time.

> **NOTE**
> In the last minutes of the test, answer all; answer anything!

Whatever you do, when the end nears, make sure to check an answer, any answer at all. The reason for this is twofold—there are no minus points for incorrect answers and most questions are multiple choice. If you have a question with one correct answer out of four alternatives, you have a 25% chance to get it right even if you have absolutely no idea what the question is about. Now, assume you have four of those questions left and some 30 seconds to go. You now have a statistical probability that you will get one extra correct answer out of answering all of those A or B, or whatever. If you are unlucky, it could still be zero; if you are lucky it could even give you two correct, which could be the difference between failure and success on exam day. What is guaranteed, however, is that if you don't answer these at all, you will get zero points on those questions.

COMMON QUESTION TYPES

The most prevalent question type you will encounter on this exam is the multiple choice question with one or more correct alternatives. When it is a multiple choice single answer with four alternatives, you will typically have two or more obviously wrong alternatives and two credible answers, one of which is correct. If you know the answer, no problem; click it and move on. If you are uncertain and can see the two plausible ones, you now have narrowed it down to a 50% chance of getting it right, so make sure you click one of the two before it is too late. In this situation you can always mark it for review. When you are ready to answer the question, just click on the radio button next to the answer you want to choose.

The most important thing to remember on a multiple choice question is to read the entire stem very carefully, word by word. If the answer seems really obvious to you, great, but make sure to look out for any negatives, double negatives, or any other twists so you don't fall into any obvious traps. A good tactic is to read the question and then try to come up with the answer *before* looking at the answer alternatives; sometimes this may keep you from being influenced by a smart distracter. Always look for clues in the stem; sometimes the way it is written will help you rule out one or more of the distracters if you just read it carefully enough. Figure 2.3 shows an example of a typical multiple choice question (note the negative in this one).

93. After deciding to use a Custom Application Directory Partition you need to perform three tasks. Which of the following is NOT one of them?

    ○ A. Enlist DNS servers into the partition
    ○ B. Assign the zone for replication scopes
    ○ C. Create the partition
    ○ D. Make sure all DC's are running the DNS Service role

Figure 2.3
A typical multiple choice exam question, with the use of a negative.

Another common question type is the "list and reorder" type of questions (you will see quite a few of those in the CertBlaster as well). The way these work is that you are given a set of items in a random order and asked to list them in the correct order. The way the Prometric exam software does this is to place the items in one of two frames separated by a column on which you will find controls. Click to highlight the item you think should be first on the list; then click the Add button or the arrow in the middle, and the item will be placed first in the second frame. Repeat this procedure with the other items until you have no items remaining in the right column. Figure 2.4 shows an example of the list and reorder window.

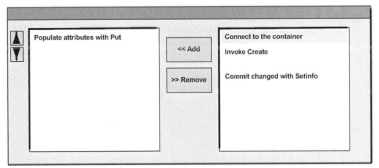

Figure 2.4
An example list and reorder window.

"Create a tree" is another question format you are likely to face on the exam. Just as in the "list and reorder" question type, you will see two columns and you will be asked to organize the information. You are asked to organize the information along a hierarchy. To move an entry from the list to the desired location in the tree, you need to select the relevant tree node by clicking it, select the entry you want to move, and then click the Add button. As soon as you add an entry to a tree node, it appears with a + sign to the left of the node name. You can click it to expand the node and see the entries you have added. If you want to move any entry, just select it and click it and then click the Remove button.

Another common question type is "drag and drop." This question format requires you to drag a label to its correct spot, either in a table or in a graphic. You will simply click the item, drag to the desired spot, and let go of the mouse. If you made an error, you can click Reset if available or just re-drag and drop the item. Figure 2.5 shows an example where you must drag the labels in the left column to the Description column. This example is actually a variant of a list and reorder type question.

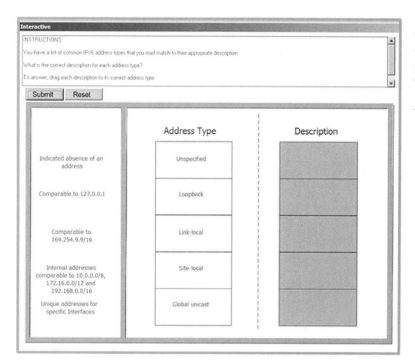

Figure 2.5
The drag and drop type question, where you drag a term from one column to its match in the other column.

Using CertBlaster for Test Preparation

Software-based test preparation is really important when it comes to MCP exams because they are all taken on the computer at the testing center. If this is your first Microsoft exam, then CertBlaster can be crucial as it will put you in the situation and familiarize you with the navigation and other important features. However, even if you're a seasoned Microsoft test taker, it will still be very useful for you to use CertBlaster to gauge, among other things, how you do within the given time limit specifically on this exam topic.

The home screen in CertBlaster contains the exams and the drills you have access to. The upper half of that screen contains the exams, as shown in Figure 2.6.

The lower portion contains the drills, one per Microsoft exam objective, as shown in Figure 2.7.

The exams consist of 50 questions, each drawn from the drills. A drill is a test bank that contains questions exclusively focused on one exam main domain. As an example, Exam 70-640 contains six main domains; therefore, you will find six drills in the 70-640 CertBlaster. Drill one will have

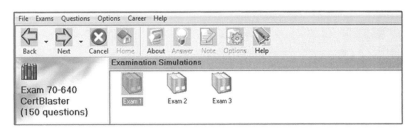

2

Figure 2.6
The top half of the CertBlaster home screen.

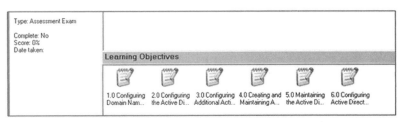

Figure 2.7
The bottom half of the CertBlaster home screen.

questions mapped to main domain one (Configuring Domain Name System (DNS) for Active Directory). Furthermore, each main domain is assigned a weight in the overall certification; the value of that weight determines the number of questions available in each drill. Finally, the Exams pull questions from the drills in numbers reflecting the relative weight of the objectives.

The CertBlaster test preparation software helps you study, cram, and simulate the exam. It has four modes:

- Assessment mode
- Study mode
- Flash mode
- Certification mode

Step 1: Assessment Mode and How It Is Personally Customized

In assessment mode you are presented with a set number of questions aimed at offering a representative sample of the types of questions you'll encounter on the exam. The assessment mode offers a time setting where you only see the questions and are expected to answer them as best you can. The main reason to take a test in assessment mode is of course to get a sense of where you stand. For that reason, CertBlaster's assessment mode enables you to save or print your customized "Personal Testing Plan" (PTP), which is generated by CertBlaster based on your responses during the test. It will list the exam objectives and sub-objectives you need to revisit in order to perfect your exam preparation. This book's chapter names (from Chapter 3 and up) are the main domains of the exam. The sub-objectives are listed underneath each question and typically appear in increasing order. Figure 2.8 shows an example.

Figure 2.8 shows question number 93; the way you know which chapter it belongs to is by looking at the last line, which lists the exam number and then 1.3. This stands for Microsoft main domain 1 (Configuring Domain Name System (DNS) for Active Directory) sub-objective 3 (Configure Zone Transfers and Replication).

93. After deciding to use a Custom Application Directory Partition you need to perform three tasks. Which of the following is NOT one of them?

A. Enlist DNS servers into the partition
B. Assign the zone for replication scopes
C. Create the partition
D. Make sure all DC's are running the DNS Service role

70-640 TS Objective 1.3 - Configure zone transfers and replication

Figure 2.8
The objectives are listed underneath each question and typically appear in increasing order.

This is why it will always be easy to go back to this book, PTP in hand, and find out which area you need to review. However, as I said in the Introduction, this is not a book where you learn the skills necessary for this exam; for that you will need a study guide. A good one is obviously Microsoft's very own training kit. The PTP also includes for each question you missed, chapter and page references back to *MCTS Self-Paced Training Kit (Exam 70-640): Configuring Windows Server® 2008 Active Directory®*.

Step 2: Study Mode

In study mode, you will be exposed to exam type questions in your own relaxing and customized learning environment. You can decide how many questions you want to handle for the sitting, you can take notes as you go through the questions, and you can see the answers and explanations if you so desire. You have unlimited time to do all this so make sure you take your time and give yourself the opportunity to understand *why* any given answer is correct. I can't stress enough that rote memorizing is not the way to pass on exam day; *comprehension* is what stays with you and enables you to navigate successfully through the twists and turns of the question types and content that you are going to face.

Step 3: Certification Mode and How To "Feel" the Exam Without Taking It

In certification mode, the exam conditions will be replicated as closely as possible. This means you will get a number of questions, type of questions, and distribution of questions over the different exam objectives to mimic as closely as possible the conditions of the exam. Obviously this is a timed exercise and you will not be able to see any of the answers or explanations. In order to feel comfortable with a CertBlaster result even in certification mode, you need a very high score (probably north of 95%). Also, be sure you got that score by *understanding* the question and answer and not by memorization alone. A score achieved through memorization will not necessarily translate to exam success, as the questions will not be identical to the ones you answer in CertBlaster.

Flash Mode

Flash mode is a last-minute convenience device. It allows you to press your spacebar, see a question, press the spacebar again to see the answer, and so forth. As you can see, this replicates the act of studying with flash cards. And although not a main element of an exam strategy, it has its place as a final touch on your way to certification. This comes last; you can do it at home or at the testing center if there is a wait.

Important Features You Will Encounter in CertBlaster

The most significant part of any CertBlaster are of course the questions. They are calibrated and mapped to the exam in a manner to help you best prepare for the types of reasoning you will need to win on exam day. In addition to this content component, some elements of the CertBlaster navigation will also help you prepare. Because these features are similar to the ones used on the exam software, they will familiarize you with the exam software feature well before exam day. The most significant of those features are the ones shown in Figure 2.9.

   ☐ Mark this Question for later   Time remaining: 00:57:10

Figure 2.9
Be sure you know how to use these elements of the test to your best advantage before you walk in the door of the exam.

These features act in the same way as they do on the actual exam. Just as on the exam, if you have skipped or marked questions for later, before it begins grading, CertBlaster will prompt you to answer such questions before it is too late (provided of course you have time left on the exam timer).

Additional CertBlaster Features That Will Help You Prepare

Study mode offers the most features and help available. Figure 2.10 shows the top navigation in Study mode.

Figure 2.10
CertBlaster's Study mode offers lots of help and guidance.

The first several options are covered in the previous section. The Home button allows you to exit the test and go back to the exam and drills page, where you can select a new exam or drill. The Hint and Answer buttons contain the same content, although the Hint feature doesn't give you the correct answer. Figure 2.11 shows what you would see after choosing an incorrect answer and then clicking the Answer button.

Clicking Note in the navigation bar will open the CertBlaster notebook, where you can type a remark regarding the question you are studying. Once you have saved your note, you will see a paper clip attached to that question. This is useful if you are studying with friends, in a group, with an instructor, or simply want to remember any special issue concerning this question. Figure 2.12 shows the Note feature in action.

After grading your test, CertBlaster then creates your Personal Testing Plan (PTP). The reason your customized PTP (based on your assessment result) is useful is because it helps you focus on your weak areas. It contains chapter and page references to the relevant MS Press book as well as references to the exam objectives (down to the sub-objective) that you need to pay attention to as a result of your assessment. To print or save your PTP, just click Next and a dialog box will prompt you. Figure 2.13 shows an example of a generic PTP.

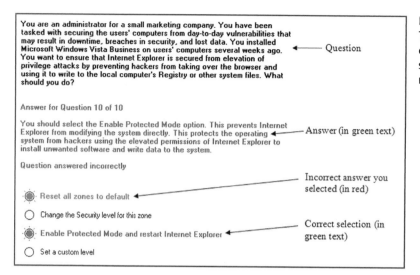

Figure 2.11
The Answer feature on Study mode shows you the correct answer.

Click OK to save   Clip on bottom right hand
                                corner of screen

Figure 2.12
The Note feature allows you to write electronic notes and attach them to specific questions.

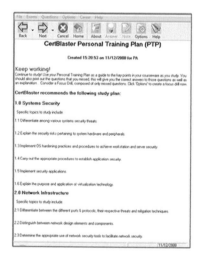

Figure 2.13
An example Personal Testing Plan.

SUMMARY

This book and software aim at enhancing your exam readiness at all levels. The goal is to give you an insight into the exam procedures and format, as well as the types of questions you will face at the exam. I hope that the 800 practice questions in this book plus the CertBlaster software (on the CD at the end of this book) will contribute to your exam readiness and help you walk in on examination day feeling prepared and confident. Good luck!

Part II
PRACTICE TESTS

3

CONFIGURING DOMAIN NAME SYSTEM (DNS) FOR ACTIVE DIRECTORY

This chapter contains 128 questions that fall under Microsoft's first main exam objective for the 70-640 exam, "Configuring Domain Name System (DNS) for Active Directory." This main objective consists of the following three sub-objectives:

- Configure zones
- Configure DNS server settings
- Configure zone transfers and replication

Microsoft has given this main exam objective, "Configuring Domain Name System (DNS) for Active Directory," a weight of 16%, which is why I have created 128 (out of a total of 800) test preparation questions for this chapter.

TEST PREPARATION QUESTIONS

1. Your company has a main office and a branch office. You need to maintain the same name-space internally for your AD DS directory as you use for your external Internet name. What is this implementation of DNS called?

   A. Perimeter networking

   B. A split-brain service

   C. DMZ

   D. Whole-brain structure

   70-640 TS Objective 1.2: Configure DNS server settings

2. You have a Windows 2008 Server network running AD DS. When you boot a computer that is part of this domain, the first process that takes place is which of the following?

   A. The authentication process

   B. The registration process

   C. The identification of SRV records from a DNS server

   D. The identification of SRV records from a DHCP server

   70-640 TS Objective 1.2: Configure DNS server settings

3. Windows Server 2008 DNS service works with which of the following addressing schemes? Select one.

A. IPv6

B. IPv4

C. Both IPv6 and IPv4

D. Neither of these

70-640 TS Objective 1.2: Configure DNS server settings

4. Windows Server 2008 DNS service had the ability to work with IPv6. Which of the following correctly describes IPv6?

A. 32-bit addressing scheme

B. 128-bit addressing scheme

C. 512-bit addressing scheme

D. 64-bit addressing scheme

70-640 TS Objective 1.2: Configure DNS server settings

5. Which of the following statements is most true about the Windows Domain Naming System?

A. It provides the Windows domain with IPv6 addressing

B. Windows DNS system is used only on the Internet

C. Windows DNS translates IP addresses into common terms

D. Windows DNS is part of AD DS

70-640 TS Objective 1.2: Configure DNS server settings

6. Which of the following statements is most true about the Windows Domain Naming System?

A. DNS is integrated with AD DS

B. DNS is intergraded with AD RMS

C. DNS is integrated with AD FS

D. DNS runs only in the perimeter network infrastructure

70-640 TS Objective 1.2: Configure DNS server settings

7. When your DNS server is communicating on the Internet, which of the following TCP/IP ports is used?

A. 51

B. 53

C. 153

D. 559

70-640 TS Objective 1.2: Configure DNS server settings

3

8. When your DNS server is running on your Windows 2008 Server domain, which TCP/IP port does it utilize?

A. 25

B. 125

C. 53

D. 21

70-640 TS Objective 1.2: Configure DNS server settings

9. When you are using Windows 2008 DNS services, which of the following statements describes how they communicate with clients and servers?

A. All clients and servers are tuned to port 53 to locate and identify computer names

B. Clients are tuned to port 53 and servers are tuned to port 54 to identify computer and server names on the network

C. Client computers will be assigned a random port as the DNS server and the server will communicate on port 53

D. Client computers are tuned to port 21 and the DNS server is tuned to port 53

70-640 TS Objective 1.2: Configure DNS server settings

10. The naming system employed by DNS is which of the following?

A. Linear

B. Static

C. Hierarchical

D. Fixed

70-640 TS Objective 1.2: Configure DNS server settings

11. The actual naming structure supported by DNS uses names that begin with a root and extend from the root when additional names are added. Which one of the following is NOT a root name?

A. Com

B. Edu

C. Cnn

D. Gov

70-640 TS Objective 1.2: Configure DNS server settings

12. In the DNS naming structure, organizations often add names from the actual DNS root. The name Microsoft.net is how many levels down from the DNS root?

A. First level

B. Second level

C. Third level

D. Fourth level

70-640 TS Objective 1.2: Configure DNS server settings

13. In the DNS naming structure, organizations often add names from the actual DNS root. The name Technet.microsoft.net is how many levels down from the name?

    A. First level

    B. Second level

    C. Third level

    D. Fourth level

    70-640 TS Objective 1.2: Configure DNS server settings

14. In Windows 2008 Server, the DNS service has been updated to use IPv6. IPv4 used four octets of binary digits to form the 32-bit IP address. IPv6 uses _____ 16-bit pieces to form a _____ IP address. Fill in the blanks.

    A. 8/156-bit

    B. 6/128-bit

    C. 8/128-bit

    D. 4/128-bit

    70-640 TS Objective 1.2: Configure DNS server settings

15. In Windows 2008 Server, the DNS service has been updated to use IPv6. IPv6 is usually displayed in which of the following forms?

    A. Binary

    B. Hexadecimal

    C. Dotted decimal notation

    D. Octets

    70-640 TS Objective 1.2: Configure DNS server settings

16. If your Windows Vista or Windows 2008 server computer is configured for DHCP and there is no available DHCP server to respond with an actual address, which of the following IPv6 addresses will your system generate?

    A. Link-local

    B. FE80::

    C. Unspecified

    D. FEC0::

    70-640 TS Objective 1.2: Configure DNS server settings

17. IPv6 provides several types of addresses. Which of the following is NOT one of the address types that IPv6 provides?

    A. Link-local

    B. Experimental

    C. Site-local

    D. Global unicast

    70-640 TS Objective 1.2: Configure DNS server settings

3

18. The increase in the number of devices requiring IP addresses has driven the development of IPv6. Which of the following is the correct number of addresses provided by IPv6?

    A. 4 billion

    B. 340 billion billion billion

    C. 340 billion billion billion billion

    D. 2^{64}

    70-640 TS Objective 1.2: Configure DNS server settings

19. Match the following address types with the correct IPv6 format.

    A. FE80::

    B. FECO::

    C. ::

    D. ::1

Unspecified	
Loopback	
Link-local	
Site-local	

    70-640 TS Objective 1.2: Configure DNS server settings

20. IPv4 has several types of addresses used for specific purposes. IPv6 also has several types of addresses. Match the IPv6 address type with the correct description.

    A. Private IP addresses, routed locally only

    B. Assigned by default when no DHCP is available

    C. Internet addresses

Link-local	
Site-local	
Global unicast	

    70-640 TS Objective 1.2: Configure DNS server settings

21. Match the four most common types of IPv6 addresses with its type description.

    A. Internal addresses comparable to 10.0.0.0/8, 172.16.0.0/12, and 192.168.0.0/16

    B. Comparable to 127.0.0.1

    C. Comparable to 169.254.9.9/16

    D. Unique addresses for specific interfaces

    E. Indicates an absence of an address

Address Type	Description
Unspecified	
Loopback	
Link-local	
Site-local	
Global unicast	

70-640 TS Objective 1.2: Configure DNS server settings

22. When you implement IPv6 and Windows Server 2008 and Windows Vista you will be supporting a secondary name resolution system. What is this secondary system for resolving names called?

   A. Peer Resolution

   B. Peer Naming System

   C. Peer Name Resolution Protocol

   D. Peer Naming Protocol

   70-640 TS Objective 1.2: Configure DNS server settings

23. Peer Name Resolution Protocol is an add-on feature for Windows Server 2008. Which of the following statements is true about PNRP?

   A. PNRP can host only a small number of names

   B. PNRP requires administrative intervention like DNS

   C. PNRP is not fault-tolerant

   D. PNRP is a distributed naming system

   70-640 TS Objective 1.2: Configure DNS server settings

24. Peer Name Resolution Protocol is an add-on feature for Windows Server 2008. Which of the following statements is true about PNRP?

   A. PNRP can scale to billions of names

   B. PNRP requires administrative intervention

   C. PNRP is not fault-tolerant

   D. PNRP uses caching to improve performance

   70-640 TS Objective 1.2: Configure DNS server settings

25. Peer Name Resolution Protocol is an add-on feature for Windows Server 2008. Which of the following statements is true about PNRP?

   A. PNRP uses caching to improve performance like DNS systems do

   B. PNRP is not fault-tolerant

   C. PNRP publication is instantaneous and does not require administrative intervention

   D. PNRP can resolve only a limited number of names

   70-640 TS Objective 1.2: Configure DNS server settings

26. DNS protects name entries with secure update. What does PNRP use to protect names from spoofing and counterfeiting?

A. PNRP uses only secure transmission technology

B. IPSec

C. CHAP

D. Digital signatures

70-640 TS Objective 1.2: Configure DNS server settings

27. To provide resolution, PNRP relies on the global IPv6 address scope and the link-local IPv6 address scope. These are referred to as which of the following?

A. Hemispheres

B. Groups

C. Scopes

D. Clouds

70-640 TS Objective 1.2: Configure DNS server settings

28. Windows Server 2008 includes PNRP server components as an add-on feature but at this time the world is still using DNS for name resolution. Why hasn't the world moved to PNRP?

A. It doesn't work on the Internet

B. The world has not moved to IPv6 yet

C. It's still in beta release

D. No one knows it has been released

70-640 TS Objective 1.2: Configure DNS server settings

29. DNS has been with us since the inception of the Internet and has been evolving with the growth of the Internet. Windows Server 2008 can provide three DNS server roles; which of the following is NOT one of them?

A. Dynamic DNS

B. Static DNS

C. Read-write DNS

D. Read-only DNS

70-640 TS Objective 1.2: Configure DNS server settings

30. Which of the following DNS server roles are usually deployed in perimeter networks and are not integrated with AD DS?

A. DDNS servers

B. Primary DNS server

C. Secondary DNS server

D. Read-only DNS server

70-640 TS Objective 1.2: Configure DNS server settings

31. Which of the following DNS servers supports only one-way replication?

    A. Read-only server

    B. Read-write DNS server

    C. Dynamic DNS server

    D. All of the above

    70-640 TS Objective 1.2: Configure DNS server settings

32. The most common protection mechanism for protecting your network by blocking entry of undesirable traffic through the manipulation of the TCP/IP port is called which of the following?

    A. Router

    B. Router-switch

    C. Firewall

    D. NAT

    70-640 TS Objective 1.2: Configure DNS server settings

33. When working with Windows 2008 AD DS, you will need to use a properly formed DNS name. This name is often referred to as an FQDN. What does FQDN stand for?

    A. Formally Qualified Domain Name

    B. Functional Quantified Domain Name

    C. Fully Qualified Doman Name

    D. Frequently Qualified Doman Name

    70-640 TS Objective 1.2: Configure DNS server settings

34. It is understood that in today's world, organizations will protect their internal networks by maintaining two namespaces for their enterprises—one internal and one public. If you use the same namespace internally for your AD DS as for your Internet name, that means you have implemented which kind of DNS service?

    A. Split-naming DNS

    B. Split-domain DNS

    C. Split-brain DNS service

    D. Dual domain DNS

    70-640 TS Objective 1.2: Configure DNS server settings

35. In regards to DNS and Microsoft Windows-based networks, which one of the following statements would NOT be true?

    A. It is possible to use Windows and non-Windows–based DNS servers

    B. With Windows DNS services and AD DS, everything becomes automatic

    C. When using non-Windows–based DNS, configuration must be done manually

    D. You cannot use non-Windows DNS servers with Windows

    70-640 TS Objective 1.2: Configure DNS server settings

36. If you are installing an AD DS in an environment where you must use non-Windows–based DNS services, the ideal network configuration would be which of the following structures?

    A. Dynamic DNS servers

    B. Split-brain DNS

    C. Whole-brain DNS

    D. None; AD DS will not work with non-Windows–based DNS servers

    70-640 TS Objective 1.2: Configure DNS server settings

37. Identify which option describes which DNS structure in the following figure.

    A. Whole-brain

    B. Split-brain

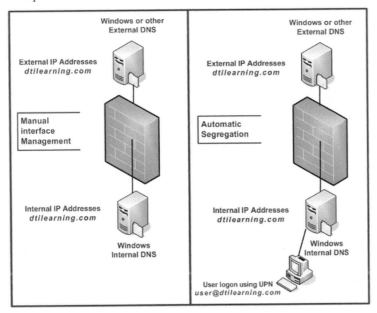

    70-640 TS Objective 1.2: Configure DNS server settings

38. Which of the following operating systems DO NOT support the registration of their own name records with DDNS in an AD DS network?

    A. Windows 2000

    B. Windows XP

    C. Windows Server 2003

    D. Windows NT

    70-640 TS Objective 1.2: Configure DNS server settings

39. Network devices that are not capable of registering their own names with DDNS may rely on what other service to perform the name registration for them?

    A. PNRP

    B. DHCP

    C. RIS

    D. WUS

    70-640 TS Objective 1.2: Configure DNS server settings

40. The name resolution process is a series of events. Place this list in the correct order starting with a request for a new web page called www.dtilearning.com.

    A. The DNS server sends a referral request to the .com name server

    B. The DNS server for dtilearning.com sends the IP address to the client

    C. A request is sent to the local DNS server

    D. A request is sent to the authoritative DNS server for dtilearning.com

    E. The client name resolver uses the IP address to request the web page

    F. The web page is sent to the user

    70-640 TS Objective 1.2: Configure DNS server settings

41. Match the following DNS zone descriptions with their correct type.

    A. The DNS containers for name resolution

    B. Records for other DNS servers

    C. Zones that contain the read-write information

    D. The zone that contains the records for a particular domain

    E. The zone that contains the records for the entire forest

Domain DNS zone	
Forest DNS zone	
Forward lookup zone	
Primary zones	
Stub zone	

    70-640 TS Objective 1.2: Configure DNS server settings

42. NetBIOS names have been used in Windows-based networking to resolve single-label names for computers. The names have been managed by WINS, but this service has been replaced in Windows Server 2008 with which of the following?

    A. Active Directory integrated zone

    B. Legacy DNS

    C. Round-robin servers

    D. GlobalNames zone

    70-640 TS Objective 1.2: Configure DNS server settings

43. DNS servers use zone transfers to replicate information from one server to another. Match the correct descriptions with the correct zone transfer.

A. AD DS multimaster replication

B. Asynchronous full transfer

C. Incremental zone transfer

AXFR	
IXFR	
Secure	

70-640 TS Objective 1.3: Configuring zone transfers and replication

44. Match the record type with the correct initials.

A. CNAME

B. MX

C. AAAA

D. SRV

E. PTR

Alias	
Host	
Mail	
Pointer	
Service	

70-640 TS Objective 1.2: Configure DNS server settings

45. Match the correct use with the record type.

A. Reverse lookups within the namespace

B. Computer objects used to resolve IP addresses to devices

C. Alternate record for a name specified in another record type

D. Routes email to a namespace

E. Location of specific TCP/IP service

Alias	
Host	
Mail	
Pointer	
Service	

70-640 TS Objective 1.2: Configure DNS server settings

46. DNS service is integrated with AD DS and DNS data is stored in an application directory partition that spans the entire forest. This makes the data available to any DNS server within the forest. By default, Windows Server 2008 creates two application directory partitions. What are these partitions called?

A. Scopes

B. Domain partitions

C. ForestDNS zones and domain DNS zones

D. GlobalNames zones

70-640 TS Objective 1.1: Configure zones

47. When a DNS server hosts a very large number of zones and records in AD DS, it may take too long to boot due to the large amount of zone data that needs to be loaded. Windows Server 2008 has a new service to help this situation. Select the name of the new service from the following choices.

A. GNZ

B. Read-only domain

C. DomainDNSZones

D. Background loading

70-640 TS Objective 1.2: Configuring DNS server settings

48. Which of the following Windows Server 2008 features will best protect records on the DNS server from unprotected network spoofs?

A. Read-only DNS data for primary zones

B. GlobalNames

C. Application directory partitions

D. ADI zones

70-640 TS Objective 1.2: Configuring DNS server settings

49. Which of the following Windows Server 2008 features will provide support for single-label names or names without parent names?

A. GNZ

B. ADI

C. SRV

D. PNRP

70-640 TS Objective 1.2: Configuring DNS server settings

50. In the event that an organization requires the use of a large number of single-label names to support applications that stem from older Windows NT-based networks, which of the following services will you need to implement?

A. WPAD

B. AD DS

C. PNRP

D. WINS

70-640 TS Objective 1.2: Configuring DNS server settings

3

51. What is the name of the protocol used by web browsers to discover the network proxy server settings?

A. WPAD

B. WINS

C. DNS

D. AD DS

70-640 TS Objective 1.2: Configuring DNS server settings

52. Which of the following protocols allows IPv4 and IPv6 networks to work together by encapsulating the IPv6 packets in an IPv4 format?

A. WPAD

B. ISTAP

C. DNS

D. AD DS

70-640 TS Objective 1.2 Configuring DNS server settings

53. It is possible for the potential routers list to be compromised when using ISATAP. This may cause IPv6 packets to be routed to malicious routers. Which of the following is designed to prevent such compromises?

A. Stub zones

B. Split-brain structures

C. Global query block lists

D. Security query block lists

70-640 TS Objective 1.2 Configuring DNS server settings

54. By default Windows Server 2008 and Windows Vista are designed to use dynamic IPv6 addresses. However, when no DHCPv6 servers are present on the network, IPv6 will automatically assign which type of address?

A. Link specific

B. Link-local

C. Site-local

D. Global

70-640 TS Objective 1.2: Configuring DNS server settings

55. Which one of the following statements is true regarding the major difference between PNRP and DNS?

A. DNS can scale many more names than PNRP

B. PNRP relies on a hierarchy of servers to resolve names

C. PNRP can scale millions of names and DNS relies on a hierarchy of servers

D. PNRP and DNS are the same except PNRP is for IPv6

70-640 TS Objective 1.2: Configuring DNS server settings

56. The first step in an AD DS logon is a DNS request for which type of DNS record?
    A. MX
    B. PTR
    C. SRV
    D. CNAME
    70-640 TS Objective 1.2: Configuring DNS server settings

57. To run the Active Directory Domain Services Installation wizard to remove a Domain Controller role, you do which of the following?
    A. Open the ADDS mmc
    B. Open Active Directory User and Computers and click Action
    C. You cannot remove a domain once it has been created
    D. Type dcpromo.exe in the Search box of the Start menu
    70-640 TS Objective 1.2: Configuring DNS server settings

58. DNS is a name resolution system used by Windows AD DS and the Internet to map IP addresses to FQDNs. Which of the following is the correct format for an FQDN?
    A. object.domain.rootname
    B. domain.namespace.rootname
    C. object.namespace.rootname
    D. rootname.namespace.object
    70-640 TS Objective 1.2: Configuring DNS server settings

59. Windows Server 2008 AD DS relies on the same structure as DNS. What is this structure called?
    A. Static
    B. Linear
    C. Single-named
    D. Hierarchical
    70-640 TS Objective 1.2: Configuring DNS server settings

60. Windows Server 2008 supports IPv6 fully and is installed by default with which of the following IPv6 address types?
    A. Loopback
    B. Link-local
    C. Site-local
    D. Global
    70-640 TS Objective 1.2: Configuring DNS server settings

3

61. Windows AD DS DNS servers can host three types of zones that are stored in the directory database. Match the descriptions with the zone types.

A. Read-only copies

B. Read-write zones that support name resolution

C. Pointers to other DNS servers

Primary	
Secondary	
Stub	

70-640 TS Objective 1.3: Configuring zone transfers and replication

62. When you install DNS with AD DS, most of the DNS configuration is done automatically. There are some manual operations that must be completed. Which of the following does NOT require manual configuration?

A. Including RLZ

B. Finalizing the DNS server

C. Registering computers running Windows 2000 operating systems

D. Reviewing DNS server content

70-640 TS Objective 1.2: Configuring DNS server settings

63. DNS server security is very important because DNS servers that are exposed to the Internet are subject to attack from malicious users. Which of the following best describes a DoS attack?

A. Disk Operating System (DOS) attack

B. Attackers try to copy records and reuse them for an attack

C. Attacks flood the DNS server with more requests than the server can respond to

D. Denial of System resources

70-640 TS Objective 1.2: Configuring DNS server settings

64. DNS Server security is sometimes compromised by an attacker who tries to obtain all the data contained on the server. This type of attack is referred to as which of the following?

A. Port scanning

B. Spoofing

C. Phishing

D. Footprinting

70-640 TS Objective 1.2: Configuring DNS server settings

65. DNS servers store records only for a specific period of time; this time period is called which of the following?

A. Scavenging

B. FLZ

C. Cache

D. TTL

70-640 TS Objective 1.2: Configuring DNS server settings

66. DNS server service in Windows Server 2008 automatically cleans all the active zones of any records in which the TTL has expired. Doing so helps to avoid providing false positives to users performing lookups. What is this process called?

    A. Clean cache

    B. Defragmenting

    C. Scavenging

    D. TTL expunge

    70-640 TS Objective 1.2: Configuring DNS server settings

67. To set up scavenging for an entire server, you must assign the setting through the server action menu. Where would you find the setting for Scavenging?

    A. Go to Initial Configuration Tasks; right-click the name in the DNS node and choose Aging

    B. Go to Initial Server Configuration > Click Roles > DNS Server > Server name

    C. Go to Server Manager; right-click the server name and choose Set Aging

    D. Go to Initial Server Configuration; right-click the server name and choose Set Aging

    70-640 TS Objective 1.2: Configuring DNS server settings

68. What does the "No-Refresh Interval" setting in the Server Aging/Scavenging properties represent?

    A. The time between the first refresh of a record stamp and the moment when the system allows the timestamp to be refreshed

    B. The time before the refresh of a record stamp and the moment when the system allows the timestamp to be refreshed

    C. The time between the most recent refresh of a record stamp and the moment when the system allows the timestamp to be refreshed

    D. The time between the most recent refresh of a record stamp and the moment when the system allows the timestamp to be removed

    70-640 TS Objective 1.3: Configure zone transfers and replication

69. What does the "Refresh Interval" setting in the Server Aging/Scavenging properties represent?

    A. The time between the first refresh of a record stamp and the moment when the system allows the timestamp to be refreshed

    B. Refresh interval is the earliest moment when a record may be updated or scavenged if no updates are applied

    C. The time between the most recent refresh of a record stamp and the moment when the system allows the timestamp to be removed

    D. Refresh interval is the earliest moment when a record may be deleted

    70-640 TS Objective 1.3: Configure zone transfers and replication

70. In the following image, circle the spot you would click to find the Clear Cache option.

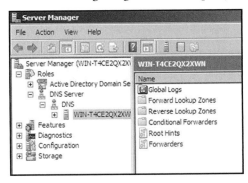

70-640 TS Objective 1.3: Configure zone transfers and replication

71. When you are finalizing the FLZ configuration for a production environment, there are several best practices that you should follow. Select one from the list that you should use if you have Windows 2000 Servers in your network.

A. Use the All Domain Controllers in This Domain for Windows 2000 Compatibility option

B. Use the Windows 2000 update application directory partitions

C. Use Windows 2000 Compatibility

D. There is no option for using Windows 2000 Compatibility

70-640 TS Objective 1.3: Configure zone transfers and replication

72. When you are finalizing the FLZ configuration for a production environment, there are several best practices that you should follow when setting up WINS. Select the correct configuration from the following.

A. On the WINS tab, assign WINS

B. On the WINS tab, assign the WINS lookup only if you are using GNZs

C. On the WINS tab, assign the WINS lookup only if you cannot use GNZs

D. The WINS tab has been removed from Windows Server 2008

70-640 TS Objective 1.3: Configure zone transfers and replication

73. The SOA records identify the zone and its related information. The following information is included in the SOA; match the description with its definition.

A. Intervals and time-based setting for the record

B. Assigned to the zone when it is created

C. The Time to Live for this record

D. The master server for the zone

E. The name of the operator of the server

Serial number	
Primary server	
Responsible person	
SOA	
TTL	

70-640 TS Objective 1.3: Configure zone transfers and replication

74. Each zone should be assigned a Responsible Person record. There are three required items for the creation of the RP record. Select from the following list the one item that is NOT needed.

A. A common group name

B. A cell phone number

C. A group mailbox in the directory

D. A text record

70-640 TS Objective 1.3: Configure zone transfers and replication

75. Most networks will require the use of RLZs. An exception to this is a small network that does not require secure communications with applications on your network. A small network is considered one with less than which of the following?

A. 75 computers

B. 150 computers

C. 500 computers

D. 1500 computers

70-640 TS Objective 1.3: Configure zone transfers and replication

76. Here are three services that you may need to create a custom record for. Select one answer that is NOT a reason to create a customer record.

A. An MX record to print to an email server

B. An FLZ zone

C. An alias

D. SRV records

70-640 TS Objective 1.3: Configure zone transfers and replication

77. Name resolution is performed with two main methods. DNS servers will either contain root hints or rely on forwards to link them to another server for the lookup. If you are configuring forwards for security purposes, what change would you make to the DNS properties shown in this image?

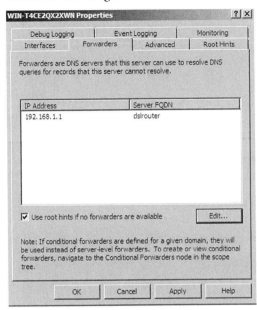

70-640 TS Objective 1.3: Configure zone transfers and replication

78. As an alternative to using forwarders, you can use conditional forwarders. How are conditional forwarders used?

    A. To forward DN requests from any user to a specific server

    B. To forward DN requests from specific users to a single server

    C. To forward DN requests from specific users to at least two servers

    D. To set up specific rules to limit DNS activity across domains

    70-640 TS Objective 1.3: Configure zone transfers and replication

79. Managing single-label names is possible by manually creating a GNZ. There are five steps in the basic process of creating a GNZ on each DC with a DNS service. Put the five steps in the correct order.

    A. Add single-label names to the DNS zone

    B. Create the GlobalNames FLZ

    C. Do not enable dynamic updates for this zone

    D. Enable GNZ support on each DNS server in the forest

    E. Set the replication scope of all DNS servers in the forest

    70-640 TS Objective 1.3: Configure zone transfers and replication

80. To create a GNZ through Server Manager support in a DNS server requires that you modify the Windows Registry using the `dnscmd` command. Which of the following is the correct format for this command?

A. `/ config /enableglocalnames`

B. `/config/ enableglobalnamessupport 1`

C. `/enableglobalnamessupport / config / 1`

D. `/enableglobalnames 1`

70-640 TS Objective 1.3: Configure zone transfers and replication

81. You don't want to use WINS in your Windows Server 2008 network, so you have enabled GNZ support. Now you need to add records. What are the GNZ names?

A. NetBIOS names

B. WINS names

C. DNS hosts

D. Aliases

70-640 TS Objective 1.2: Configure DNS server settings

82. When adding GNZ records, what requirements do you need to adhere to in order to conserve the GNZ names?

A. They cannot be longer than 256 characters

B. They cannot be longer than 255 characters

C. They cannot be longer than 26 characters

D. They cannot be longer than 15 characters

70-640 TS Objective 1.2: Configure DNS server settings

83. When adding GNZ name records, there are three parts to each entry when using a command line. What are the three parts of the command-line entry for GNZ names?

A. Domain name/global name/NetBIOS name

B. Computer name/domain name/host name

C. DNS server name/domain name/FQDN

D. DNS server name/single global name/corresponding DNS name

70-640 TS Objective 1.2: Configure DNS server settings

84. When you are adding GNZ name records from the command line, which of the following is the correct syntax to use for the `dnscmd` command?

A. `dnsservername / recordadd globalnames singlelabelname cname correspondingdnsname`

B. `dnsservername / recordadd globalnames cname correspondingdnsname`

C. `dnsservername / recordadd globalnames singlelabelname correspondingdnsname`

D. `dnsservername / recordadd globalnames singlelabelname cname`

70-640 TS Objective 1.2: Configure DNS server settings

3

85. When supporting a multitude of single-label names, you may not have support when using GNZ because of the sheer number of entries. You should install WINS. What is the minimum number of WINS servers you should install?

A. 1

B. 2

C. 3

D. 6

70-640 TS Objective 1.2: Configure DNS server settings

86. When configuring your Windows Server 2008 to provide WINS support for your single-label names, the servers you install should be configured for which of the following?

A. Synchronization

B. Pull synchronization

C. Push-pull synchronization

D. Push synchronization

70-640 TS Objective 1.2: Configure DNS server settings

87. When configuring your Windows Server 2008 to provide WINS support for your single-label names, you should set two values in the DHCP server. Select the correct settings you need to implement.

A. 044 WINS/NBNS and 045 WINS

B. 044 WINS/NBNS and 046 WINS/NBT

C. 046 WINS/NBNS and 046 WINS/NBT

D. 046 WINS/NBNS and 044 WINS/NBT

70-640 TS Objective 1.2: Configure DNS server settings

88. When you link DNS and WINS together you provide for your Windows network which of the following?

A. FQDN

B. FQDN and DNS names

C. FQDN and single-label name resolution

D. Root-level names

70-640 TS Objective 1.2: Configure DNS server settings

89. Which was the first Microsoft Operating System that enabled all of its DNS clients to utilize dynamic DNS?

A. NT 3.1

B. Windows 98

C. Windows 2000

D. Windows XP

70-640 TS Objective 1.2: Configure DNS server settings

90. In traditional Windows Server networks, a minimum of two DNS servers should be specified in the DHCP setting. This would provide client computers with the DNS addresses they need to resolve name requests. Remote clients would resolve over the WAN. With the integration of DNS with the directory store, DNS data is now available from the local DC. Which DHCP options are needed to affect this change in Windows Server 2008?

    A. All DCs run the DNS server role by default

    B. Add the name resolution service

    C. Add the name resolution service and the 006 DNS server value to the scope

    D. 0006 DNS servers

    70-640 TS Objective 1.3: Configure zone transfers and replication

91. Custom application partitions in DNS are created to provide name resolution across domains. The application directory is created from the command line. What information is needed to create the custom application directory with the `dnscmd` command?

    A. Domain one name and domain two name

    B. DNSServer name and its IP address

    C. `dnsservername` and `partitionfqdn`

    D. The name of the partition

    70-640 TS Objective 1.3: Configure zone transfers and replication

92. To create an application directory you need to be a member of which group?

    A. Domain administrator

    B. Local administrator

    C. Enterprise administrator

    D. DNS administrator

    70-640 TS Objective 1.3: Configure zone transfers and replication

93. After deciding to use a Custom Application Directory Partition, you need to perform three tasks. Which of the following is NOT one of them?

    A. Enlist DNS servers into the partition

    B. Assign the zone for replication scopes

    C. Create the partition

    D. Make sure all DCs are running the DNS Service role

    70-640 TS Objective 1.3: Configure zone transfers and replication

94. To enlist a DNS server into a Custom Application Directory partition, you can use the following `dnscmd` command.

    A. `enlistdirectory`

    B. `enlistdirectoryfqdn`

    C. `enlistdirectorypartition`

    D. `partitionfqdn`

    70-640 TS Objective 1.3: Configure zone transfers and replication

3

95. When managing different aspects of DNS servers, the most powerful command-line tool is dnscmd. Which of the following dnscmd switches would initiate a scavenging operation?

A. /config

B. /clearcache

C. /scaverg

D. /startscavarging

70-640 TS Objective 1.2: Configure DNS server settings

96. You want to create a backup of your DNS server's setting from the command line. Which of the following commands do you use?

A. dnscmd / backup

B. dnscmd /statistics

C. dnscmd /exportsettings

D. export /dnssetting

70-640 TS Objective 1.2: Configure DNS server settings

97. From time to time you will need to clear the DNS cache in your DNS server. Which of the following command-line switches, when used with dnscmd, will clear the cache?

A. /dnsclr

B. /cacheclear

C. /clear

D. /clearcache

70-640 TS Objective 1.2: Configure DNS server settings

98. Which of the following command-line tools is NOT generally used for DNS server administration or maintenance?

A. nslookup

B. ipconfig

C. dnscmd

D. dnslint

70-640 TS Objective 1.2: Configure DNS server settings

99. Match the description of purpose with its correct command-line tool.

A. Manages aspects of DNS

B. Diagnoses name resolution issues

C. IP configuration information

D. Performs query testing

dnscmd	
dnslint	
nslookup	
ipconfig	

70-640 TS Objective 1.2: Configure DNS server settings

100. The DNS Manager is used to perform initial configuration of a new server. Where is this tool located?
   A. Admin Tools
   B. Server Manager
   C. Windows Add Components
   D. Administrative Tools program group on the Server Manager
   70-640 TS Objective 1.2: Configure DNS server settings

101. The switch /flushdns is used with which of the following command-line tools?
   A. dnscmd
   B. cmd
   C. nslookup
   D. ipconfig
   70-640 TS Objective 1.2: Configure DNS server settings

102. The switch /config is used as an option in which of the following command-line tools?
   A. nslookup
   B. ipconfig
   C. dnscmd
   D. dnslint
   70-640 TS Objective 1.2: Configure DNS server settings

103. dnslint is used to diagnose DNS name resolution issues. To use dnslint to request domain name resolution tests, you would use which of the following commands?
   A. dnslint /test
   B. dnslint /fqdn
   C. dnslint /d
   D. dnslint /nametest
   70-640 TS Objective 1.2: Configure DNS server settings

104. The command-line tool ipconfig has some optional switches that are used for IPv6. Which of the following switches renews a dynamic IPv6 address from DHCP?
   A. ipconfig /renewv6
   B. ipconfig /renewIPv6
   C. ipconfig /renew6
   D. ipconfig /new
   70-640 TS Objective 1.2: Configure DNS server settings

3

105. The command-line tool ipconfig has some optional switches that are used for IPv6. Which of the following switches releases an IPv6 address from a DHCP client?

A. ipconfig/release

B. ipconfig/releasev6

C. ipconfig/release6

D. ipconfig/releaseip6

70-640 TS Objective 1.2: Configure DNS server settings

106. dnslint is used to diagnose DNS name resolution issues. To use dnslint to request domain name resolution tests to verify records specifically related to Active Directory, you would use which of the following commands?

A. dnslint/ad

B. dnslint/ql

C. dnslint/d

D. dnslint/list

70-640 TS Objective 1.2: Configure DNS server settings

107. You can use ipconfig to force the registration of a dynamic DNC client with the DNS server. Which of the following commands renews a DDNS registration?

A. ipconfig/ddns

B. ipconfig/register

C. ipconfig/registerddns

D. ipconfig/registerdns

70-640 TS Objective 1.2: Configure DNS server settings

108. Name resolution in Windows can be performed by two main methods. DNS Servers use root hints or forwarders to link them to other servers to perform lookups. By default, which method is enabled in Windows DNS?

A. Both root hints and forwards are enabled

B. Root hints are the default

C. Forwarders

D. Neither is set as default

70-640 TS Objective 1.3: Configure zone transfers and replication

109. When you install a DNS server, it creates two application directory partitions with AD DS in a forest. Which partitions are installed by default?

A. One for the forest and one for the root name

B. One for the forest and one for the domain data

C. One for the domain and one for the site data

D. One for the main domain and one for the child domain

70-640 TS Objective 1.3: Configure zone transfers and replication

110. By default in Windows Server 2008, how does a domain name resolution between two child domains pass?

A. Directly between the child domains

B. Through a custom application directory

C. Through root hints or forwarders

D. Through the forest root domain

70-640 TS Objective 1.3: Configure zone transfers and replication

111. You have 20 computers located in a remote site and you want them to be able to log on without having to resolve the DNS servers over the WAN connection. What configuration options do you have?

A. Have the DCs in the remote location run DHCP

B. Have the DCs in the remote location run the DNS server role

C. You have to install a DNS server at the remote location

D. You need a read-only DC at the remote site

70-640 TS Objective 1.3: Configure zone transfers and replication

112. Network administrator traditionally provides a minimum of how many DNS server options in the DHCP scope setting?

A. 1

B. 2

C. 3

D. 4

70-640 TS Objective 1.2: Configure DNS server settings

113. When comparing IPv4 and IPv6 addresses there are some comparable features that you should be aware of. In the following chart, match the IPv6 address types with the comparable IPv4 addresses.

A. 10.0.0.0, 172.16.0.0, 192.168.0.0

B. APIPA

C. 127.0.0.1

D. Public Addresses

E. 0.0.0.0

Unspecified ::	
Loopback ::1	
Link-local FE80::	
Site-local FEC0::	
Global unicast	

70-640 TS Objective 1.2: Configure DNS server settings

3

114. When configuring a DNS setting, each SOA record requires that certain information be added during initial configuration. Which of the following needs to be added?

A. DNS update intervals

B. Name records updates

C. Date and time settings

D. Contact information of the party responsible for the zone

70-640 TS Objective 1.2: Configure DNS server settings

115. DNS servers can be configured to provide high availability by creating multiple records for the same resource, each with a different IP address. This is called which of the following?

A. Load balancing

B. IP balancing

C. Round robin

D. Hyper-v

70-640 TS Objective 1.2: Configure DNS server settings

116. Non-dynamic DNS servers rely on manually updating name and zone records. These servers are referred to as which of the following?

A. Bind servers

B. Non-Windows DNS servers

C. Legacy DNS

D. UNIX DNS servers

70-640 TS Objective 1.2: Configure DNS server settings

117. Match the correct description of each of the following DNS terms.

A. Resolver contacts a name server to perform a name lookup, and the name server returns a result or an error

B. Provides an IP address to obtain an FQDN

C. Contacts a name server for name lookup

D. Query in which a name server contacts a second name server to perform a name lookup

Term	Description
Name recursion	
Iterative	
Recursive	
Reverse lookup	

70-640 TS Objective 1.2: Configure DNS server settings

118. DNS servers have a built-in mechanism for name resolution call root hints. DNS servers that provide resolution to the Internet can rely on root hints to locate authoritative server for root names. How are these hints updated?

    A. Through clients

    B. Manually by network and server administrators

    C. Through Windows updates

    D. Through security updates

    70-640 TS Objective 1.2: Configure DNS server settings

119. How would you make the decision as to whether to use WINS or GNZ services?

    A. Use GNZs when you need a large number of single-label names resolved

    B. Use GNZs when you have a select list of names

    C. Use GNZs when you have a select list of names and WINS when you have a multitude of names

    D. Use WINS when a small number of single-label names are used

    70-640 TS Objective 1.2: Configure DNS server settings

120. If you need to create and configure a zone for single-label name management in a Windows Server 2008 DNS server, where do you start?

    A. Administrative Tools Program group

    B. Server manager

    C. Server manager > Select Primary Zone

    D. Server manager > Forward Lookup Zone > Primary Zone

    70-640 TS Objective 1.2: Configure DNS server settings

121. Which of the following tasks cannot be performed with the DNS manager tool?

    A. Add and remove forward zones

    B. Add and remove reverse zones

    C. Monitor contents of the server cache

    D. Debug option for trace logging to a text file

    70-640 TS Objective 1.2: Configure DNS server settings

122. The DNS installation and configuration involves various tasks. Put the following list in sequential order to show how your DNS server should be set up.

    A. Create RLZs

    B. Add custom records to FLZ as needed

    C. Set the scavenging configuration

    D. Finalize the FLZs

    E. Add DNS security

    70-640 TS Objective 1.2: Configure DNS server settings

123. Windows Server 2008 supports three zone types. Match the zone type with the correct description.

A. Copy of the authoritative server for a namespace

B. Is authoritative for the namespace it contains

C. Pointer to other authoritative servers for the namespace

Primary zone	
Secondary zone	
Stub zone	

70-640 TS Objective 1.2: Configure DNS server settings

124. Zone types can be stored as text files. In the New Zone wizard, indicate where you would make this primary zone a text file.

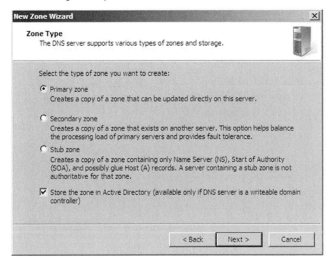

70-640 TS Objective 1.2: Configure DNS server settings

125. What are the names of the two default partitions that host DNS data when DNS is integrated with AD DS?

A. ForestZone and DomainDNS

B. ForestDNSZones and Child DomainDNS

C. ForestDNSZones and DomainZones

D. ForrestDNSZones and DomainDNSZones

70-640 TS Objective 1.2: Configure DNS server settings

126. DNS depends on name records. These records can be created manually or by using Dynamic DNS. Older devices may not support DDNS and instead rely on which of the following technologies to update the DNS name records?

    A. DHCP

    B. Scope

    C. DNS

    D. dnscmd

    70-640 TS Objective 1.2: Configure DNS server settings

127. DNS links all the devices in a Windows Server 2008 network running AD DS. All the network devices are linked to the directory and to the DNS name resolution service. Place the following list in the correct order to describe what happens when you boot a computer that is part of a domain.

    A. DNS identifies the SRV to find the closest DC

    B. The computer authenticates to the DC

    C. The computer boots

    70-640 TS Objective 1.2: Configure DNS server settings

128. DNS is at the very heart of the TCP/IP protocol. Without DNS, using the Internet would not be an enjoyable experience by any means. When DNS communicates with devices on your network or on the Internet, it relies on which TCP/IP port?

    A. 125

    B. 23

    C. 52

    D. 53

    70-640 TS Objective 1.2: Configure DNS server settings

4

CONFIGURING THE ACTIVE DIRECTORY INFRASTRUCTURE

This chapter contains 200 questions that fall under Microsoft's second main exam objective for the 70-640 exam, "Configuring the Active Directory Infrastructure." This main objective consists of the following six sub-objectives:

- Configure a forest or a domain
- Configure trusts
- Configure sites
- Configure Active Directory replication
- Configure the global catalog
- Configure operations masters

Microsoft has given this main exam objective a weight of 25%, which is why I have created 200 (out of a total of 800) test preparation questions for this chapter.

TEST PREPARATION QUESTIONS

1. Active Directory Data Store AD DS stores its data on the Domain Controllers. What is the name of the file?

A. Adds.dit

B. Ntds.adds

C. Ntds.dit

D. Ad.dit

70-640 TS Objective 2.1: Configure a forest or a domain

2. Match the five technologies that provide the identity and access solutions with the Windows components.

Identity	Active Directory Domain Services
Applications	AD Lightweight Directory Services
Trust	AD Certificates Services
Integrity	AD Rights Management
Partnership	AD Federation Services

70-640 TS Objective 2.1: Configure a forest or a domain

3. Which one of the following is NOT a component of an Active Directory Infrastructure?
   A. Data store
   B. Domain
   C. Forest
   D. Tree
   E. Leaf

70-640 TS Objective 2.1: Configure a forest or a domain

4. When you are creating a network topology and are considering the use for sites, which of the following statements correctly defines a site?
   A. A site is a container for objects
   B. A site is a collection of AD domains
   C. A site is an object that represents a portion of the network with good connectivity
   D. A site is the namespace of a forest

70-640 TS Objective 2.1: Configure a forest or a domain

5. The features that are available in an Active Directory domain are determined by the functional level. How many functional levels are available in Windows Server 2008?
   A. 3
   B. 6
   C. 4
   D. 2

70-640 TS Objective 2.1: Configure a forest or a domain

6. Which of the following containers also offers you a scope with which to manage the objects by linking GPOs?
   A. Users
   B. Containers
   C. OUs
   D. Built-in

70-640 TS Objective 2.1: Configure a forest or a domain

7. Which of the following Windows Server 2008 technologies runs the Kerberos Key Distribution Center service?

   A. AD Cs

   B. AD FS

   C. AD LDS

   D. AD DS

   70-640 TS Objective 2.1: Configure a forest or a domain

8. The forest is the collection of all the AD domains. What is the first domain installed in a forest called?

   A. Directory schema

   B. Schema

   C. Root

   D. Forest root domain

   70-640 TS Objective 2.1: Configure a forest or a domain

9. The identity and access solution infrastructure is responsible for protecting confidential information and access to resources on the network. Which of the following represents the security policy and permissions on a particular resource?

   A. TGT

   B. Kerberos

   C. DC

   D. ACL

   70-640 TS Objective 2.1: Configure a forest or a domain

10. Microsoft previously released a number of components that, when combined, produced a complete IDA platform. With the release of Server 2008, Microsoft has combined how many of these previously separate components into an integrated IDA platform?

    A. 4

    B. 5

    C. 6

    D. 7

    70-640 TS Objective 2.1: Configure a forest or a domain

11. When a person or service logs onto an IDA infrastructure in order to validate the identity of the user, the user must provide secrets known only to the user and the system. This process is called which of the following?

    A. Authorization

    B. Authentication

    C. Access

    D. Permissions

    70-640 TS Objective 2.1: Configure a forest or a domain

12. In an AD DS domain, what is the name of the protocol that is used to authenticate identities?

    A. Security

    B. SAM

    C. Kerberos

    D. TGT

    70-640 TS Objective 2.1: Configure a forest or a domain

13. After Kerberos identifies a user or computer, it generates a package of information that is used to identify the authenticated user or computer. Which choice identifies this package?

    A. Windows Security Model

    B. Authenticated User

    C. Ticket Granting Ticket

    D. Authentication

    70-640 TS Objective 2.1: Configure a forest or a domain

14. To provide an adequate level of fault-tolerance in the event that a DC fails, it is recommended that you have how many DCs in each domain in your forest?

    A. 2

    B. 3

    C. 4

    D. 6

    70-640 TS Objective 2.1: Configure a forest or a domain

15. What is the correct command-line entry to add or remove a Domain Controller in Windows Server 2008?

    A. `dcpromotion`

    B. `cdpromo`

    C. `dcpromo.exe`

    D. `promoce.exe`

    70-640 TS Objective 2.1: Configure a forest or a domain

16. If you have a text file that contains a section heading called `[DCINSTALL]`, what is that text file used for?

    A. Unattended install

    B. Unattended installation answer file

    C. DC installation

    D. AD DS installation info file

    70-640 TS Objective 2.1: Configure a forest or a domain

17. When you are using `dcpromo` to install a DC, you can provide options at the command line by using which of the following?

    A. `dcpromo /unattendOption`

    B. `dcpromo /option`

    C. `dcpromo /optionUnattended`

    D. `dcpromo /value`

    70-640 TS Objective 2.1: Configure a forest or a domain

18. An option to installing a DC from the command line is using an answer file to hold the values needed for the installation. The answer file is called to the installation program using which of the following options of the `dcpromo` command?

    A. `/answer file "path"`

    B. `/attended:"path to the file"`

    C. `/unattend:"path to the file"`

    D. `/: "path to the file"`

    70-640 TS Objective 2.1: Configure a forest or a domain

19. When you are preparing to install the first Windows 2008 server in an existing domain, you need to prep the existing DC first. Which of the following will you type at the command prompt?

    A. `ad/forstprep`

    B. `adprep/forest`

    C. `adprep/forestprep`

    D. `adprep/rodcprep`

    70-640 TS Objective 2.1: Configure a forest or a domain

20. Put the following list into the correct order to prepare the forest schema for adding the first Windows 2008 server into an existing Windows 2000 or 2003 forest or domain.

    A. At the command prompt, change directories to the `ADprep` folder

    B. Log on as a member of the Enterprise Admin, Schema Admins, Domain Admins

    C. Enter `adprep/forestprep`

    D. Copy `\Sources\Adprep` to the schema master

    70-640 TS Objective 2.1: Configure a forest or a domain

21. To install a Windows Server 2008 domain into an existing Windows 2000 or 2003 domain you need to prepare the domains for the new DC. After you copy the `adprep` folder from the Windows Server 2008 DVD, what do you do next?

    A. Open a command prompt and enter `adprep`

    B. Open a command prompt and enter `adprep/gprep`

    C. Open a command prompt and enter `adprep/domainprep`

    D. Open a command prompt and enter `adprep/domainprep/gpprep`

    70-640 TS Objective 2.1: Configure a forest or a domain

22. When using the advanced mode option during the installation of a Domain Controller, you have an option that will allow you to install a new DC from replicated data created by existing Domain Controllers. This option is called which of the following?

    A. Source Domain Controller

    B. Source Install

    C. Install from Source

    D. Install from Media

    70-640 TS Objective 2.1: Configure a forest or a domain

23. When you want to create a new child domain from an existing domain, you need to prepare AD before creating the Windows Server 2008 Domain Controller. Which of the following commands will you run before creating the child domain?

    A. adprep

    B. adprep/forestprep

    C. adprep/domainprep

    D. forestprep

    70-640 TS Objective 2.1: Configure a forest or a domain

24. During the creation of an RODC several configuration parameters are specified. Which of the following are not required?

    A. The user who will complete the next phase of installation

    B. Name

    C. Active Directory Site

    D. Domain Admin creates an account

    70-640 TS Objective 2.1: Configure a forest or a domain

25. To create the prestaged account for an RODC, you use Active Directory User and Computer snap-in. Right-click on the DC OU and choose which of the following?

    A. Create Read-Only DC Account

    B. Attach RODC

    C. Create DC

    D. Pre-Create Read-Only Domain Controller Account

    70-640 TS Objective 2.1: Configure a forest or a domain

26. After prestaging the account for the RODC, the RODC will be attached to the account. This is completed from a command prompt that launches a wizard. To attach a server to an RODC account, you type which of the following?

    A. dcpromo/attach

    B. dcpromo/useexistingaccount

    C. dcpromo/useexistingaccount:attach

    D. dcpromo

    70-640 TS Objective 2.1: Configure a forest or a domain

27. When adding DC to an existing forest, all the data from the directory partitions must be replicated to the new DC. To make this more efficient you can use the IFM option. To create the IFM data, you run the ntdsutil.exe command. Which of the following commands are used in the next step in the creation of the IFM media?

    A. activate ntds

    B. activate instance

    C. activate instance ifm

    D. activate instance ntds

    70-640 TS Objective 2.1: Configure a forest or a domain

28. You can create four types of IFM media. Match the correct command with the description of the IFM media that it creates.

    A. IFM without SYSVOL for a writable DC or an AD LS

    B. IFM without SYSVOL for a read-only DC

    C. IFM with SYSVOL for a writable DC

    D. IFM with SYSVOL for an RODC

Command	Description
create sysvol full	
create full	
create sysvol rodc	
create RODC	

    70-640 TS Objective 2.1: Configure a forest or a domain

29. Domain Controllers can be removed by using which of the following?

    A. dcpromo.exe/remove

    B. dcpromo.exe

    C. ntdsutil/remove

    D. You cannot remove a DC form a command prompt

    70-640 TS Objective 2.1: Configure a forest or a domain

30. To remove a Domain Controller from a network while it is not connected to the network, you must use which of the following options?

    A. dcpromo/remove

    B. dcpromo/force

    C. dcpromo/forcefulremoval

    D. dcpromo/forceremoval

    70-640 TS Objective 2.1: Configure a forest or a domain

31. Active Directory DS uses five single master operations; two of these are performed for the entire forest. Select from the following the two roles performed for the entire forest.

    A. RID

    B. Domain naming

    C. Infrastructure

    D. PDC Emulator

    E. Schema

    70-640 TS Objective 2.1: Configure a forest or a domain

32. AD DS contains five operation single master roles; three of these roles are performed in each domain. From the list, select the three roles that are performed in each domain by single master Domain Controllers.

    A. PDC Emulator

    B. Infrastructure

    C. Domain naming

    D. Schema

    E. Relative identifier (RID)

    70-640 TS Objective 2.1: Configure a forest or a domain

33. When you have a multidomain infrastructure, objects may refer to objects in other domains. The multimember attribute contains the distinguished name. If a member is moved or renamed, which of the single master roles is responsible for updating the member attribute?

    A. Domain naming

    B. Schema

    C. RID

    D. Infrastructure

    E. PDC Emulator

    70-640 TS Objective 2.1: Configure a forest or a domain

34. The SID of a security principal must be unique. Because AD DCs create SIDs, which of the single master roles is responsible for ensuring that the SIDs assigned are unique?

    A. Domain naming

    B. Schema

    C. RID

    D. Infrastructure

    E. PDC Emulator

    70-640 TS Objective 2.1: Configure a forest or a domain

35. Timestamps are very important in the AD DS environment. AD, Kerberos, FRS, and DFS=R all rely on timestamps. Which of the single operation roles is responsible for providing a master time source for the domain?

    A. Domain naming

    B. RID

    C. Schema

    D. PDC Emulator

    E. Infrastructure

    70-640 TS Objective 2.1: Configure a forest or a domain

36. To help in planning your role placement you need to know which DCs are performing single master operation roles. Each role requires the use of an AD administrative tool. To identify the PDC Emulator role, which of the following tools would you use?

    A. AD Users and Computers snap-in

    B. AD Domains and Trusts snap-in

    C. AD Schema snap-in

    D. AD FSMO snap-in

    70-640 TS Objective 2.1: Configure a forest or a domain

37. To help in planning your role placement you need to know which DCs are performing single master operation roles. Each role requires the use of an AD administrative tool. To identify the RID master role, which of the following tools would you use?

    A. AD Domains and Trusts snap-in

    B. AD Schema snap-in

    C. AD FSMO snap-in

    D. AD Users and Computers snap-in

    70-640 TS Objective 2.1: Configure a forest or a domain

38. To help in planning your role placement you need to know which DCs are performing single master operation roles. Each role requires the use of an AD administrative tool. To identify the Infrastructure master role, which of the following tools would you use?

    A. AD Domains and Trusts snap-in

    B. AD Schema snap-in

    C. AD Users and Computers snap-in

    D. AD FSMO snap-in

    70-640 TS Objective 2.1: Configure a forest or a domain

39. To help in planning your role placement you need to know which DCs are performing single master operation roles. Each role requires the use of an AD administrative tool. To identify the Domain Naming role, which of the following tools would you use?

    A. AD Users and Computers snap-in

    B. AD Domains and Trusts snap-in

    C. AD Schema snap-in

    D. AD FSMO snap-in

    70-640 TS Objective 2.1: Configure a forest or a domain

40. To help in planning your role placement you need to know which DCs are performing single master operation roles. Each role requires the use of an AD administrative tool. To identify the Schema master role which of the following tools would you use?

    A. AD Users and Computers snap-in

    B. AD Domains and Trusts snap-in

    C. AD Schema snap-in

    D. AD FSMO snap-in

    70-640 TS Objective 2.1: Configure a forest or a domain

41. When providing for downtime of a Domain Controller the role may be transferred to another DC and transferred back to the original DC. When providing for downtime of a Domain Controller, the role may be transferred to another DC and transferred back to the original DC. In which of the following roles can you transfer back? (Choose two.)

    A. PCD emulator

    B. RID

    C. Doman naming

    D. Schema

    E. Infrastructure

    70-640 TS Objective 2.1: Configure a forest or a domain

42. Which of the following domain functional levels is NOT supported by Windows Server 2008?

    A. Windows Server 2008

    B. Windows Server 2000/NT

    C. Windows Server 2000

    D. Windows Server 2003

    70-640 TS Objective 2.1: Configure a forest or a domain

43. If you are adding a Windows Server 2008 server to a domain that has a Windows 2000 and Windows 2003 Domain Controller, which functional level should you choose?

    A. Windows Server 2000

    B. Windows Server 2003

    C. Either Windows Server 2000 or 2003

    D. Windows Server 2008

    70-640 TS Objective 2.1: Configure a forest or a domain

44. Upgrading your functional domain level offers advantages by making available features that are not available with the older server operating systems. Which of the following features are available only with Windows Server 2008 domain functional level?

    A. DC rename

    B. Selective authentication

    C. Authorization manager policies

    D. Fine-gained password policies

    70-640 TS Objective 2.1: Configure a forest or a domain

45. Upgrading your functional domain level offers advantages by making available features that are not available with the older server operating systems. Which of the following features are available only with Windows Server 2008 domain functional level?

    A. DC rename

    B. Selective authentication

    C. Last interactive logon information

    D. Authorization manager policies

    70-640 TS Objective 2.1: Configure a forest or a domain

4

46. Upgrading your functional domain level offers advantages by making available features that are not available with the older server operating systems. Which of the following features are available only with Windows Server 2008 domain functional level?

    A. DC rename

    B. Advanced encryption

    C. Selective authentication

    D. Authorization manager policies

    70-640 TS Objective 2.1: Configure a forest or a domain

47. Upgrading your functional domain level offers advantages by making available features that are not available with the older server operating systems. Which of the following features are available only with Windows Server 2008 domain functional level?

    A. DC rename

    B. Selective authentication

    C. Authorization manager policies

    D. DFS-R

    70-640 TS Objective 2.1: Configure a forest or a domain

48. Windows Server 2008 supports three forest-level functional levels. Which of the following is the default forest functional level in Windows Server 2008?

    A. Windows 2000 Native

    B. Windows Server 2003

    C. Windows Server 2008

    D. There is no default; you select it during `dcpromo`

    70-640 TS Objective 2.1: Configure a forest or a domain

49. Some of the recommendations for how the domain and root structure for AD DS should be designed have changed. Most recent recommendations now suggest which of the following?

    A. Build your forest with a single domain to create a dedicated forest root

    B. Use a dedicated forest root domain

    C. Build a forest with a single domain

    D. There is no general recommendation as far as the root domain

    70-640 TS Objective 2.2: Configure trusts

50. Which of the following should be considered when creating the structure of your domain?

    A. The business units

    B. Business organizational model

    C. Domain characteristics

    D. Departments, divisions, and so on

    70-640 TS Objective 2.2: Configure trusts

51. Domains are defined by certain characteristics. Which of the following is NOT a domain characteristic?

    A. Multiple DNS namespaces

    B. A single domain partition replicated to all DCs

    C. A single Kerberos policy

    D. A single DNS namespace

    70-640 TS Objective 2.2: Configure trusts

52. Password and account lockout polices have been updated with Windows Server 2008. Which one of the following statements is true regarding Windows Server 2008 password policy?

    A. Windows Server 2008 will support more than one password policy in all functional levels

    B. Windows Server 2008 supports fine-grained password policies at the Windows Server 2008 functional level

    C. Windows Server 2008 in functional level Server 2003 will support multiple passwords in a single domain

    D. To support multiple password policies you need to create multiple domains

    70-640 TS Objective 2.2: Configure trusts

53. The addition of a domain to a forest has additional costs associated with it in both hardware and software. Which of the following are increases that should be considered when you are considering adding a domain to a forest?

    ■ More Domain Controllers are needed; two per domain are recommended

    ■ Moving users can be more difficult than moving between OUs

    ■ Cross-domain access of resources may require additional DCs

    ■ Group policy objects need to be duplicated in each domain

    A. All of the choices are correct

    B. One of the choices is correct

    C. Two of the choices are correct

    D. None of the choices is correct

    70-640 TS Objective 2.2: Configure trusts

54. Arrange the following domains into a single-tree forest.

70-640 TS Objective 2.2: Configure trusts

55. You have to arrange the following domains into trees. The domains contain both contiguous and noncontiguous DNS namespace. How would you arrange the following domains?

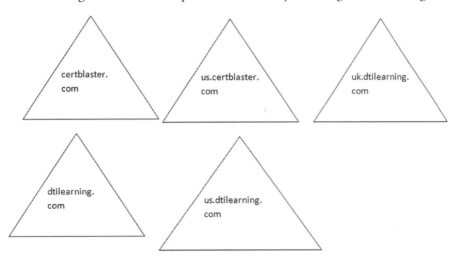

70-640 TS Objective 2.2: Configure trusts

56. Indicate whether these statements indicate inter-forest migration or intra-forest migration.

A. Preserves existing accounts

B. Consolidate domains

C. Same forest

D. Moves objects

E. Nondestructive

F. Separate forest

70-640 TS Objective 2.2: Configure trusts

57. Which of the following describes inter-forest migration and which describes intra-forest migration?

A. Domain restructuring procedure that preserves the existing source domain and copies accounts into a target domain

B. Moving objects from a source domain to a target domain in the same forest

70-640 TS Objective 2.2: Configure trusts

58. The Active Directory Migration tool is used to migrate objects between a source and a target. Which of the following statements are true about the Active Directory Migration tool?

   1. ADMT is used to migrate domains in the same forest

   2. ADMT is used to migrate domain in different forests

   A. Statement 1 is true

   B. Statement 2 is true

   C. Neither statement is true

   D. Both statements are true

   70-640 TS Objective 2.2: Configure trusts

59. The image depicts a security screen used to set permissions. By which of the following acronyms is the security screen referred to?

   A. SID

   B. SD

   C. ACE

   D. DACL

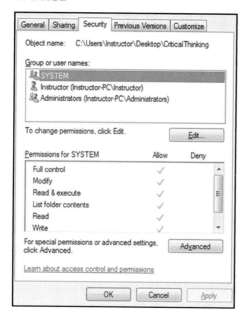

   70-640 TS Objective 2.2: Configure trusts

60. Match the correct term with its description.

A. Describes auditing

B. Domain unique values assigned to accounts of all security principles

C. Link a specific permission with the SID of the security principle

D. Describes resource access permissions

E. Describes the permissions, ownership, rights, and auditing procedure for a resource

F. Compares the SIDs in the user token to the SID in the ACE

Term	Description
SIDs	
SD	
SACL	
DACL	
ACE	
LSASS	

70-640 TS Objective 2.2: Configure trusts

61. After accounts are copied to the target domain during migration, new SIDs are created for the accounts in the target domain. Since the new SIDs are not the same as the SIDs of the source accounts, you have to address this problem. Select the correct solution.

A. Security translation

B. SIDHistory

C. Copy the file, folder, and other permissions to the target destination

D. Use ADMT to translate the SIDs

70-640 TS Objective 2.2: Configure trusts

62. Group membership is a concern during migration of accounts. Inter-forest and intra-forest migrations are handled differently. Match the correct type of migration to the corresponding list.

A. Populate the universal group with SIDHistory

B. Change universal to global after migration to target groups

C. Create universal groups and change them to global after migration

Inter-Forest	Intra-Forest
Migrate global groups	
Migrate users	
Use ADMT to add new accounts	

70-640 TS Objective 2.2: Configure trusts

63. During the migration process of moving objects, including users and computers, from one domain or forest to another, there are a number of concerns and issues. From the following list, select which issues are of greatest concern during the migration process.
    - Password policy migration
    - Built-in groups, domain admin, and local admin groups
    - Service accounts
    A. One of these is a great concern
    B. Two of these are of great concern
    C. All of these are of great concern
    D. None of these is of great concern
    70-640 TS Objective 2.2: Configure trusts

64. Which of the following statements is true concerning trust relationships between domains in a Windows AD DS domain?
    A. One domain authenticates the user's identity
    B. Two domains must authenticate the user's identity to have a trust
    C. Both domains must identify the user's identity to establish a trust
    D. User identities are established by a trusting third party
    70-640 TS Objective 2.2: Configure trusts

65. Under respective pyramid, write the correct label (trusted or trusting) to identify the trusting and trusted domains in this simple trust relationship.

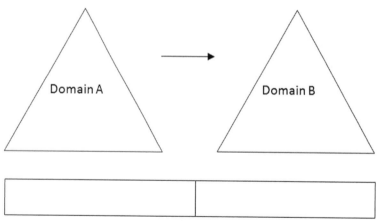

70-640 TS Objective 2.2: Configure trusts

66. The authentication process within a domain uses Kerberos v5. When a user logs on to a computer using Kerberos v5, there several steps involved in the process. Place the following steps in the correct order.

    A. The KDC gives the user a session ticket

    B. The Key Distribution Center (KDC) gives the user a ticket-granting ticket (TGT)

    C. The user requests access to a service

    D. The user presents a Ticket Granting Ticket (TGT) to the KDC

    E. The system forwards the authentication request to the DC

    F. The user logs on

    70-640 TS Objective 2.2: Configure trusts

67. The forest shown in the following diagram consists of two trees, the dtilearing.com tree and the dti.com tree. The root domain of each tree has an automatic two-way transitive trust. Draw an arrow to show the trust relationship between the trees in the forest.

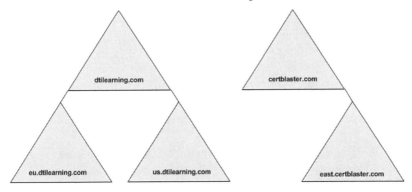

    70-640 TS Objective 2.2: Configure trusts

68. Which of the following types of trusts are NOT created manually?

    A. Shortcut

    B. External

    C. Realm

    D. Tree-root

    E. Forest

    70-640 TS Objective 2.2: Configure trusts

69. How would you start the wizard shown in the following image?

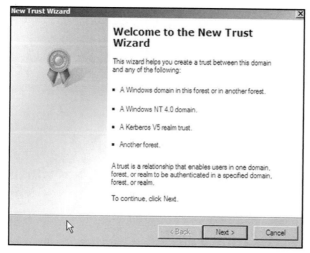

A. Open the AD Users and Groups snap-in > Right-click the domain and select Properties > Click New Trust

B. Open the AD Trusts snap-in > Open the Domains Properties page > Select New Trust wizard

C. Open AD Domains and Trusts > Right-click the domain and click Properties > Click the Trusts tab > Click New Trust

D. Open Domain and Trusts > Click the Action Menu > Select Trust wizard

70-640 TS Objective 2.2: Configure trusts

70. In the following diagram, create a one-way shortcut trust between dti.com and eu.dtilearn-ing.com by drawing the appropriate arrows.

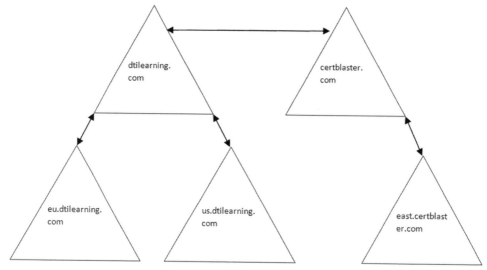

70-640 TS Objective 2.2: Configure trusts

71. What type of trust creates a non-transitive one-way relationship between a domain in your forest and a domain that is not in your Windows domain?

    A. Shortcut trust

    B. External trust

    C. Realm trust

    D. Forest trust

    70-640 TS Objective 2.2: Configure trusts

72. What type of trust will you use when you need to create a cross-platform interoperability with a UNIX realm that uses Kerberos v5?

    A. Shortcut trust

    B. External trust

    C. Realm trust

    D. Forest trust

    70-640 TS Objective 2.2: Configure trusts

73. What type of trust is shown in the following diagram?

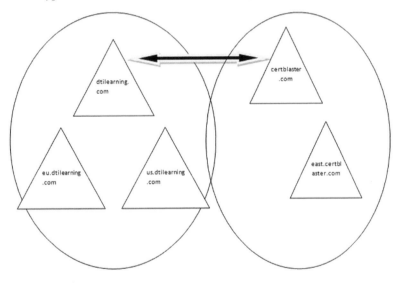

dtilearning.com Forest   certblaster.com Forest

    A. Realm trust

    B. Shortcut trust

    C. Forest trust

    D. External trust

    70-640 TS Objective 2.2: Configure trusts

74. When a user from one domain logs into a workstation on a different domain, the authentication request must traverse the trust path, which can possibly affect performance and authentication times. Also if a DC is not available in the trust path, the workstations will not be able to log in. To prevent this problem, which of the following trusts would you use to create a trust relationship directly between the child domain and the forest trust path?

A. External

B. Shortcut

C. Realm

D. Forest

70-640 TS Objective 2.2: Configure trusts

75. When working with domains that are not in your forest, you may need to create a trust relationship between a domain in your forest and a Windows domain that is not in your forest. Which of the following types of trust will you use?

A. External

B. Shortcut

C. Realm

D. Forest

70-640 TS Objective 2.2: Configure trusts

76. When authentication in a non-Windows Kerberos domain is used to authenticate Windows clients, the Kerberos tickets do not contain all the authorization needed by the Windows domain. To allow non-Windows–based authentication from a Kerberos domain, you would use which of the following trusts?

A. External

B. Shortcut

C. Realm

D. Forest

70-640 TS Objective 2.2: Configure trusts

77. To verify whether a trust relationship between two Windows domains is functioning properly, you can validate its relationship using the following steps. Put the sequence in the correct order.

A. Select Trust

B. Click Validate

C. Click Properties

D. Click Yes

E. Right-click the domain

F. Open AD Domains and Trusts

G. Click Properties

H. Click the Trust tab

70-640 TS Objective 2.2: Configure trusts

78. If you need to remove a trust, you can do it manually. These are the steps to remove a trust manually; put them into the correct order.

A. Click the Trusts tabs

B. Click Yes

C. Enter authorized credentials

D. Right-click the domain

E. Select the trust to be removed

F. Open AD Domains and Trusts

G. Click Remove

70-640 TS Objective 2.2: Configure trusts

79. When you configure a trust relationship between domains, it is necessary to control user access to the resources. Which one of the following statements is true concerning a trust relationship?

A. Trust relationships grant access to all resources

B. It is not possible for users to gain access to resources in your domain after establishing a trust relationship

C. Trust relationships are secured with ACLs

D. Trust relationships grant no access to resources explicitly, but it is possible that creating a trust will result in access to domain resources

70-640 TS Objective 2.2: Configure trusts

80. You are using Selective Authentication for a trust in your domain so that users cannot access resources in the trusting domain except when you give them which of the following permissions?

Using a check mark, indicate the correct permission in the ACL in the following image.

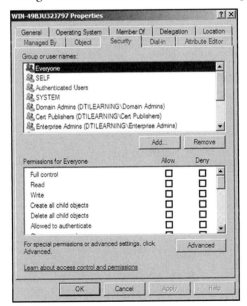

70-640 TS Objective 2.2: Configure trusts

81. Active Directory represents network topology with objects called which of the following?

    A. Users

    B. Computers

    C. OLS

    D. Sites

    70-640 TS Objective 2.3: Configure sites

82. Which of the following statements best describes replication?

    A. Communication between sites

    B. Transferring information between sites

    C. Transferring changes between users

    D. Transferring changes between DCs

    70-640 TS Objective 2.3: Configure sites

83. Active Directory consists of two types of network connections. Which of the following best describes the types of connections?

    A. High and low

    B. Broadband and baseband

    C. Immediate and intermediate

    D. Highly connected and less highly connected

    70-640 TS Objective 2.3: Configure sites

84. The Active Directory site represents which of the following?

    A. Highly connected

    B. Highly notified

    C. Highly and less highly connected

    D. Any network segment

    70-640 TS Objective 2.3: Configure sites

85. When you define a site in AD, the DCs within the site will replicate in which manner? Select the best answer.

    A. As scheduled

    B. Replication within the site is not needed

    C. Almost instantly

    D. Every eight minutes

    70-640 TS Objective 2.3: Configure sites

86. Active Directory is distributed across the network with multiple Domain Controllers providing the same services of authentication and directory access. When you want to encourage certain clients to authenticate their own sites, that is called which of the following? Select the best answer from the list.

A. Service placement

B. Service localization

C. Site planning

D. Replication

70-640 TS Objective 2.3: Configure sites

87. Which of the following statement is true concerning the Active Directory site structure?

A. Active Directory site will map directly to the network sites

B. Active Directory sites are used only to control replication

C. Active Directory sites are used only for service localization

D. Active Directory sites are used to control replication and to enable service locations

70-640 TS Objective 2.3: Configure sites

88. In regard to the design and placement of AD sites, several factors should be considered in your planning. Which of the following factors are important?

- Service placement
- Connection speed
- User population

A. One of the factors is important in determining site requirements

B. Two of the factors are important in determining site requirements

C. All of the factors are important in determining site requirements

D. None of the factors listed is important in determining site requirements

70-640 TS Objective 2.3: Configure sites

89. Concerning sites, when an Active Directory forest is created, which of the following statements is true?

A. Two sites are created, one for the root and one for the first domain

B. One site is created and is named the same as the first domain

C. One site is created and named the same as your DNS name for the root

D. One site is created called Default-First-Site-Name

70-640 TS Objective 2.3: Configure sites

90. Which of the following statements would NOT be a reason to create an additional site?

A. A slow link

B. A large number of users in a remote location

C. Replication is dominating bandwidth

D. Remote users need access to a centrally located data center

70-640 TS Objective 2.3: Configure sites

91. There are two objects created when you define an Active Directory site; what are they?

    A. A site object and an IP address

    B. A link and a subnet

    C. A replication zone and a subnet

    D. A site object and a subnet object

    70-640 TS Objective 2.3: Configure sites

92. Shown is the Active Directory Sites and Services dialog box. Draw a check mark where you would click to create a new site.

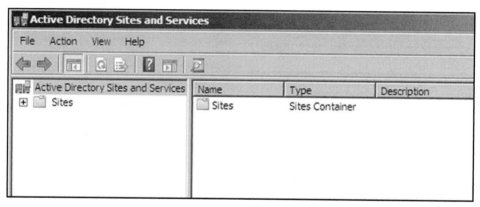

    70-640 TS Objective 2.3: Configure sites

93. What is the following dialog box used for?

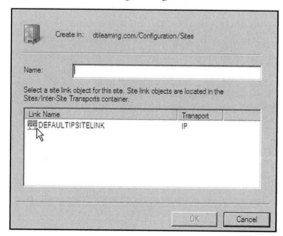

    A. Creating a new subnet

    B. Creating a new site object

    C. Directing traffic

    D. Controlling replication

    70-640 TS Objective 2.3: Configure sites

94. What is the following dialog box used for?

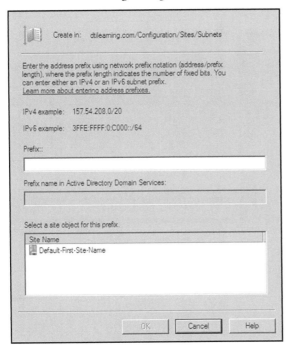

A. This is the Default-First-Name-Site box
B. This is the Rename Site dialog box
C. This is the New DNS Name dialog box
D. This is the New Object-Subnet dialog box
70-640 TS Objective 2.3: Configure sites

95. The site subnet IP addresses are defined as a range of addresses using network prefix notation. Which of the following is the correct way to enter a subnet representing 10.0.6.1 to 10.0.6.254 with a 255.255.255.0 subnet?
A. 10.0.6.1-254/255.255.0.0
B. 10.0.6.0 /255.255.0.0
C. 10.0.6.0 / 24
D. 10.0.6.1 -254 / 16
70-640 TS Objective 2.3: Configure sites

96. After correctly entering the network prefix, the next step in creating the site is selecting the site object. How many sites can a subnet be associated with?
A. 2
B. 4
C. 3
D. 1
70-640 TS Objective 2.3: Configure sites

97. Concerning sites and subnets, what would you use the following dialog box for?

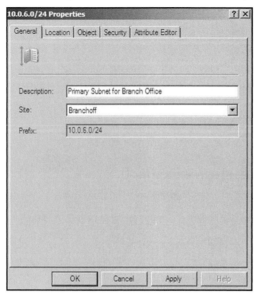

A. To associate a site with a subnet
B. To define a new subnet
C. To define a new site
D. To change the site to which the subnet is linked

70-640 TS Objective 2.3: Configure sites

98. Draw a check mark on the location of the default domain controller that is created with the Active Directory forest.

70-640 TS Objective 2.3: Configure sites

99. Which of the following statements is NOT true?

   A. The Servers container in a site should only contain Domain Controllers

   B. Promoting a server to a DC in a site will automatically place the server into the server container of that site

   C. All servers in a site should be in the Servers container under the site

   D. You can pre-create servers in the server container under the site

   70-640 TS Objective 2.3: Configure sites

100. How do you launch the Move Server dialog box from the Active Directory Sites and Services snap-in?

   A. Right-click Sites and select Move

   B. Right-click Default-First-Name and select Move

   C. Right-click Servers and select Move

   D. Right-click on the Domain Controller and select Move

   70-640 TS Objective 2.3: Configure sites

101. Which one of the following statements is NOT true concerning Domain Controllers and sites in Active Directory?

   A. Place a DC in the site that is associated with the DC's IP address

   B. If a server has more than one network interface it can only be in one site

   C. Client logons in sites with no DC are handled by other DCs in the domain

   D. If a site has no DC, users will not be able to log on

   70-640 TS Objective 2.3: Configure sites

102. Draw a check mark where you would click to remove a Domain Controller from a site.

   70-640 TS Objective 2.3: Configure sites

103. How does a client find the servers available in the site?

   A. The client checks the server's IP address

   B. The client locates the server in DNS by the A records

   C. The client's Hosts file is updated with the server's IP addresses

   D. The DC adds a SRV record to DNS that advertised the services

   70-640 TS Objective 2.3: Configure sites

104. Match the Windows Server 2008 service with the correct port number.

    A. LDAP

    B. Kerberos

    C. Kerberos Password protocol

    D. GC Services

Port	Service Name
389	
88	
464	
3268	

    70-640 TS Objective 2.3: Configure sites

105. How does a Windows client connect and authenticate to the domain for the first time? Place the steps in the correct order.

    A. Client authenticates with the first DC that responds

    B. DNS lists all DCs in the site

    C. Client queries for DCs in site-specific _tcp folder

    D. Client attempts contact with all DCs

    E. Client stores the site name

    F. First DC to respond checks IP address for site affiliation

    G. DNS returns all matching DCs in the domain

    H. Client queries the _tcp folder for SRV records

    I. Client receives an IP address from DHCP

    70-640 TS Objective 2.3: Configure sites

106. It is possible that a site may not have a Domain Controller. This would be a situation where the site was set up for service localization. This site is authenticated by a nearby Domain Controller in a process referred to as which of the following?

    A. Site distribution

    B. Site coverage

    C. Direct authentication

    D. Automatic coverage

    70-640 TS Objective 2.3: Configure sites

107. There are three major naming contexts that hold objects in the directory database. Match the correct name to its description in this list.

Naming Conventions	Definition
A. Domain	NC contains all the objects stored in a domain and GPCs
B. Configuration	Objects that represent the logical structure of the forest, includes sites, subnets, and services
C. Schema	Defines the object classes and their attributes for the directory

70-640 TS Objective 2.3: Configure sites

108. Which of the following is true about every Domain Controller within a domain?

A. Each Domain Controller has a copy of the domain NC

B. Each Domain Controller has a copy of the domain NC and the configuration

C. Each Domain Controller has a copy of the domain NC and the schema

D. Each Domain Controller has a copy of the domain NC, the configuration, and the schema

70-640 TS Objective 2.3: Configure sites

109. In which version of Windows Server did the RODCs become available?

A. Windows Server 2000

B. Windows Server 2003

C. Windows Server NT

D. Windows Server 2008

70-640 TS Objective 2.3: Configure sites

110. Generally RODCs have complete replicas containing every attribute in the Domain NC, configuration, and schema. There is one attribute that's not replicated to RODC. Which attribute is generally not replicated to an RODC?

A. GPCs

B. Sites

C. Subnets

D. Passwords

70-640 TS Objective 2.3: Configure sites

111. The Global Catalog or GC is a partition that stores information about objects in the forest. Which of the following statements best describes what the GC represents?

A. The GC provides a complete copy of every attribute of every object in the forest

B. The GC maintains a complete copy of one of the domains in the forest

C. The GC contains a subset of attributes optimized for searching across domains

D. The GC contains a set of attributes used for searching within its own domain

70-640 TS Objective 2.3: Configure sites

112. Another term used to describe the Global Catalog or GC is which of the following?

    A. GPC

    B. NC

    C. PAS

    D. NTDS

    70-640 TS Objective 2.3: Configure sites

113. It has been cited that you should configure a GC on a Domain Controller whenever you have applications that perform directory queries. These applications use which port number?

    A. 3268

    B. 326

    C. 368

    D. 268

    70-640 TS Objective 2.3: Configure sites

114. How is the first global catalog server in a new forest created?

    A. The first GC is created by running dcpromo.exe

    B. The first GC is created by clicking on the Servers object

    C. The first GC is created with the Active Directory Domain Services Installation Wizard

    D. The first GC is created when you create the first domain in the forest

    70-640 TS Objective 2.3: Configure sites

115. You need to configure the Global Catalog setting in the Default First site. Draw a check mark where you would right-click in AD Sites and Services.

    70-640 TS Objective 2.3: Configure sites

116. How do you remove the Global Catalog role from a Domain Controller?

    A. Right-click the Server container and select Properties, then uncheck the GC box

    B. Click on the server and select Action > Remove

    C. Right-click on the Server under the Server container and uncheck the GC box

    D. Right-click the NTDS Setting node and select Properties. In the General tab, remove the check in GC

    70-640 TS Objective 2.3: Configure sites

117. You have a Domain Controller that you would like to promote to a Global Catalog server. After you open Active Directory Sites and Services, which of the following steps would you take?

A. Right-click the NTDS Setting node and select Properties; in the General tab select the check in Global Catalog

B. Right-click the server node and select properties; on the Connections tab select Global Catalog

C. Right-click on the Site and select Properties; then check the Global Catalog box

D. Click on the Server node and then go to Action > Select Global Catalog

70-640 TS Objective 2.3: Configure sites

118. Universal groups include users and groups from multiple domains in a forest. Universal group membership is replicated in the GC. If you don't have a GC in a site, a member of a universal group may be unable to log in. This can be fixed by enabling universal group membership caching. How do you enable universal group membership caching?

A. Open Active Directory Sites and Services, select the site, right-click, select Properties, and enable UGMC

B. Open Active Directory Sites and Services, expand the node, select the server, right-click it to open the properties, and enable UGMC

C. Open Active Directory Sites and Services, select the site, in the Details pane select Servers, right-click, and enable UGMC

D. Open Active Directory Sites and Services, select the site, in the Details pane right-click the NTDS Site setting, choose Properties, and check Enable UGMC

70-640 TS Objective 2.3: Configure sites

119. If you don't have a GC server in a site and you have enabled Universal Group Membership Caching on the DC, how often will the DC update universal group membership information from the designated GC server?

A. Every 24 hours

B. Every 8 hours

C. With each AD replication

D. With every client log on

70-640 TS Objective 2.3: Configure sites

120. This is the Properties dialog box where Universal Group Membership Caching is enabled. How do you open this dialog box?

   A. Open Active Directory Sites and Services, select the site, right-click, and select Properties

   B. Open Active Directory Sites and Services, expand the node, select the server, and right-click it to open the properties

   C. Open Active Directory Sites and Services, select the site, in the Details pane select Servers, and right-click

   D. Open Active Directory Sites and Services, select the site, in the Details pane right-click the NTDS Site Setting, and choose Properties

   70-640 TS Objective 2.3: Configure sites

121. Fill in the correct AD partitions from the list to make this a complete and true statement concerning replication.

   The _____ partitions of the directory are replicated to all DCs in a domain and the _____ are replicated to all DCs in the forest.

   A. Domain

   B. Configuration

   C. Schema

   70-640 TS Objective 2.3: Configure sites

122. Which of the following AD partitions are NOT by default replicated to all DCs?

   A. Domain

   B. Application

   C. Configuration

   D. Schema

   70-640 TS Objective 2.3: Configure sites

123. If you need to examine the application directory partitions in your forest you would use which of the following tools?

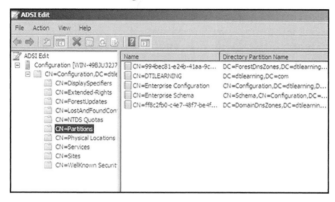

   A. Active Directory Sites and Services

   B. Active Directory Users and Computers

   C. Active Directory Domains and Trusts

   D. Active Directory Services interface

   70-640 TS Objective 2.3: Configure sites

124. Active Directory application directories are created automatically by most of the applications that require them. Application directories can also be created manually by using which one of the following command-line tools?

   A. Netdom.exe

   B. Ntdsutil.exe

   C. Ldp.exe

   D. Ntds.exe

   70-640 TS Objective 2.3: Configure sites

125. You can expose application directory partitions with ADSI edit. Which of the following tools can you use to manage application directory partitions directly?

   A. Dcpromo

   B. Ntdsutil.exe and Ldp.exe

   C. Regsvr32.exe

   D. CSVDE.exe and Ldp.exe

   70-640 TS Objective 2.3: Configure sites

126. If you want to view the application directory partition in your forest, you can use the ADSI Edit. Which of the following are the correct steps you take to view the application directory partitions?

    A. Open ADSI Edit, and in the Select a Well Known Naming Context, choose CN

    B. Open ADSI Edit, Connect To, select Configuration, and select the CN folder

    C. Open ADSI Edit, Connect To, Configuration, Expand Configuration

    D. Open ADSI Edit, Connect To, Configuration, Expand Configuration, select the CN=Partitions

    70-640 TS Objective 2.3: Configure sites

127. In the ADSI Edit window, draw a check mark at the point you would click to select the next step in viewing the forest application directory partitions.

    70-640 TS Objective 2.3: Configure sites

128. Installing an RODC is completed in several steps. Put the following list in the correct order to install an RODC.

    A. One writable DC must be a Windows 2008 server

    B. Install the RODC

    C. Set the forest functional level to Windows Server 2003 or higher

    D. Run adprep/rodcprep on any DCs running Windows Server 2003

    70-640 TS Objective 2.4: Configure Active Directory replication

129. In the absence of a DC in a remote or branch office, authentication and service ticket activities are directed to a centralized hub site, possibly over a WAN link. Which of the following activities will generate activity over the WAN link to the hub site?

    A. Authentication

    B. Service tickets

    C. Connecting to a file and print service

    D. All of the above

    70-640 TS Objective 2.4: Configure Active Directory replication

130. Which of the following are NOT considered risks to placing a DC in a remote office?

 A. Security

 B. Administration

 C. AD integrity

 D. Unreliable performance

 70-640 TS Objective 2.4: Configure Active Directory replication

131. Which of the following is a true statement concerning RODCs?

 A. Replication is from the RODC only to the hub site DC

 B. RODC cannot replicate to any DCs

 C. Replication is one-way from an RODC to a selected DC

 D. Replication is one-way from a writable Domain Controller to an RODC

 70-640 TS Objective 2.4: Configure Active Directory replication

132. When upgrading an existing forest to include DCs that are running Windows Server 2008, you must configure permissions that allow RODCs to replicate DNS application directory partitions. How is this configuration accomplished?

 A. Open a command prompt and run `adprep`

 B. Open a command prompt and open the \sources\adprep folder

 C. Run `adprep/rodcprep`

 D. Open a command prompt and run `rodcprep`

 70-640 TS Objective 2.4: Configure Active Directory replication

133. You are preparing an existing forest to include a Windows Server 2008 to install an RODC. You'll need to run `adprep`. Where would you look for `adprep`?

 A. Service Manager

 B. Adprep folder

 C. On the Windows Server 2008 cdrom\sources\adprep

 D. On the Windows Server 2008 \Sources\Adprop

 70-640 TS Objective 2.4: Configure Active Directory replication

134. You are installing an RODC in a new branch office that your company is preparing to open. Select from the following list all true statements concerning the new RODC installation (choose four).

 A. The RODC must replicate with a writable Windows Server 2008 DC

 B. The Windows Server 2008 that the RODC replicates can be in any site

 C. The RODC will perform DNS functions only if the Windows Server 2008 that it replicates acts as a DNS server

 D. RODC cannot perform DNS functions

 E. RODC can only run on Windows Server 2008

 F. RODC can run on a core installation of Windows Server 2008

 70-640 TS Objective 2.4: Configure Active Directory replication

135. If an RODC is caching users' credentials, authenticating users, and processing service tickets, it must use which of the following?

A. Password allowed list

B. Two-way replication

C. Local Administrator account

D. Password replication policy

70-640 TS Objective 2.4: Configure Active Directory replication

136. The Password Replication Policy of an RODC is controlled by two attributes of the RODC computer account. What are these attributes known as?

A. RODC User and Computer groups

B. RODC cached users and computer groups

C. Password Replication Policy Allowed List and Password Replication Policy Denied List

D. Allowed RODC Password Replication Group and Denied RODC Password Replication Group

70-640 TS Objective 2.4: Configure Active Directory replication

137. To help in the administration of Password Replication Policy on an RODC there are two reports that assist in the administration of user and computer accounts on the RODC. Select the two reports from the list.

A. Password Replication Policy statics

B. RODC passwords that have been authenticated to the site hub

C. Accounts whose passwords are stored on the RODC

D. Accounts that have been authenticated to this RODC

E. RODC accounts that have been authenticated to the site hub

70-640 TS Objective 2.4: Configure Active Directory replication

138. It is possible to prepopulate credentials in the RODC. By adding a user to the allow list on the RODC, you allow the credentials to be cached until the authentication is replicated from a writable DC. This happens when the user logs in for the first time. Use prepopulated credentials to ensure that users and computers are processed locally by the RODC even when they are authenticating for the first time. Where do you prepopulate credentials?

A. Prepopulated credentials are set up in the writable DC in Users and Computers

B. Prepopulated credentials are set up by manually authenticating the user or computer account when you add them to the allowed list

C. Password Replication Policy tab

D. Password Replication Policy, Advanced tab

70-640 TS Objective 2.4: Configure Active Directory replication

139. With each functional level Windows Server adds new capabilities of Active Directory. At which Windows functional level can you use DFS-R to replicate SYSVOL?

    A. Windows 2000 Native

    B. Windows Server 2003 Native

    C. Windows 2008 or Windows 2003

    D. Windows 2008

    70-640 TS Objective 2.4: Configure Active Directory replication

140. SYSVOL replication by default uses File Replication Service (FRS), but you have an option to convert replication to DFS-R, or Distributed File System Replication. There are four stages of DFS-R migration; place the four stages in the correct order from start to eliminate.

    A. SYSVOL is copied to SYSVOL_DFSR

    B. FRS is used to replicate SYSVOL

    C. SYSVOL folder replication is stopped

    D. SYSVOL\sysvol share is changed to SYSVOL_DFSR\sysvol

    70-640 TS Objective 2.4: Configure Active Directory replication

141. To move a Domain Controller through the four stages of migration from SYSVOL-FRS to SYSVOL-DFS-R you use a command-line tool. Which tool is used to migrate FRS to DFS-R?

    A. Dfsrmeg.exe

    B. Dfsrmig.exe

    C. DFSadmin.exe

    D. DFSRadmin.exe

    70-640 TS Objective 2.4: Configure Active Directory replication

142. To understand Active Directory Replication you should understand some basic terms that describe replication in the domain. Match the term with its meaning.

    A. Accuracy

    B. Consistency

    C. Keeping traffic levels reasonable

Term	Meaning
Integrity	
Convergence	
Performance	

    70-640 TS Objective 2.4: Configure Active Directory replication

143. Concerning Active Directory replication, a Domain Controller replicates changes from another Domain Controller because of which of the following?

    A. Topology

    B. Objects

    C. Connector Objects

    D. Replication

    70-640 TS Objective 2.4: Configure Active Directory replication

144. Connection objects in Active Directory are one-way and they represent inbound-only replication. Which of the following is true concerning connector objects?

    A. Replication in AD is always push technology

    B. Replication in AD is usually push technology

    C. Replication in AD is always pull technology

    D. Replication in AD is push-pull technology

    70-640 TS Objective 2.4: Configure Active Directory replication

145. Replication paths between Domain Controllers in Active Directory create a replication topology through their connection objects. Which of the following statements is true about replication topology?

    A. You have to create the replication topology manually

    B. Automatic topology created by Active Directory will not be very efficient

    C. If one Domain Controller fails, replication will stop

    D. You do not have to create the replication topology manually

    70-640 TS Objective 2.4: Configure Active Directory replication

146. Replication paths between Domain Controllers in Active Directory create a replication topology through their connection objects. Which of the following statements is true about replication topology?

    A. If one DC fails in the topology, the replication will stop

    B. You have to create replication topology manually

    C. Replication topology is two-way so replication continues if a Domain Controller fails

    D. Automatic topology created by Active Directory will not be efficient

    70-640 TS Objective 2.4: Configure Active Directory replication

147. Replication paths between Domain Controllers in Active Directory create a replication topology through their connection objects. Which of the following statements is true concerning replication topology?

    A. You have to create replication topology manually

    B. Automatically created topology will not be very efficient

    C. Topology between connection objects is one-way

    D. Active Directory creates a topology that has no more than three hops between any two DCs

    70-640 TS Objective 2.4: Configure Active Directory replication

148. On each Active Directory Domain Controller, a component helps to optimize replication between Domain Controllers. What is the component called?

    A. Replication Checker

    B. Consistency Checker

    C. Knowledge Checker

    D. Knowledge Consistency Checker

    70-640 TS Objective 2.4: Configure Active Directory replication

149. The Knowledge Consistency Checker, or KCC, helps to generate and optimize replication automatically between Domain Controllers. What happens if a Domain Controller becomes unresponsive? Select the best answer.

    A. The KCC will submit an alert notifying the administrator

    B. The KCC will rearrange the topology, adding or deleting connector objects as needed

    C. The KCC will rearrange the topology temporarily without deleting or adding any connector objects

    D. The KCC will wait until the Domain Controller comes back online

    70-640 TS Objective 2.4: Configure Active Directory replication

150. Which of the following is true concerning the creation of manual connection objects?

    A. Manual connections objects are common and used all the time

    B. Manual connection objects created with the Active Directory Sites and Service snap-in

    C. Manual connections are typically used for Operations masters

    D. Manual connections are created with the AD Schema snap-in

    70-640 TS Objective 2.4: Configure Active Directory replication

151. Intra-site replication is the replication of changes within a single site. Once a change to a partition is made, it is replicated to its partners. Notification is the process that notifies partners that changes are available. What are these notification delays called?

    A. Initial and partial notification delays

    B. Partial and subsequent notification delays

    C. Initial and primary notification delays

    D. Initial and subsequent notification delays

    70-640 TS Objective 2.4: Configure Active Directory replication

152. Intra-site replication is the replication of changes within a single site. Once a change to a partition is made it is replicated to its partners. Notification is the process that notifies partners that changes are available. How long does the upstream partner wait until it notifies the next replication partner that a change is available?

    A. One sec

    B. Three sec

    C. One min

    D. Eight min

    70-640 TS Objective 2.4: Configure Active Directory replication

4

153. Notification is the process of informing downstream partners that changes are available. Once the downstream partner requests the changes from the upstream partner, which of the following agents takes over the transfer?

    A. Transfer agent

    B. Directory transfer agent

    C. Directory agent

    D. Directory replication agent

    70-640 TS Objective 2.4: Configure Active Directory replication

154. What is the rate of change between replication partners in a site?

    A. Eight sec

    B. One min

    C. Fifteen sec

    D. Three hops

    70-640 TS Objective 2.4: Configure Active Directory replication

155. Active Directory replication topology will ensure that there are no more than three hops between all Domain Controllers in a site. If each partner waits the standard rate of change between each change, how long will it take before all changes are fully replicated within the site?

    A. One min

    B. Two min

    C. Thirty sec

    D. Five min

    70-640 TS Objective 2.4: Configure Active Directory replication

156. To avoid the possibility that a downstream replication partner doesn't receive notification of a change because the upstream partner is off-line, the downstream partner will perform which of the following processes?

    A. Posting

    B. Polling

    C. Frequent checking

    D. Frequency checking

    70-640 TS Objective 2.4: Configure Active Directory replication

157. To avoid the possibility that a downstream replication partner doesn't receive notification of a change because the upstream partner is off-line, the downstream partner will poll the upstream partner. The default interval for polling a partner for intra-site partners is which of the following?

    A. Once per hour

    B. Every 30 min

    C. Once every eight hours

    D. Daily

    70-640 TS Objective 2.4: Configure Active Directory replication

158. In the event that an upstream partner fails to respond to repeated polling requests, it may be that the Domain Controller is off-line. In this situation the downstream partner will perform which of the following actions?

A. Notify the network owner

B. Send an alert by email to the net admin

C. Launch the KCC

D. Launch the AD Sites and Services tool

70-640 TS Objective 2.4: Configure Active Directory replication

159. The KCC builds intra-site replication topology that connects the site. Between sites you create site links to represent the network paths for replication. Which of the following builds the connections between site links?

A. Inter-site topology tool

B. IT tool

C. ITP

D. ISTG

70-640 TS Objective 2.4: Configure Active Directory replication

160. The KCC builds connection objects between Domain Controllers within sites to enable replication. The ISTG builds connections between servers to enable replication between sites. What are these connections referred to as?

A. Site objects

B. Intra-site objects

C. Site link objects

D. Replication links

70-640 TS Objective 2.4: Configure Active Directory replication

161. When you create a forest, one site link is created. What is the site link called that is created?

A. FORESTLINK

B. FORESTSITELINK

C. DEFAULTLINK

D. DEFAULTIPSITELINK

70-640 TS Objective 2.4: Configure Active Directory replication

162. Which of the following correctly describes how the replication between sites occurs?

A. A site link tells Active Directory that it can replicated between those sites and the ISTG will create the connection objects to set the replication path

B. A site link is determined by the ISTG and the connection object it added to make replication more efficient

C. The ISTG sets the site links and the replication path by default

D. The DEFAULTIPSITELINK sets the replication path and the ISTG determines the schedule of replication between sites

70-640 TS Objective 2.4: Configure Active Directory replication

163. Inside the Inter-Site Transport container what is the container called that contains the site links?

    A. UDP

    B. TCP

    C. IP

    D. SL

    70-640 TS Objective 2.4: Configure Active Directory replication

164. Changes between sites are replicated with one of two available protocols. Which of the following is the most commonly used protocol for intra-site replication?

    A. Directory Service Procedure Call

    B. Directory Procedure Call

    C. Directory Service Remote Procedure Call

    D. Inter-Site Messaging: SMTP

    70-640 TS Objective 2.4: Configure Active Directory replication

165. Which of the following inter-site replication protocols requires using a certificate authority?

    A. Directory Service Procedure Call

    B. Directory Procedure Call

    C. Directory Service Remote Procedure Call

    D. Inter-Site Messaging: SMTP

    70-640 TS Objective 2.4: Configure Active Directory replication

166. Which replication protocol will require that both sites be in different domains because the protocol does not support domain name context?

    A. Inter-Site Messaging

    B. Directory Service Remote Procedure Call

    C. User Datagram Protocol

    D. Internet Protocol

    70-640 TS Objective 2.4: Configure Active Directory replication

167. When ISTG creates a replication topology between sites, it selects one Domain Controller to be responsible for all replication into and out of the site for a partition. What is this server called?

    A. Bulkhead server

    B. Bridging server

    C. Bridgehead server

    D. Push-pull server

    70-640 TS Objective 2.4: Configure Active Directory replication

168. When replication occurs between two sites changes made to the domain partition within the site will be replicated to which server in the site?

A. Bulkhead server

B. Bridging server

C. Bridgehead server

D. Push-pull server

70-640 TS Objective 2.4: Configure Active Directory replication

4

169. The bridgehead server is the server responsible for replicating changes to partitions from one site to another site. How are bridgehead servers selected?

A. Automatically by the ISTG

B. Automatically by the KCC

C. Manually

D. Both automatically and manually

E. The bridgehead server is selected automatically by the ISTG

70-640 TS Objective 2.4: Configure Active Directory replication

170. A bridgehead server that is manually selected is referred to as which of the following?

A. Manual bridgehead server

B. Designated bridgehead server

C. Typical bridgehead server

D. Preferred bridgehead server

70-640 TS Objective 2.4: Configure Active Directory replication

171. If you have three sites, Atlantic, Pacific, and Headquarters, and Atlantic and Headquarters sites are linked and Pacific and Headquarters are linked, then the link between Atlantic and Pacific would be referred to as being which of the following?

A. Transitive

B. Intransitive

C. Cotransitive

D. Spoke and hub

70-640 TS Objective 2.4: Configure Active Directory replication

172. Site link transitivity can be disabled by going to the inter-site transport container and clicking on the IP folder properties and doing which of the following?

A. Deleting the folder

B. Deleting the connector object

C. Deselecting Bridge All Site Links

D. Selecting Do Not Bridge All Site Links

70-640 TS Objective 2.4: Configure Active Directory replication

173. Site link bridges are used to create transitive links between sites. Site link bridges are needed in which one of the following situations?

    A. When you connect bridgehead servers

    B. When you configure inter-site replication

    C. With ISTG

    D. When you disable link transitivity

    70-640 TS Objective 2.4: Configure Active Directory replication

174. Site link costs are used to manage replication. When there is more than one path for replication how the link cost is configured will determine the flow of replication traffic. Which of the following is true concerning costs?

    A. High costs are for fast links

    B. Lower costs are used to indicate slower links

    C. All links are configured by default at a cost of 0

    D. Higher cost are used for slow links

    70-640 Objective 2.4: Configure Active Directory replication

175. Site link costs are used to manage replication. When there is more than one path for replication how the link cost is configured will determine the flow of replication traffic. Which of the following is true concerning costs?

    A. Low costs are used for slow links

    B. Links are configured with a cost of 0 by default

    C. High costs are used for fast links

    D. Lower costs used for fast links

    70-640 TS Objective 2.4: Configure Active Directory replication

176. Site link costs are used to manage replication. When there is more than one path for replication how the link cost is configured will determine the flow of replication traffic. Which of the following is true concerning costs assigned to site links?

    A. High costs are for fast links

    B. Lower costs are used to indicate slower links

    C. All links are configured by default at a cost of 100

    D. Higher costs are used for slow links

    70-640 TS Objective 2.4: Configure Active Directory replication

177. Inter-site replication is based solely on polling with no notifications so the bridgehead server will poll its upstream replication partner to find out whether changes are available. What is the default polling interval?

    A. 1 hour

    B. 2 hours

    C. 3 hours

    D. 4 hours

    70-640 TS Objective 2.4: Configure Active Directory replication

178. Inter-site replication is based solely on polling with no notifications so the bridgehead server will poll its upstream replication partner to find out whether changes are available. What is the minimum polling interval that can be configured for the bridgehead server?

    A. 1 min

    B. 8 min

    C. 15 min

    D. 20 min

    70-640 TS Objective 2.4: Configure Active Directory replication

179. You can restrict inter-site replication to specific times by setting the schedule attribute of a site link. By default how does replication occur?

    A. Once a day

    B. 12 times a day

    C. 24 hours a day

    D. Twice a day

    70-640 TS Objective 2.4: Configure Active Directory replication

180. Windows provides two tools for monitoring replication. Match the correct tool with its description.

    A. Performs tests and reports on replication and security of AD DS

    B. Reports the status of replication on a DC

Tool	Description
Repadmin.exe	
Dcdiag.exe	

    70-640 TS Objective 2.4: Configure Active Directory replication

181. The Directory Service Diagnosis tool includes many reports that are related to replication. Match the correct name to the report description in the list.

    A. IDs errors in the knowledge consistency checker

    B. Reports on operation errors in the file replication system

    C. Checks for timely replication between DCs

    D. Checks for failures that would prevent or delay inter-site replication

Inter-site	
KCCEvent	
Replications	
FrsEvent	

    70-640 TS Objective 2.4: Configure Active Directory replication

4

182. There are two operations master roles that must be unique in the forest. Select two roles from the list that must be performed by only one Domain Controller in the entire forest.

    A. Domain Naming master role

    B. RID master role

    C. Infrastructure master role

    D. PDC Emulator role

    E. Schema master role

    70-640 TS Objective 2.6: Configure operations masters

183. When a Group Policy object is modified by two DCs at the same time, conflicts between versions can cause problems with replication. This situation is avoided by using one domain mast operation server. Which master role manages GOP updates within a domain?

    A. Infrastructure master

    B. Schema master

    C. PDC Emulator

    D. RID master

    70-640 TS Objective 2.6: Configure operations masters

184. Applications, tools, and clients written to support Windows NT4.0 request a writable Domain Controller. Which of the following master roles support Windows NT4.0 domain applications?

    A. Infrastructure master

    B. Schema master

    C. RID master

    D. PDC Emulator

    70-640 TS Objective 2.6: Configure operations masters

185. In situations where a user's password is changed or reset the Domain Controller that makes the changes replicates the changes first to which of the following master roles?

    A. Infrastructure master

    B. PDC Emulator

    C. Schema master

    D. RID master

    70-640 TS Objective 2.6: Configure operations masters

186. Which of the master roles holds the network browse list that is used to list the workgroups and domains in Networks or My Network Places?

    A. Infrastructure master

    B. PDC Emulator

    C. Schema master

    D. RID master

    70-640 TS Objective 2.6: Configure operations masters

187. When you open a network in a Windows Client computer and then open a domain, which domain wide operations master role holds the list of computers shown in the network's window?

A. PDC Emulator

B. Infrastructure master

C. Domain Naming master

D. RID master

70-640 TS Objective 2.6: Configure operations masters

188. When forest root domains are first created all five operation master roles are performed by the Domain Controller. As Domain Controllers are added, roles are assigned to other Domain Controllers. As a best practice the schema master role should be placed with which other master role?

A. RID master

B. PDC Emulator

C. Infrastructure master

D. Domain Naming master

70-640 TS Objective 2.6: Configure operations masters

189. When forest root domains are first created all five operation master roles are performed by the Domain Controller. As Domain Controllers are added, roles are assigned to other Domain Controllers and you should place the RID master with which of the following master roles?

A. Schema master

B. Domain Naming master

C. Infrastructure master

D. PDC Emulator

70-640 TS Objective 2.6: Configure operations masters

190. When forest root domains are first created all five operation master roles are performed by the Domain Controller. As Domain Controllers are added and roles are assigned to other Domain Controllers, which one of the following roles should NOT be placed on a DC that is a Global Catalog Server?

A. Schema master

B. Domain Naming master

C. Infrastructure master

D. PDC Emulator

70-640 TS Objective 2.6: Configure operations masters

191. When forest root domains are first created all five operation master roles are performed by the Domain Controller. As Domain Controllers are added and roles are assigned, the RID master and PDC emulator can be placed on the same DC as which of the following DCs?

    A. Schema master

    B. Domain Naming master

    C. Infrastructure master

    D. GC

    70-640 TS Objective 2.6: Configure operations masters

192. When you first create the forest root domain with the first Domain Controller, how many operation master roles are performed by the Domain Controller?

    A. Three

    B. Four

    C. Five

    D. None

    70-640 TS Objective 2.6: Configure operations masters

193. It is important to recognize operation master roles that may cause impact on normal network functionality. Failure of which of the following operation master roles will have the most immediate impact on normal operations?

    A. RID master

    B. Infrastructure

    C. Schema

    D. PDC Emulator

    70-640 TS Objective 2.6: Configure operations masters

194. It is important to recognize operation master roles that may cause impact on normal network functionality. Failure of which of the following operation master roles will have impact on names of group membership from other domains?

    A. RID master

    B. Infrastructure

    C. Schema

    D. PDC Emulator

    70-640 TS Objective 2.6: Configure operations masters

195. It is important to recognize operation master roles that may cause impact on normal network functionality. Failure of which of the following operation master roles will prevent Domain Controllers from creating new SIDs?

    A. Domain naming master

    B. Schema master

    C. RID master

    D. Infrastructure master

    70-640 TS Objective 2.6: Configure operations masters

196. It is important to recognize operation master roles that may cause impact on normal network functionality. Failure of which of the following operation master roles will prevent you from creating new users?

A. Domain naming master

B. Schema master

C. RID master

D. Infrastructure master

70-640 TS Objective 2.6: Configure operations masters

197. Which of the following Operation master roles would be least likely to cause a disruption in everyday operations and little disruption to normal network functionality?

A. PDC Emulator

B. Schema master

C. RID master

D. Infrastructure master

70-640 TS Objective 2.6: Configure operations masters

198. Which of the following Operation master roles would be least likely to cause a disruption in everyday operations and little disruption to normal network functionality?

A. RID master

B. Infrastructure master

C. Domain naming master

D. PDC Emulator

70-640 TS Objective 2.6: Configure operations masters

199. When you establish your forest how many roles are performed by the first Domain Controller?

A. Three

B. Five

C. None

D. One

70-640 TS Objective 2.6: Configure operations masters

200. When you add the first domain to a forest how many roles are performed by the first Domain Controller in that domain?

A. Three

B. Two

C. Five

D. None

70-640 TS Objective 2.6: Configure operations masters

5

CONFIGURING ADDITIONAL ACTIVE DIRECTORY SERVER ROLES

This chapter contains 72 questions that all fall under Microsoft's third main exam objective for the 70-640 exam, "Configuring Additional Active Directory Server Roles." This main objective consists of the following four sub-objectives:

- Configure Active Directory Lightweight Directory Service (AD LDS)
- Configure Active Directory Rights Management Service (AD RMS)
- Configure the Read-Only Domain Controller (RODC)
- Configure Active Directory Federation Services (AD FS)

Microsoft has given this exam objective a weight of 9%, which is why I created 72 (out of a total of 800) test preparation questions for this chapter.

TEST PREPARATION QUESTIONS

1. Active Directory Lightweight Directory Services differs from Microsoft SQL Server data-base in some important ways. AD LDS is an LDAP directory and SQL is a relational data-base. List the following statements under the heading that defines which type of database they describe.

Fast read and search	Non-schema	Schema structure
Fast writes	Centrally located data	Structured
Decentralized	Hierarchical	

LDAP Directory	Relational Database

70-640 TS Objective 3.1: Configure Active Directory Lightweight Directory Service (AD LDS)

2. Which of the following statements is true about Active Directory Lightweight Directory Services?

A. AD LDS is based on Microsoft SQL Server

B. AD LDS is a total copy of all the files and features of Active Directory

C. AD LDS is an application

D. When you install AD LDS it completely reconfigures the operating system

70-640 TS Objective 3.1: Configure Active Directory Lightweight Directory Service (AD LDS)

3. Which of the following statements is true about Active Directory Lightweight Directory Services?

A. AD LDS is based on the same code as AD but is much easier to work with

B. When you install AD LDS it completely reconfigures the operating system

C. AD LDS is based on Microsoft SQL Server

D. AS LDS is a master role

70-640 TS Objective 3.1: Configure Active Directory Lightweight Directory Service (AD LDS)

4. Which of the following statements is true about Active Directory Lightweight Directory Services?

A. AD LDS is based on LDAP

B. AD LDS is a total copy of all the files and features of Active Directory

C. AD LDS is a server role

D. When you install AD LDS it completely reconfigures the operating system

70-640 TS Objective 3.1: Configure Active Directory Lightweight Directory Service (AD LDS)

5. Which of the following is true of AD LDS?

A. It supports Group policy

B. It includes a Global Catalog

C. It uses public key infrastructures

D. Directory partitions use X.500 naming conventions

70-640 TS Objective 3.1: Configure Active Directory Lightweight Directory Service (AD LDS)

6. Which of the following is true of AD LDS?

A. It supports trusts

B. It supports SRV records

C. It supports MAPI

D. It runs on Windows Vista

70-640 TS Objective 3.1: Configure Active Directory Lightweight Directory Service (AD LDS)

7. Which of the following statements is NOT a feature of AD LDS?

A. It uses multimaster replication for data consistency

B. It supports schema extensions

C. It can install replicas from removable media

D. It can use security principles to access Windows server network

70-640 TS Objective 3.1: Configure Active Directory Lightweight Directory Service (AD LDS)

8. You have installed AD LDS on your Windows Server 2008 member server. What is the folder that holds the AD LDS files named?

    A. %Systemroot%\ALDS

    B. %Systemroot%\LDS

    C. %Systemroot%\ADAM

    D. ADAMNTD

    70-640 TS Objective 3.1: Configure Active Directory Lightweight Directory Service (AD LDS)

9. What is the AD LDS directory store called?

    A. Adamn.dit

    B. Adamntd

    C. Adamntds.idf

    D. Adamntds.dit

    70-640 TS Objective 3.1: Configure Active Directory Lightweight Directory Service (AD LDS)

10. Which one of the following statements is true concerning AD LDS installations?

    A. On a server core installation of AD LDS, the same files and folders are installed as in a full installation of Windows Server 2008

    B. On an AD LDS installation the full Server 2008 install has fewer files than the core installation

    C. The installation of AD LDS on a server core has fewer files than an installation on a full installation of Windows Server 2008

    D. The core installation has the additional tool called AD Schema Analyzer

    70-640 TS Objective 3.1: Configure Active Directory Lightweight Directory Service (AD LDS)

11. List the following tools next to their correct descriptions.

    AD LDS Setup   AC Schema snap-in

    AD Sites and Services   ADSI Edit

Tool	Description
	Modify schema for AD LDS instances
	Configure and manage replication scopes
	Create AD LDS instances
	Manage AD LDS content

70-640 TS Objective 3.1: Configure Active Directory Lightweight Directory Service (AD LDS)

12. List the following tools next to their correct uses.

CSVE   DSAMain

DSACLS   DSDBUtil

Tool	Use
	Import data into AD LDS
	Control access control lists on AD LDS objects
	Mount AD Store backups
	Perform db maintenance

70-640 TS Objective 3.1: Configure Active Directory Lightweight Directory Service (AD LDS)

13. List the following tools next to their correct uses.

Dcdiag   LDIFDE

DSMgmt   LDP

Tool	Use
	Diagnose AD LDS instances
	Support application partition and policy management
	Import data into AD LDS instances
	Modify content and AD LDS instances through LDAP

70-640 TS Objective 3.1: Configure Active Directory Lightweight Directory Service (AD LDS)

14. AD LDS is installed by first installing the binaries and then the instances to use the service. The instance creation has several steps. Place the following steps into the correct order.

A. Create a data drive for the server

B. Name the instance

C. Define the ports to use

70-640 TS Objective 3.1: Configure Active Directory Lightweight Directory Service (AD LDS)

15. Both AD LDS and AD DS use the same ports. What is the default LDAP port?

A. 3269

B. 636

C. 389

D. 3389

70-640 TS Objective 3.1: Configure Active Directory Lightweight Directory Service (AD LDS)

16. Which of the following is the default LDAP Secure Sockets Layer port?

A. 389

B. 3268

C. 3269

D. 636

70-640 TS Objective 3.1: Configure Active Directory Lightweight Directory Service (AD LDS)

17. What are the AD DS ports for communication with the Global Catalog?

A. 3268 and 3269

B. 3326 and 3327

C. 636 and 639

D. 389 and 636

70-640 TS Objective 3.1: Configure Active Directory Lightweight Directory Service (AD LDS)

18. What is the secure communication port that AD DS uses for secure LDAP to access Global Catalog?

A. 389

B. 639

C. 3326

D. 3269

70-640 TS Objective 3.1: Configure Active Directory Lightweight Directory Service (AD LDS)

19. As a best practice, what is the best port to use for the first instance of AD LDS?

A. 500

B. 5,000

C. 5,001

D. 50,000

70-640 TS Objective 3.1: Configure Active Directory Lightweight Directory Service (AD LDS)

20. When the AD LDS Setup wizard detects that ports 389 and 636 are already in use, what range of ports will it suggest?

A. 500

B. 5,000

C. 5,001

D. 50,000+

70-640 TS Objective 3.1: Configure Active Directory Lightweight Directory Service (AD LDS)

21. Application partitions for AD LDS can be created in three ways. Which of the following is NOT one of the ways?

A. When you install the application

B. With dcpromo

C. When you create the instance

D. Using LDP.exe

70-640 TS Objective 3.1: Configure Active Directory Lightweight Directory Service (AD LDS)

22. A service account is used to run the instance you create. Which of the following are password policies that should NOT be employed for this service account?

A. Set the password to never expire

B. Assign a complex password

C. Do not allow users to change passwords

D. Name the account different than the instance

70-640 TS Objective 3.1: Configure Active Directory Lightweight Directory Service (AD LDS)

23. A service account is usually created to run the instance. Which of the following service account guidelines should NOT be followed for a service account on a domain?

A. Use a complex password

B. Create a local account

C. Name the account the same as the instance

D. Set the password to never expire

70-640 TS Objective 3.1: Configure Active Directory Lightweight Directory Service (AD LDS)

24. List and reorder the default AD LDS LDIF files to match their purposes.

MS-ADAM-Upgrade-1   MS-adamschemaw2k8

MS-asamschemaw2ke   MS-AdamSynMetadata

Filename	Purpose
	Upgrade the AD LDS schema
	Prerequisite for synchronizing an instance with AD 2k3
	Prerequisite for synchronizing an instance with AD 2k8
	Prerequisite for synchronizing data with AD DS forest and AD LDS

70-640 TS Objective 3.1: Configure Active Directory Lightweight Directory Service (AD LDS)

25. List and reorder the default AD LDS LDIF files to match their purposes.

MS-AZMan   MS-User

MS-InetOrgPerson   MS-UserProxy

Filename	Purpose
	Required to support Windows Authorization Manage
	Required to create inetOrgPerson
	Required to create user classes and attributes
	Required to create a simple userProxy class

70-640 TS Objective 3.1: Configure Active Directory Lightweight Directory Service (AD LDS)

26. List and reorder the default AD LDS LDIF files to match their purposes.

MS-ADLDS-DisplaySpecifiers   MS-UserProxy   MS-UserProxyHull

Filename	Purpose
	Required for the AD Sites and Services operation
	Required to create a full userProxy class
	Required to create a simple userProxy class

70-640 TS Objective 3.1: Configure Active Directory Lightweight Directory Service (AD LDS)

27. You can create unattended AD LDS instance creations. Which of the following commands would you use to create an unattended instance creation on a server core installation?

A. dcpromo

B. adpromo

C. adamInstall

D. adsmsetup

70-640 TS Objective 3.1: Configure Active Directory Lightweight Directory Service (AD LDS)

28. You can create unattended AD LDS instance creations. Which of the following commands would you use to create an unattended instance creation on a full installation?

A. dcpromo.exe

B. adamInstall.exe

C. adpromo.exe

D. adsmsetup.exe

70-640 TS Objective 3.1: Configure Active Directory Lightweight Directory Service (AD LDS)

29. Which one of the following statements is NOT true concerning answer files used for AD LDS instance creation?

A. Passwords are displayed in clear text

B. Passwords are included with the file

C. Passwords are communicated in cipher text

D. Passwords are removed as soon as the file is used

70-640 TS Objective 3.1: Configure Active Directory Lightweight Directory Service (AD LDS)

30. After typing the answer file for the AD LDS creation, you should save the file in which of the following locations?

A. %systemroot%\ "Name of instance"

B. %systemroot%\ LDS folder

C. %systemroot%\ ADAM folder

D. DriveRoot\ ADAM folder

70-640 TS Objective 3.1: Configure Active Directory Lightweight Directory Service (AD LDS)

31. When you are ready to create your AD LDS instance, you need which rights to run the AdamInstall?

    A. Local administrator

    B. Domain administrator

    C. Enterprise administrator

    D. Schema administrator

    70-640 TS Objective 3.1: Configure Active Directory Lightweight Directory Service (AD LDS)

32. To create your AD LDS instance with the answer file, you type which of the following commands?

    A. `ADLDSinstall /answer:`*`filename.txt`*

    B. `Adinstall / answer:`*`filename.txt`*

    C. `Adaminstall / answerfile:`*`filename.txt`*

    D. `Adaminstall /answer:`*`filename.txt`*

    70-640 TS Objective 3.1: Configure Active Directory Lightweight Directory Service (AD LDS)

33. LDAP directories can be migrated to AD LDS by using which of the following commands?

    A. `LDP`

    B. `LDIFDE`

    C. `LDAP`

    D. `LDIF`

    70-640 TS Objective 3.1: Configure Active Directory Lightweight Directory Service (AD LDS)

34. To import data into AD LDS, you will need which of the following rights to perform the migration?

    A. Local administrator rights

    B. Domain administrator rights

    C. Schema rights and local rights

    D. Local administrative rights and administrative rights to the instance

    70-640 TS Objective 3.1: Configure Active Directory Lightweight Directory Service (AD LDS)

35. While exporting legacy instances, passwords can be imported. Which of the following switches will encrypt all passwords?

    A. `-p`

    B. `-r`

    C. `-h`

    D. `Sasl`

    70-640 TS Objective 3.1: Configure Active Directory Lightweight Directory Service (AD LDS)

36. While exporting legacy instances, passwords can be imported and encrypted. Which of the following encryption types is used?

A. MD5

B. SASL

C. SSL

D. MS-CHAP

70-640 TS Objective 3.1: Configure Active Directory Lightweight Directory Service (AD LDS)

37. AD LDS instance creation creates log files in the %systemroot%\Debug folder. What are these log files called?

A. ADAMSetup.log

B. ADAMSetup_loader.log

C. ADAMError.log

D. ADAMSetup.log and ADAMSetup_loader.log

70-640 TS Objective 3.1: Configure Active Directory Lightweight Directory Service (AD LDS)

38. Active Directory Right Management Services was formerly known as which of the following?

A. Digital Rights Management

B. Rights Management Services

C. Key Management Server

D. Management Rights

70-640 TS Objective 3.2: Configure Active Directory Rights Management Service (AD RMS)

39. The implementation of AD RMS may be done in stages. Take the following three statements and place them in the correct order that an organization may take to implement AD RMS.

A. Distributing materials outside of the network perimeter

B. Implementing access rights for documents produced in-house

C. Content sharing with partners

70-640 TS Objective 3.2: Configure Active Directory Rights Management Service (AD RMS)

40. AD RMS consists of several components that perform specific functions. List and reorder the correct function to match the component responsible for that function.

AD DS Forest   SQL Servers   AD RMS Clients

AD RMS Root Cluster   IIS Servers

Function	Component
	Authentication
	Certification and licensing
	Configuration and logging
	Hosts AD RMS URL
	Consumption of AD RMS

70-640 TS Objective 3.2: Configure Active Directory Rights Management Service (AD RMS)

41. On the first install of an AD RMS server you create an AD RMS root cluster that handles certification and licensing requests. How many root clusters can exist in an AD DS forest?

    A. 1

    B. 2

    C. 3

    D. ∞

    70-640 TS Objective 3.2: Configure Active Directory Rights Management Service (AD RMS)

42. After the AD RMS infrastructure is in place you can enable word processors, presentations, email, and other applications to use AD RMS for protection. As documents are created, what happens to the user rights?

    A. They are added to the document

    B. They are embedded directly into the document

    C. They are packaged with the document in an email

    D. They are available only if the document stays within the network

    70-640 TS Objective 3.2: Configure Active Directory Rights Management Service (AD RMS)

43. A new feature of AD RMS is that the AD RMS servers are self-enrolled when they are created, unlike former versions, which required access to the Microsoft Enrollment Center. What does this allow that earlier version of Windows Rights Management did not?

    A. Server Licensor Certificates

    B. Microsoft Live Sign-in

    C. Internet access not needed

    D. Vista clients

    70-640 TS Objective 3.2: Configure Active Directory Rights Management Service (AD RMS)

44. What are the processor and RAM requirements for the AD RMS installation system?

    A. One Pentium, 3.4 GHz, 512MB

    B. One Pentium, 4.3 GHz, 512MB

    C. Two Pentium, 3.4 GHz, 512MB

    D. Two Pentium, 4.3 GHz, 1024MB

    70-640 TS Objective 3.2: Configure Active Directory Rights Management Service (AD RMS)

45. What are the recommended hardware requirements for the AD RMS installation system?

    A. One Pentium, 3.4 GHz, 512MB

    B. One Pentium, 4.3 GHz, 512MB

    C. Two Pentium, 3.4 GHz, 512MB

    D. Two Pentium, 4.3 GHz, 1024MB

    70-640 TS Objective 3.2: Configure Active Directory Rights Management Service (AD RMS)

46. What are the recommended hardware requirements for hard disk space for the AD RMS installation system?

    A. 20GB

    B. 40GB

    C. 80GB

    D. 10GB

    70-640 TS Objective 3.2: Configure Active Directory Rights Management Service (AD RMS)

47. What are the minimum hardware requirements for hard disk space for the AD RMS installation system?

    A. 20GB

    B. 40GB

    C. 80GB

    D. 10GB

    70-640 TS Objective 3.2: Configure Active Directory Rights Management Service (AD RMS)

48. If a DC is not placed in a remote or branch office, authentication and service ticket activities are directed to a centralized hub site over a WAN link. Which of the following activities will generate activity over the WAN link to the hub site?

    A. Authentication

    B. Service tickets

    C. Connecting to a file and print service

    D. All of the above

    70-640 Objective 3.3: Configure the Read-Only Domain Controller (RODC)

49. Which of the following are NOT considered reasons for placing an RODC in a remote office?

    A. Security

    B. Administration

    C. AD integrity

    D. Unreliable performance

    70-640 Objective 3.2: Configure Active Directory Rights Management Service (AD RMS)

50. Installing an RODC is completed in several steps. Put the following list in the correct order to install an RODC.

    A. Ensure that one writable DC is a Windows 2008 server

    B. Install the RODC

    C. Run `adprep/rodcprep` on any DCs running Windows Server 2003

    D. Set the Forest Functional Level to Windows Server 2003 or higher

    70-640 Objective 3.2: Configure Active Directory Rights Management Service (AD RMS)

51. Which of the following is a true statement concerning RODCs?

    A. Replication is from the RODC only to the hub site DC

    B. RODC cannot replicate to any DCs

    C. Replication is one-way from an RODC to a selected DC

    D. Replication is one-way from a writable domain controller to an RODC

    70-640 Objective 3.3: Configure the Read-Only Domain Controller (RODC)

52. RODCs cache user credentials, authenticate users, and process service tickets to save WAN bandwidth and increase user response time. Therefore, RODCs must use which of the following?

    A. Password allowed list

    B. Two-way replication

    C. Local administrator account

    D. Password replication policy

    70-640 Objective 3.3: Configure the Read-Only Domain Controller (RODC)

53. The Read-Only Domain Controller (RODC) password replication policy is controlled by which of the following two attributes of the RODC computer account?

    A. RODC User and Computer groups

    B. RODC cached users and computer groups

    C. Password Replication Policy Allowed List and Password Replication Policy Denied List

    D. Allowed RODC Password Replication Group and Denied RODC Password Replication Group

    70-640 Objective 3.3: Configure the Read-Only Domain Controller (RODC)

54. The purpose of a firewall is to keep unwanted traffic out of a perimeter network. Traditional perimeter networks will have how many layers of protection?

    A. 1

    B. 2

    C. 3

    D. 0

    70-640 TS Objective 3.4: Configure Active Directory Federation Services (AD FS)

55. The purpose of a firewall is to keep unwanted traffic out. The external firewall will use one key set of ports. List and reorder the ports to match them with the service.

    443   25   80   53

Port	Service
	DNS traffic
	HTTP
	HTTP and SSL
	SMTP

    70-640 TS Objective 3.4: Configure Active Directory Federation Services (AD FS)

56. Which choice best describes Active Directory Federation Services?

    A. Forest trusts

    B. Intransitive Forest trusts

    C. Extends trust with LDAP TCP ports

    D. Extends Forest trusts with HTTP ports

    70-640 TS Objective 3.4: Configure Active Directory Federation Services (AD FS)

57. AD FS is an AD technology that extends a service similar to the Forest trust through common HTTP ports. Which port does AD FS use?

    A. HTTP and port 80

    B. LDAP TCP/IP

    C. HTTP port 443

    D. IP Port 3389

    70-640 TS Objective 3.4: Configure Active Directory Federation Services (AD FS)

58. AD FS can be employed to implement partnerships with other organizations. What are the requirements for connecting to an organization with AD FS?

    A. The other organization must rely on AD DS directories

    B. The other organization needs only to have a Windows domain

    C. The other organization needs to have AD DS with AD FS deployed

    D. The other organization needs to support Windows clients

    70-640 TS Objective 3.4: Configure Active Directory Federation Services (AD FS)

59. One of the key features of using AD FS is how it authenticates a client. Which of the following does AD FS use when authenticating clients?

    A. It manages an internal and external authentication store

    B. Each organization manages its own authentication store

    C. It uses the original authentication the client performed in its own network

    D. It uses ADDS for authentication of users

    70-640 TS Objective 3.4: Configure Active Directory Federation Services (AD FS)

60. Organizations that use AD FS to form business-to-business partnerships fall into two groups. Match the groups with their descriptions by writing the group next to the correct category.

    Resource organizations   Account organizations

	Companies that have external websites and want to simplify authentication to resources
	Companies that enter into AD FS partnerships for resource organizations that manage the accounts

    70-640 TS Objective 3.4: Configure Active Directory Federation Services (AD FS)

61. AD FS supports three designs that depend on the type of business partnership you need to establish. Match the three designs with their correct descriptions.

A. Federated Web SSO with Forest trust

B. Web SSO

C. Federated Web SSO

	Links applications within an extranet to the internal directory stores of account organization
	Uses two AD DS forests
	All users for an extranet application are external without AD DS accounts

70-640 TS Objective 3.4: Configure Active Directory Federation Services (AD FS)

62. AD FS uses several components to support the AD FS process. Claims are statements each partner makes about its users. Claims can be obtained in all of the following ways except one; select the one that's NOT an ADFS claim.

A. The FS server queries the internal directory store for claims

B. The account organization provides the claims to the resource federation server

C. Users create claims when they access the resource

D. The federation service queries the AD DS for the claims

70-640 TS Objective 3.4: Configure Active Directory Federation Services (AD FS)

63. AD FS uses several components to support the AD FS process. Cookies are used during the web sessions that are authenticated through AD FS. There are three types of cookies used by AD DS. Which of the following is NOT a cookie used by AD FS?

A. Authentication cookies

B. Third-party cookies

C. Account partner cookies

D. Sign-out cookies

70-640 TS Objective 3.4: Configure Active Directory Federation Services (AD FS)

64. AD FS certificates are used to secure communications. List and reorder the correct certificate type to the server role. Some server roles will require more than one type of certificate.

Server authentication and token-signing   Server authentication

Server Role	Certificates(s)
Federation servers	
Federation service proxies	
AD FS web agents	

70-640 TS Objective 3.4: Configure Active Directory Federation Services (AD FS)

65. List the following Account Federation descriptions next to their correct terms.

A. The AF server that is hosted in the account organizations internal network

B. The FSP that is hosted in the account organization's perimeter network

C. The AD DS directory that contains the accounts of the users accessing the applications

Term	Description
Account Federation Server	
AF server proxy	
Account partner	

70-640 TS Objective 3.4: Configure Active Directory Federation Services (AD FS).

66. Match the following Account Federation terms with their correct descriptions.

Term	Description
Federated application	ASP.NET application
Federated user	User granted claims in the account directory
Federation	Two organizations with a federation trust
Federation trust	One-way trust between a resource organization and account organization

70-640 TS Objective 3.4: Configure Active Directory Federation Services (AD FS)

67. List the following Account Federation terms next to their correct descriptions.

Client account discovery web page   Client logon page

Client certificate

Term	Description
	Lists partner organizations and identifies organizations during logon
	AD FS uses two-way authentication between federation server and proxies
	Web page that gives feedback to users

70-640 TS Objective 3.4: Configure Active Directory Federation Services (AD FS)

5

68. List the following Account Federation terms next to their correct descriptions.

Resource account   Resource group
Resource federation server   Resource partner/organization
Resource federation service proxy

Term	Description
	Using Windows Integrated authentication to create resource accounts for each user
	Server that performs claims mappings and issues access security tokens
	Located in the perimeter network of the resource organization
	Located in the resource forest to map incoming claims
	Organization that hosts the federated applications

70-640 TS Objective 3.4: Configure Active Directory Federation Services (AD FS)

69. List the following Account Federation terms next to their correct descriptions.

Security token   Server authentication certificate
Security token service   Server farm

Term	Description
	Digitally signed object with the claim
	AD FS web service that issues tokens
	Enables two-way authentication between federation server and proxies
	Group of federation servers acting together

70-640 TS Objective 3.4: Configure Active Directory Federation Services (AD FS)

70. List the following Account Federation terms next to their correct descriptions.

SOA   Token-signing certificate
SSO   Trust policy

Term	Description
	Standards-based and language-agnostic architectures that rely on web services to support distributed services
	Simplifies access with single logon for users
	Certificate used to sign security tokens from the resource federation server
	How partners, certificates, claims, and account stores are identified

70-640 TS Objective 3.4: Configure Active Directory Federation Services (AD FS)

71. Match the following Account Federation terms with their correct descriptions.

Term	Description
Uniform Resource Identifier	Used by AD FS to identify partners and account stores
Verification certificate	Public key of a token-signing certificate
WS-*	Standards-based Internet service that forms part of an SOA
WS-Security	SOA specification on digitally signing and encrypting SOAP message
WS-Federation	Web server specifications for federation implementation

5

72. What are the hardware requirements for AD FS deployment?
    A. 133 MHz with 512MB RAM
    B. 533 MHz with 512MB RAM
    C. 1 GHz with 512MB RAM
    D. 1 GHz with 1024MB RAM
    70-640 TS Objective 3.4: Configure Active Directory Federation Services (AD FS)

6

CREATING AND MAINTAINING ACTIVE DIRECTORY OBJECTS

This chapter contains 192 questions that all fall under Microsoft's fourth main exam objective for the 70-640 exam, "Creating and Maintaining Active Directory Objects." This main objective consists of the following seven sub-objectives:

- Automate creation of Active Directory accounts
- Maintain Active Directory accounts
- Create and apply Group Policy objects (GPOs)
- Configure GPO templates
- Configure software deployment GPOs
- Configure account policies
- Configure audit policy by using GPOs

TEST PREPARATION QUESTIONS

1. Which of the following methods of creating users would not be the best option when creating a large number of users?

   A. LDIFDE

   B. CSVDE

   C. AD Users and Computers snap-in

   D. Account templates

   70-640 TS Objective 4.1: Automate creation of Active Directory accounts

2. Which of the following is NOT a prepopulated user account template category?

   A. Password

   B. Group membership

   C. Logon hours

   D. Home folder

   70-640 TS Objective 4.1: Automate creation of Active Directory accounts

3. Which of the following is NOT prompted for by the User wizard as part of the user template?

   A. Name

   B. Logon name

   C. Password setting

   D. Group membership

   70-640 TS Objective 4.1: Automate creation of Active Directory accounts

4. Windows Server 2008 supports a collection of command-line tools called DS commands. Match the command with its description.

Command	Description
A. dsadd	1. Performs a query based on parameters
B. dsget	2. Moves an object to a new container
C. dsmod	3. Returns specified attributes of an object
D. dsmove	4. Modifies specified attributes of an object
E. dsrm	5. Creates an object in the directory
F. dsquery	6. Removes an object

   70-640 TS Objective 4.1: Automate creation of Active Directory accounts

5. Which of the following DS commands would you use to create a user object?

   A. dsget

   B. dsadd

   C. dsmod

   D. dsuser

   70-640 TS Objective 4.1: Automate creation of Active Directory accounts

6. How can you find help for parameters for DSADD USER?

   A. Enter DSADD USER/?

   B. Enter /?

   C. Enter DSADD USER/

   D. Enter DSASSUSER/?

   70-640 TS Objective 4.1: Automate creation of Active Directory accounts

7. CSVDE is a command-line tool used to import or export AD objects from a comma-delimited file. Comma-delimited files are also known as which of the following?

   A. Txt file

   B. .cvs file

   C. .csv file

   D. Cdt file

   70-640 TS Objective 4.1: Automate creation of Active Directory accounts

8. CSVDE is a command-line tool used to import or export AD objects from which of the following file types?

    A. Txt file

    B. .csv file

    C. .cvs file

    D. Cdt file

    70-640 TS Objective 4.1: Automate creation of Active Directory accounts

9. CSVDE is a command-line tool used to import or export AD objects. CSVDE uses several different parameters to specify different modes. Match the correct parameter to its corresponding function. The parameters are default, -k, and -i.

Parameter	Function
	Export
	Import
	Ignore errors

    70-640 TS Objective 4.1: Automate creation of Active Directory accounts

10. Which of the following attributes cannot be imported by using the CSVDE command?

    A. Logon name

    B. Last and first name

    C. User object in AD

    D. Password

    70-640 TS Objective 4.1: Automate creation of Active Directory accounts

11. To find out more information about CSVDE, you can use Windows Server 2008 Help and Support or use which of the following parameters?

    A. csvde/Help

    B. csvde/Help?

    C. Csvde/?

    D. Csvde/help and support

    70-640 TS Objective 4.1: Automate creation of Active Directory accounts

12. Ldifde.exe uses a draft Internet standard for file format that can be used to perform batch operations. Which one of the following standards does Ldifde.exe use?

    A. Lightweight Directory Access Protocol Data Exchange Format

    B. Lightweight Directory Access Protocol Data Interchange Format

    C. Lightweight Directory Access Interchange

    D. Lightweight Directory Access Format

    70-640 TS Objective 4.1: Automate creation of Active Directory accounts

13. When importing users with LDIFDE, the file format consists of blocks of lines that comprise an operation. Each operation is separated by a blank line. Each operation begins with which one of the following attributes?

    A. DN

    B. CN

    C. SN

    D. sAMA

    70-640 TS Objective 4.1: Automate creation of Active Directory accounts

14. To find out more information about using LDIFDE, you can use which of the following parameters?

    A. LDIFDE/?

    B. LDIFDE/Help

    C. LDIFDE/Help?

    D. LDIFDE/help and support

    70-640 TS Objective 4.1: Automate creation of Active Directory accounts

15. LDIFDE uses a variety of parameters to specify different modes. Match the correct command parameter to its corresponding use.

Parameter	Use
-j path	Import mode
-i	Filename
-s	Domain controller to bind for query
-v	Verbose mode
-f	Log file location

    70-640 TS Objective 4.1: Automate creation of Active Directory accounts

16. LDIFDE uses a variety of parameters to specify different modes. Match the correct command parameter with its corresponding use.

Parameter	Use
-r Filter	Root of the LDAP search
-p	LDAP search filter
-o list	Search scope
-d RootDN	Comma-separated list of attributes
-l list	Comma-separated list of attributes

    70-640 TS Objective 4.1: Automate creation of Active Directory accounts

17. Windows PowerShell is a new feature in Windows Server 2008. How do you install PowerShell?

A. It is installed during the standard installation

B. Open Service Manager and choose the Add Features link

C. Use Add/Remove Programs

D. Download it from Microsoft TechNet downloads

70-640 TS Objective 4.1: Automate creation of Active Directory accounts

18. Windows PowerShell is a command-line shell and scripting language that includes over how many command-line tools?

A. 100

B. 110

C. 130

D. 120

70-640 TS Objective 4.1: Automate creation of Active Directory accounts

19. You are about to install Windows PowerShell in your new Windows Server 2008 Domain Controller. Draw a check mark where you would click to add PowerShell.

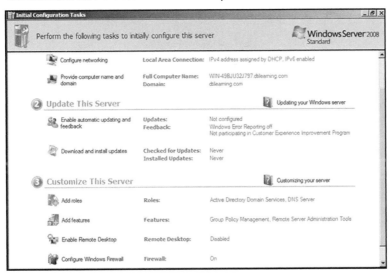

70-640 TS Objective 4.1: Automate creation of Active Directory accounts

20. After installing Windows PowerShell in a Windows Server 2008 computer, how do you access the program?

A. Open the Administrative Tools folder

B. Type CMD

C. Type RUN

D. Choose Start > All Programs

70-640 TS Objective 4.1: Automate creation of Active Directory accounts

21. How can you recognize when you are in a PowerShell console?

A. It looks the same as a CMD.exe

B. You cannot run Cmd.exe commands

C. The background is blue

D. The prompt includes IS

70-640 TS Objective 4.1: Automate creation of Active Directory accounts

22. In PowerShell, you issue directives by using which of the following?

A. Dirs

B. Directives

C. Atletts

D. Cmdlets

70-640 TS Objective 4.1: Automate creation of Active Directory accounts

23. Which PowerShell cmdlet produced the output shown in the image?

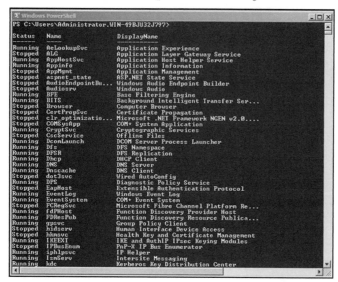

A. Get-Service

B. Get-Status

C. Get-Dir

D. Dir

70-640 TS Objective 4.1: Automate creation of Active Directory accounts

24. When using Windows, PowerShell directives are issued by using cmdlets. These are single-feature commands that have a common syntax. What is the syntax used by cmdlets in PowerShell?

A. Noun-Noun

B. Noun-Verb

C. Verb-Noun

D. Verb

70-640 TS Objective 4.1: Automate creation of Active Directory accounts

25. When getting started with Windows PowerShell, the best place to get help is which of the following cmdlets?

A. GET?

B. Get-Help

C. Get-?

D. Get-service

70-640 TS Objective 4.1: Automate creation of Active Directory accounts

26. What command was piped together with the Get-Service cmdlet to produce the output in the image?

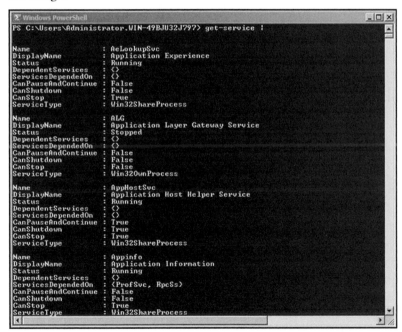

A. Format-List

B. Detail

C. Format

D. List

70-640 TS Objective 4.1: Automate creation of Active Directory accounts

27. The most basic Windows PowerShell script to create a user in Active Directory has four steps. What is the correct order of these four steps?

    A. Commit changes with SetInfo

    B. Invoke create

    C. Connect to the container

    D. Populate attributes with Put

    70-640 TS Objective 4.1: Automate creation of Active Directory accounts

28. Windows PowerShell can be used to import users from a database. Which one of the following file types can be used to import a file with user account information using PowerShell?

    A. Xls

    B. Xlsx

    C. Cvs

    D. Csv

    70-640 TS Objective 4.1: Automate creation of Active Directory accounts

29. VBScript is a language that is used for automating various administrative tasks. VBScript can be created with Notepad and saved with which of the following extensions?

    A. Vbs

    B. Vb

    C. Vsb

    D. Script

    70-640 TS Objective 4.1: Automate creation of Active Directory accounts

30. VBScript is a language that is used for automating various administrative tasks. To execute a script you can double-click on the vbs file and open the script with which of the following? Select the best answer.

    A. Cscript

    B. Wscript.exe

    C. Script.vbs

    D. Vbs.exe

    70-640 TS Objective 4.1: Automate creation of Active Directory accounts

31. The User Properties dialog box has various tabs for reading and modifying user attributes. Match the tabs with their uses in the following list.

Account Tab	Logon Names, Passwords, and Account Flags
Profile tab	Name properties, contact information
Member Of tab	Detailed contact information
General tab	Logon script and home folder
Address tab	Group membership

    70-640 TS Objective 4.1: Automate creation of Active Directory accounts

32. What new Windows Server 2008 feature is visible in the following image?

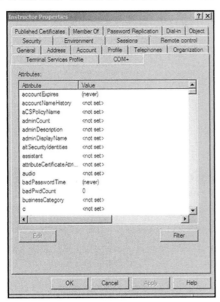

    A. Advanced tab

    B. Advanced Properties

    C. Attribute Editor

    D. Advanced Editor

    70-640 TS Objective 4.1: Automate creation of Active Directory accounts

33. How would you turn on the Attribute Editor in Windows Server 2008?

    A. Click View > Attribute Editor

    B. Click the View menu and select the Advanced Features option

    C. Click Attribute and check the Attribute Editor check box

    D. Click System properties and select the Attributes tab

    70-640 TS Objective 4.1: Automate creation of Active Directory accounts

34. The AD Users and Computers snap-in allows you to manage multiple user objects simultaneously. To manage more than one object, you would do which of the following?

    A. Select the first object, hold down the Ctrl key, and select additional objects

    B. Select the objects and click the Multiple selector

    C. Select one object and press the Windows key to select more objects

    D. Select one object and press the Shift key to select more objects

    70-640 TS Objective 4.1: Automate creation of Active Directory accounts

35. Limited user objects are available for editing when multiple user accounts are being edited at the same time. Which of the following properties are available when you are managing attributes of multiple users?

A. General

B. Remote

C. COM+

D. Account

E. Address

F. Profile

G. Organization

H. Member of

70-640 TS Objective 4.1: Automate creation of Active Directory accounts

36. Which one of the following user object names is the pre-Windows 2000 logon name, which must be unique for the entire domain?

A. userPrincipalName (UPN)

B. relative distinguished name (RDN)

C. displayName

D. sAMAccountName

70-640 TS Objective 4.1: Automate creation of Active Directory accounts

37. Which of the following user object names are the DNS name and the logon name of the user?

A. sAMAccountName

B. userPrincipalName (UPN)

C. relative distinguished name (RDN)

D. displayName

70-640 TS Objective 4.1: Automate creation of Active Directory accounts

38. Which of the following user object names may be equal to the Common Name or CN but must be unique within its OU or container?

A. sAMAccountName

B. userPrincipalName (UPN)

C. relative distinguished name (RDN)

D. displayName

70-640 TS Objective 4.1: Automate creation of Active Directory accounts

39. Which of the user object names appears in the Exchange global address list?

A. sAMAccountName

B. userPrincipalName (UPN)

C. relative distinguished name (RDN)

D. displayName

70-640 TS Objective 4.1: Automate creation of Active Directory accounts

40. If you want to determine which workstation users can log on to, where would you click? Draw a check mark where you would click.

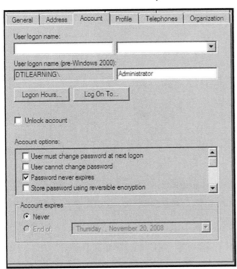

70-640 TS Objective 4.1: Automate creation of Active Directory accounts

41. When a user forgets his or her password and you have to reset it, you should follow best practices to do so. Which check box do you check in the Account Options area of the dialog box shown here to follow best practices?

70-640 TS Objective 4.1: Automate creation of Active Directory accounts

42. Which of the following DS commands do you use to reset a password?

A. dsmod user UserDN

B. dsmod user UserDN -pwd

C. dsmod user UserDN -pwd NewPassword

D. dsmod user UserDN -pwd -mustchpwd

70-640 TS Objective 4.1: Automate creation of Active Directory accounts

43. Which of the following DS commands do you use to reset a password and force the user to change his or her password?

   A. dsmod user UserDN -pwd NewPassword -mustchpwd yes

   B. dsmod user UserDN -pwd

   C. dsmod user UserDN -pwd NewPassword

   D. dsmod user UserDN -pwd -mustchpwd

   70-640 TS Objective 4.1: Automate creation of Active Directory accounts

44. What is an account lockout policy?

   A. When a user is locked out after being terminated

   B. When too many logon failures occur within a specified time limit

   C. When logon time restrictions are enforced

   D. When a user attempts to log on and is already logged on to another workstation

   70-640 TS Objective 4.1: Automate creation of Active Directory accounts

45. How do you unlock an account that has been locked pursuant to a lockout policy?

   A. Right-click the account, select Lockout, and click the check box

   B. Right-click the account, select the Account tab, and select the Password tab

   C. Right-click the account, select the Account tab, and click Reset

   D. Right-click the account, select Properties and then the Account tab, and then uncheck the Unlock Account check box

   70-640 TS Objective 4.1: Automate creation of Active Directory accounts

46. Since user accounts are security principal identities, they should be disabled when they are not being used. The dsmod command to disable an account is which of the following?

   A. dsmod user unserDN -disable

   B. dsmod user unserDN -disabled

   C. dsmod user unserDN -disabled yes

   D. dsmod user unserDN -disable yes

   70-640 TS Objective 4.1: Automate creation of Active Directory accounts

47. Since user accounts are security principal identities, they should be disabled when they are not being used. The dsmod command used to enable an account is which of the following?

   A. dsmod user unserDN -disabled no

   B. dsmod user unserDN -enable

   C. dsmod user unserDN -disabled

   D. dsmod user unserDN -enable no

   70-640 TS Objective 4.1: Automate creation of Active Directory accounts

48. Which of the following is true about deleting a user account?

    A. A user account is removed completely from the directory as soon as it is disabled

    B. A user account is removed from the directory 30 days after it is deleted

    C. A user account is never completely removed from the directory

    D. A user account cannot be re-created by simply creating a new account with the same name

    70-640 TS Objective 4.1: Automate creation of Active Directory accounts

49. Which of the following statements correctly describes what happens when a user's deleted Active Directory account is deprovisioned in stages?

    A. A user account is removed completely from the directory as soon as it is disabled

    B. A subset of the user's account is tombstoned for 60 days

    C. A user account is removed from the directory 30 days after it is deleted

    D. A subset of the user's account always remains in the directory

    70-640 TS Objective 4.1: Automate creation of Active Directory accounts

50. Which of the following is true about user accounts in Active Directory?

    A. User accounts can be reused but they will be assigned a new SID

    B. User accounts can be recycled and can retain the SID and group memberships

    C. User accounts should never be reused

    D. Security policy will not allow user accounts to be reactivated after 60 days

    70-640 TS Objective 4.1: Automate creation of Active Directory accounts

51. To delete a user account with DS, you would use which one of the following commands?

    A. dsmod userDN dsrm

    B. dsmod dsrm userDN

    C. dsrm

    D. dsrm UserDN

    70-640 TS Objective 4.1: Automate creation of Active Directory accounts

52. Which of the following statements is true concerning moving a user account in the Active Directory Users and Computers snap-in?

    A. You can drag it

    B. You can select the account and select Get from the Action menu

    C. You can drag and drop it in the snap-in or right-click the user and select the Move command

    D. You cannot move a user from within the snap-in

    70-640 TS Objective 4.1: Automate creation of Active Directory accounts

53. To move a user account in Active Directory using DS, you would use which of the following syntax examples?

A. `dsmove UserDN -newparent TargetOUDN`

B. `move username targetOUDN`

C. `DNname -newparent TargetOu`

D. `dsmove UserDN`

70-640 TS Objective 4.1: Automate creation of Active Directory accounts

54. To create groups in Active Directory, you right-click the OU and choose New and Group. When naming the new group, there are two properties to configure. Which of the following best describes the use of these two properties?

A. The common name and the domain name

B. The cn name and the NetBIOS name

C. The cn name and the sAMAccountName

D. The group name and the domain name

70-640 TS Objective 4.1: Automate creation of Active Directory account.

55. From the New Object Group dialog box, which types of groups can be selected under Group Type?

A. Domain Local and Security

B. Security and Distribution

C. Security and Global

D. Distribution and Universal

70-640 TS Objective 4.1: Automate creation of Active Directory accounts

56. Which of the following is NOT true about distribution groups?

A. Distribution groups are not security enabled

B. Distribution groups have SIDs

C. Distribution groups are used for email applications

D. They cannot be given permissions

70-640 TS Objective 4.1: Automate creation of Active Directory accounts

57. From the New Object Group dialog box, which types of groups are available to choose from under Group Scope?

A. Security, Domain, and Global

B. Security, Universal, and Local

C. Security, Domain, and Universal

D. Domain Local, Global, and Universal

70-640 TS Objective 4.1: Automate creation of Active Directory accounts

58. Write the objects from the object list under the correct heading to define the members of the Domain Local Group Scope.

Object List
Users
Computers
Global groups
Domain Local groups
Universal groups

Members from the Same Domain	Members from Another Domain and Same Forest	Members from a Trusted External Domain

70-640 TS Objective 4.1: Automate creation of Active Directory accounts

59. Write the objects from the object list under the correct heading to define the members of the Universal Group Scope.

Object List
Users
Computers
Global groups
Domain Local groups
Universal groups

Members from the Same Domain	Members from Another Domain and Same Forest	Members from a Trusted External Domain

70-640 TS Objective 4.1: Automate creation of Active Directory accounts

60. Write the objects from the object list under the correct heading to define the members of the Global Group Scope.

Object List
Users
Computers
Global groups
Domain Local groups
Universal groups

Members from the Same Domain	Members from Another Domain and Same Forest	Members from a Trusted External Domain

70-640 TS Objective 4.1: Automate creation of Active Directory accounts

61. What is this dialog box used for?

A. Adding groups to user accounts

B. Adding or removing a member to/from a group

C. Renaming a group

D. Changing a group's scope

70-640 TS Objective 4.1: Automate creation of Active Directory accounts

62. Using the figure, draw a check mark where you would click to add a computer to a group.

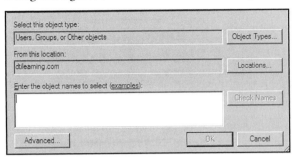

70-640 TS Objective 4.1: Automate creation of Active Directory accounts

63. The process of adding groups to other groups, or creating a hierarchy of groups to support the business model, is called nesting. The best practice for nesting is known by which of the following acronyms?

A. AGDLA

B. AGDULA

C. ADGLA

D. ALDGA

70-640 TS Objective 4.1: Automate creation of Active Directory accounts

64. The dsadd command can be used to create groups in Active Directory. Which of the following is the correct command to add a group?

A. dsadd add group Group

B. dsadd group DN

C. dsadd DN

D. dsadd group GroupDN

70-640 TS Objective 4.1: Automate creation of Active Directory accounts

65. CSVDE can be used to create a group in Active Directory. CSVDE uses data imported from a file. Which of the following file types does CSVDE use to import data?

A. Tab-delimited

B. CVS file

C. Comma-separated

D. Excel

70-640 TS Objective 4.1: Automate creation of Active Directory accounts

66. LDIFDE is a tool that's used to import and export files in Active Directory. LDIFDE can be used to create groups using which of the following file types?

A. LDAP

B. Lightweight Directory Access Protocol Data Interchange Format

C. Lightweight Directory Access Protocol Format

D. Lightweight Directory Access Protocol Data interchange

70-640 TS Objective 4.1: Automate creation of Active Directory accounts

67. When joining a computer with a domain it is recommended that you take which one of the following actions?

A. Create a custom OU to host computer objects

B. Use the Computer container

C. Use the default Computer OU

D. Create a new OU within the default Computer container

70-640 TS Objective 4.1: Automate creation of Active Directory accounts

68. You have been granted the "Create Computer Objects" permission and have right-clicked on the OU and selected Computers from the New menu. Next you enter the name of your computer. What is this process called?

A. Granting Computer Access policy

B. Delegation of Administrative privilege

C. Prestaging the account

D. Joining a domain

70-640 TS Objective 4.1: Automate creation of Active Directory accounts

69. To join a Windows Vista or Server 2008 computer with a domain, you need to click on the Computer Name tab. This is done by using which of the following methods?

A. Right-clicking My Computer and selecting the Computer Name tab

B. Right-clicking Computer and selecting the Computer Name tab

C. Right-clicking Computer, selecting Properties and, in Computer Name, clicking Change Settings

D. Selecting the Advanced Workgroup setting, and then changing Domain Settings

70-640 TS Objective 4.1: Automate creation of Active Directory accounts

70. Best practices dictate that computers be prestaged and not be placed in the default Computer container. To reduce the possibility of computers being joined with the domain before a Computer object is created, Windows can be instructed to redirect computers joined with the domain without prestaged accounts. How is this redirection accomplished?

A. Right-click on the computer container you want to use as the default and select the Use Default check box

B. Select the Computer container and enter the DN of the redirected OU

C. Use regedit.msc

D. Use redircmp.exe

70-640 TS Objective 4.1: Automate creation of Active Directory accounts

71. By default any authenticated user is allowed to create computer objects in the default computer container. Which attribute of the domain permits this?

A. Ms-DS-machineAccountQuota

B. Ms-machineAccountComputerObj

C. Ms-machineAccount

D. Ms-machineAccountCtrl

70-640 TS Objective 4.1: Automate creation of Active Directory accounts

72. By default any authenticated user is allowed to create computer objects in the default computer container. What is the maximum number of computer accounts a user can create by default?

    A. 1

    B. 2

    C. 5

    D. 10

    70-640 TS Objective 4.1: Automate creation of Active Directory accounts

73. Computers can be imported into Active Directory with CSVDE. The comma-separated values data exchange command uses a comma-delimited text file called a .csv file to import computers into AD. When importing computers, you need to include the userAccountControl attribute and set it to which of the following values?

    A. 2048

    B. 4096

    C. 256

    D. 65536

    70-640 TS Objective 4.1: Automate creation of Active Directory accounts

74. Computer objects can be created with dsadd. Which of the following will create a computer object in AD using dsadd?

    A. dsadd add Computer

    B. dsadd Computer DN

    C. dsadd computer ComputerDN

    D. dsadd computerobject Computer DN

    70-640 TS Objective 4.1: Automate creation of Active Directory accounts

75. Creating computer objects with Windows PowerShell involves four steps. What is the correct order of the following steps?

    A. Populate the mandatory attributes

    B. Use the Create method

    C. Connect to the container

    D. Commit changes

    70-640 TS Objective 4.1: Automate creation of Active Directory accounts

76. Creating computer objects with VBScript involves four steps. What is the correct order of the following steps?

    A. Use the Create method

    B. Populate the mandatory attributes

    C. Commit changes

    D. Connect to the container

    70-640 TS Objective 4.1: Automate creation of Active Directory accounts

77. Importing computer objects with LDIFDE used the Lightweight Access Protocol Data Interchange Format. This format uses text files containing operations that are specified by blocks of lines separated by blank lines. Each operation starts with which one of the following?

   A. A letter

   B. DN

   C. CN

   D. ObjectClass

   70-640 TS Objective 4.1: Automate creation of Active Directory accounts

78. The netdom command can perform various functions. To use the netdom command to add a Computer object, you type which one of the following commands?

   A. netdom add ComputerDN

   B. netdom ComputerName /domain:DN

   C. netdom CN=Computer_Name

   D. netdom add Computername / domain:DomainName

   70-640 TS Objective 4.1: Automate creation of Active Directory accounts

79. CSVDE is a command-line tool that can be used to import or export computer objects from a specific type of file. Which choice identifies that file type?

   A. .csv file

   B. Txt file

   C. .cvs file

   D. Cdt file

   70-640 TS Objective 4.1: Automate creation of Active Directory accounts

80. CSVDE is a command-line tool used to import or export computer objects into Active Directory. CSVDE uses several parameters to specify different modes. Match the correct parameter with its corresponding function.

Parameter	Function
default	Export
-f	Import
ik	Ignore errors
-i	Filename

   70-640 TS Objective 4.1: Automate creation of Active Directory accounts

81. What are Organizational Units?

A. OUs are used to assign permissions

B. OUs are collections of objects used for administration

C. OUs are collections of groups

D. OUs are folders used to assign permissions

70-640 TS Objective 4.2: Maintain Active Directory accounts

82. Arrange the steps to create an organizational unit into the correct order by writing into the left column the numbers 1 through 6.

	Name the OU.
	Right-click the Domain or OU where you want to add the new OU.
	Complete the Description and Managed by information.
	Open the AD Users and Computers snap-in.
	Select Protect from Accidental Deletion.
	Right-click and go to Properties.

70-640 TS Objective 4.2: Maintain Active Directory accounts

83. Windows Server 2008 has a new feature. In the New Object dialog box, circle the new feature.

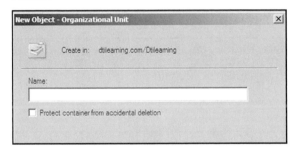

70-640 TS Objective 4.2: Maintain Active Directory accounts

84. What are the two permissions added to protect the OU container from accidental delegation?

A. Deny::Delete and Everyone::Deny::Delete

B. Everyone::Deny and Everyone::Deny::Delete

C. Authenticate::Users and Deny::Delete::OU

D. Everyone::Deny::Delete and Everyone::Deny::Delete::Subtree

70-640 TS Objective 4.2: Maintain Active Directory accounts

85. There are several steps necessary to delete an OU that has the Protect Container from Accidental Deletion option selected. Place the following list into the correct order by writing into the left column the numbers 1 through 5.

	Click OK.
	Select the OU Properties.
	Select the Object tab.
	Clear the check box.
	Turn on Advanced Features in the AD User and Computer snap-in.

70-640 TS Objective 4.2: Maintain Active Directory accounts

86. Place the steps needed to create a new user in Active Directory in the correct order by writing into the left column the numbers 1 through 8.

	Open the AD Users and Computers snap-in.
	Select UPN suffix.
	Fill in the logon name.
	Set an initial password.
	Select User Must Change Password.
	Expand your domain and open the target OU or container.
	Right-click the node and select New User.
	Follow the correct naming conventions.

70-640 TS Objective 4.2: Maintain Active Directory accounts

87. Place the steps needed to create a new group in Active Directory in the correct order by writing into the left column the numbers 1 through 8.

	Open Group Properties.
	Right-click the container and select New Group.
	Choose Group Type.
	Select Group Scope.
	Open the AD Users and Computers snap-in.
	Expand the node to navigate to the container.
	Enter the properties for the group.
	Follow the correct naming conventions.

70-640 TS Objective 4.2: Maintain Active Directory accounts

88. Computers are AD objects and have accounts just like users. When computers log on they are assigned a name. How are computer usernames created in Active Directory?

    A. From a combination of the computer name and the password used to create the account

    B. The password assigned when the computer was added to AD is the username

    C. The computer name with a + sign added to the end

    D. The computer name with a $ sign added to the end

    70-640 TS Objective 4.2: Maintain Active Directory accounts

89. Place the steps needed to create a new computer in Active Directory in the correct order by writing into the left column the numbers 1 through 7.

	Open the AD Users and Computers snap-in.
	Right-click and open Properties.
	Expand the node to navigate to the container.
	Enter properties for the computer.
	Type the Computer name.
	Specify the user or group to join the computer to the domain.
	Right-click the container and select New Computer.

    70-640 TS Objective 4.2: Maintain Active Directory accounts

90. Which of the following computer account properties items will NOT be entered automatically when the computer joins the domain?

    A. Description

    B. DNS name

    C. Operating system

    D. DC type

    70-640 TS Objective 4.2: Maintain Active Directory accounts

91. Where do you click to find the Add/Remove Columns dialog box in the Active Directory Users and Computers snap-in?

    A. File menu

    B. Action menu

    C. View menu

    D. Help menu

    70-640 TS Objective 4.2: Maintain Active Directory accounts

92. Which View option was selected to produce the view shown in the figure?

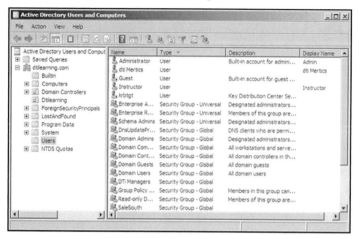

A. Large Icons

B. Small Icons

C. List

D. Detail

70-640 TS Objective 4.2: Maintain Active Directory accounts

93. In the following figure, the Type column is sorted in ascending order. How do you sort a column using the AD Users and Computers snap-in?

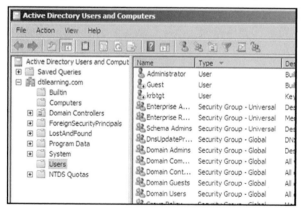

A. From the View menu

B. Select View > Sort > Ascending

C. Double-click the column heading

D. Click the column heading

70-640 TS Objective 4.2: Maintain Active Directory accounts

94. Which version of Windows Server introduced Save Queries in the AD Users and Computers snap-in?

    A. Windows Server 2008

    B. Windows Server 2003

    C. Windows Server 2000

    D. NT Server

    70-640 TS Objective 4.2: Maintain Active Directory accounts

95. What is the first step in creating a saved query?

    A. Open AD Users and Computers from My Computer

    B. Open AD Users and Computers from the Service manager

    C. Open AD Users and Computers from the MMC snap-in

    D. Open ADUCSQ.msc

    70-640 TS Objective 4.2: Maintain Active Directory accounts

96. An Active Directory Users and Computers console with saved queries is shown in the following image. Which choice best describes how the console was opened?

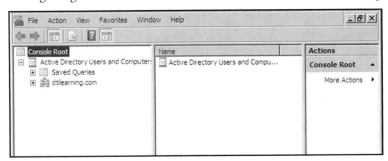

    A. From an MMC snap-in

    B. From Service Manager Roles

    C. From AD Users and Computers within the Service Manager

    D. From Service Manager Configuration

    70-640 TS Objective 4.2: Maintain Active Directory accounts

97. You are creating a new query in Active Directory and need to open the New Query dialog box. Which choice represents the best way to access this dialog box?

    A. Use the AD Users and Computers Security tab

    B. Use the AD Users and Computers View menu

    C. Use an AD Users and Computers Saved Query

    D. Use the Domain node of AD Users and Computers

    70-640 TS Objective 4.2: Maintain Active Directory accounts

98. List the steps to create a new Saved Query into the correct order by entering numbers 1 through 10 reflecting the first to last step.

	Open AD Users and Computers from a snap-in.
	Enter a description.
	Select New.
	Select Query.
	Right-click Saved Query.
	Click Browse.
	Define the query.
	Type a name.
	Select Type AD object.
	Select OK.

70-640 TS Objective 4.2: Maintain Active Directory accounts

99. After creating a new saved query, where will the query be found?

A. Use the AD Users and Computer snap-in; under Saved Query

B. From Service Manager > Roles > Saved Query

C. From AD Users and Computers; choose Service Manager > Saved Query

D. From Service Manager Configuration > Saved Query

70-640 TS Objective 4.2: Maintain Active Directory accounts

100. Which of following actions will NOT give you the Select Users, Contacts, Computers, or Groups dialog box?

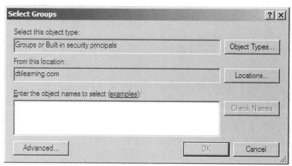

A. Adding a member to a group

B. Adding a new user

C. Assigning a permission

D. Creating a linked property

70-640 TS Objective 4.2: Maintain Active Directory accounts

101. When you're using the Select Users, Contacts, Computers, or Groups dialog box and you know the names of the objects to be added, you can enter them into the Enter the Object Names To Select text box. If multiple names are to be used, you separate them with which of the following?

A. Tabs

B. Semicolons

C. Periods

D. Asterisks

70-640 TS Objective 4.2: Maintain Active Directory accounts

102. When adding members to a group using the Select Users, Contacts, Computers, or Groups dialog box, which of the following is not searched for by default?

A. Computers

B. Users

C. Groups

D. Contacts

70-640 TS Objective 4.2: Maintain Active Directory accounts

103. When using the Select Users, Contacts, Computers, or Groups dialog box to specify a name on the Managed By tab, which of the following are NOT searched for by default?

A. Computers

B. Users

C. Groups

D. Contacts

70-640 TS Objective 4.2: Maintain Active Directory accounts

104. When using the Select User, Contacts, Computers, or Groups dialog box you can search for things such as disabled accounts, non-expiring passwords, and stale accounts. What option will allow you to expand your search for these items?

A. Object Types

B. Locations

C. Check Names

D. Advanced

70-640 TS Objective 4.2: Maintain Active Directory accounts

105. The Find box allows you to find items in Active Directory; what is another name for the Find box?

A. Active Directory Search box

B. Active Directory Query locator

C. Active Directory Query tool

D. None of the above

70-640 TS Objective 4.2: Maintain Active Directory accounts

106. When using the Find box to search for AD objects, you should narrow the scope as much as possible. For the most advanced control over your query, you choose which of the following from the Find drop-down menu?

    A. Advanced search

    B. Custom search

    C. Complete search

    D. Full search

    70-640 TS Objective 4.2: Maintain Active Directory accounts

107. If you want to make a desktop shortcut to open the Find User, Contact, and Groups box, what would you make the target of the shortcut?

    A. Rundll32

    B. Rundill32 query

    C. Runndll32 query OpenQueryWindow

    D. Rundll32 dsquery, OpenQueryWindow

    70-640 TS Objective 4.2: Maintain Active Directory accounts

108. Dsquery is one of the DS commands used to locate objects in Active Directory. What would you type if you need to get information about using the `dsquery` command?

    A. `ds command help`

    B. `dscmd/`

    C. `dcquery /help`

    D. `dsquery.exe /?`

    70-640 TS Objective 4.2: Maintain Active Directory accounts

109. In many situations there are tasks, like resetting passwords, that administrators may ask other individuals or groups to take responsibility for. What is this distributed administration called in Windows Server 2008?

    A. Distributed administrative ability

    B. Delegation of administrated control

    C. Task delegation

    D. Authorization demotion

    70-640 TS Objective 4.2: Maintain Active Directory accounts

110. You have the Properties dialog box open for an object and want to view the ACL of an object. You don't see a Security tab in the Properties dialog box; what is wrong?

    A. The Advanced Features view is not selected

    B. View Advanced Features tab is where the ACL is located

    C. Click the Advanced tab from the General tab

    D. There are no ACEs for that object

    70-640 TS Objective 4.2: Maintain Active Directory accounts

111. You are looking for the DACL of an object. Which tab should you select from the Advanced Security Settings dialog box for the AD object?

    A. Advanced

    B. Permissions

    C. Effective permissions

    D. Owner

    70-640 TS Objective 4.2: Maintain Active Directory accounts

112. You have the Permissions tab of the Advanced Security Setting dialog box open to view the DACL and you want to see the granular ACEs of the permission entry. Which tab should you select to see the granular ACEs?

    A. Permissions

    B. Owners

    C. Effective permissions

    D. Advanced

    70-640 TS Objective 4.2: Maintain Active Directory accounts

113. Permissions assigned to manage access rights are important to understand. If you have rights to change a password, you must know and enter which one of the following to change the password?

    A. The username

    B. The previous password

    C. The current password

    D. None of the above

    70-640 TS Objective 4.2: Maintain Active Directory accounts

114. Permissions assigned to manage access rights are important to understand. If you have rights to reset a password, you must know and enter which one of the following to change the password?

    A. The previous and new passwords

    B. The previous password

    C. The current password

    D. None of the above

    70-640 TS Objective 4.2: Maintain Active Directory accounts

6

115. You are assigned the task of delegating responsibility for resetting passwords to the customer support team. All the members of the team are in the Support group. Place the following steps in the correct order by adding the numerals 1 through 10.

	Open the user object properties.
	Click the Security tab.
	Click Add.
	Click OK.
	Open the AD Users and Computers snap-in.
	Select Advanced from the View menu.
	Select the Support Groups security principal.
	Configure the Allow::Reset Password
	Click the Advanced button.
	Close the dialog boxes.

70-640 TS Objective 4.2: Maintain Active Directory accounts

116. Complete the following statement by selecting the correct answer as it relates to inheritance. Explicit permissions _____override permissions that are inherited from parent objects.

A. Sometimes

B. Usually

C. Never

D. Always

70-640 TS Objective 4.2: Maintain Active Directory accounts

117. You want to use the Delegation of Control wizard. After opening the Active Directory Users and Computers snap-in what is your next step?

A. View Delegation Control

B. File > New Delegation

C. Advanced > Delegation of Control wizard

D. Right-click Domain or OU

70-640 TS Objective 4.2: Maintain Active Directory accounts

118. Reorder the following list of procedures for using the Delegation of Control wizard into the correct order by adding numerals.

	Specify the task to delegate.
	Select the group to grant privileges to.
	Open the AD Users and Computers snap-in.
	Right-click the node to delegate control.
	Apply ACEs to enable delegation.
	Add Users or Groups.

70-640 TS Objective 4.2: Maintain Active Directory accounts

119. What is the command-line tool used to set permissions and delegate?

A. Dcal.exe

B. Addscals.exe

C. Dscals/?

D. Dscals.exe

70-640 TS Objective 4.2: Maintain Active Directory accounts

120. How would you reset the permissions on the object displayed in the following figure?

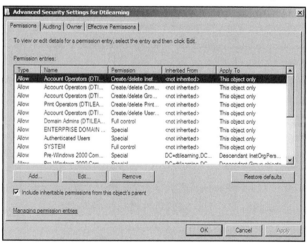

70-640 TS Objective 4.2: Maintain Active Directory accounts

121. How can the default permissions be reset from the command line?

A. Using dscals /s

B. Using dscals/r

C. Using dscals/reset

D. Using dscals/recover

Objective 4.2: Maintain Active Directory accounts

122. When creating additional user accounts, which of the following is NOT a preconfigured user account template category?

A. Group membership

B. Logon hours

C. Password

D. Home folder

70-640 TS Objective 4.2: Maintain Active Directory accounts

123. The User Properties dialog box has various tabs for reading and modifying attributes of users. Which tab in the Properties dialog box contains information for maintaining logon names, passwords, and account flags?

A. Account tab

B. General tab

C. Profile tab

D. Members Of tab

70-640 TS Objective 4.2: Maintain Active Directory accounts

124. The User Properties dialog box has various tabs for reading and modifying attributes of users. Which tab in the Properties dialog box contains information about the name properties that are configured when the account is created, including basic information and contact information?

A. Account tab

B. General tab

C. Profile tab

D. Members Of tab

70-640 TS Objective 4.2: Maintain Active Directory accounts

125. The User Properties dialog box has various tabs for reading and modifying attributes of users. Which tab in the Properties dialog box contains detailed contact information?

A. Addresses tab

B. General tab

C. Profile tab

D. Members Of tab

70-640 TS Objective 4.2: Maintain Active Directory accounts

126. The User Properties dialog box has various tabs for reading and modifying attributes of users. Which tab in the Properties dialog box contains logon scripts and home folder locations?

A. Addresses tab

B. General tab

C. Profile tab

D. Members Of tab

70-640 TS Objective 4.2: Maintain Active Directory accounts

127. The User Properties dialog box has various tabs for reading and modifying attributes of users. Which tab in the Properties dialog box is used to add or remove memberships?

A. Addresses tab

B. General tab

C. Profile tab

D. Members Of tab

70-640 TS Objective 4.2: Maintain Active Directory accounts

128. Active Directory Users and Computers allows you to select multiple user accounts for modification. Match the list of objects to the list of user properties.

Objects	User Properties
A. Profile	1. Description, Office, Phone, Fax, Web Page, and Email
B. Address	2. UPN Suffix, Logon hours, Restrictions, Account options, and Account Expiration
C. Organization	3. Street, PO, City, State, ZIP, and Country
D. General	4. Path, Logon Script, and Home Folder
E. Account	5. Title, Department, Company, and Manager

70-640 TS Objective 4.2: Maintain Active Directory accounts

129. A user forgets his password and needs it reset. What is the best practice to use when resetting the password?

A. Ask the user the password that he would like to use and enter it for him

B. Create a new account with a default password

C. Use a default password

D. Set a new password and check User Must Change Password at Next Logon

70-640 TS Objective 4.2: Maintain Active Directory accounts

130. It's important to make sure that user accounts are being used correctly. When creating user accounts before they are needed, which of the following should be done?

A. Use a very strong password

B. Use a default password that is widely known so the account can be activated quickly when needed

C. Set the account to User Must Change Password at Next Logon

D. Disable the account

70-640 TS Objective 4.2: Maintain Active Directory accounts

131. You can use a DS command from the command line to reset a password. Which of the following is the correct DS command to reset a password?

A. dsmod user UserDN -pwd NewPassword

B. dsmod user UserDN -pwd -mustchpwd

C. dsmod user UserDN -pwd

D. dsmod user UserDN

70-640 TS Objective 4.2: Maintain Active Directory accounts

132. The DS command can be used to force a user to reset her password at the next logon. Which of the following is the correct DS command to reset a password and force the user to change her password at the next logon?

    A. dsmod user UserDN -pwd -mustchpwd

    B. dsmod user UserDN -pwd NewPassword -mustchpwd yes

    C. dsmod user UserDN -pwd

    D. dsmod user UserDN -pwd NewPassword

    70-640 TS Objective 4.2: Maintain Active Directory accounts

133. When a user attempts to log on with the wrong password it is called a logon failure. Too many logon failures within a specified time period will lock the account. Which choice best describes this action?

    A. Disabled logon

    B. Authentication denial

    C. Domain access restriction

    D. Lock-out policy

    70-640 TS Objective 4.2: Maintain Active Directory accounts

134. You have a user who attempts too many failed logon attempts within the lockout policy's specified time and has been locked out of his account. How do you unlock the account?

    A. Right-click the account, select Lockout, and clear the check box

    B. Right-click the account, select Account tab, and select the Password tab

    C. Right-click the account, select Properties, select the Account tab, and uncheck the Unlock Account check box

    D. Right-click the account, select the Account tab, and click Reset

    70-640 TS Objective 4.2: Maintain Active Directory accounts

135. When creating user accounts before they are needed, you can use the dsmod command to disable the account. Which of the following DS commands is used to disable a user account?

    A. dsmod user unserDN -disable

    B. dsmod user unserDN -enabled no

    C. dsmod user unserDN -disabled yes

    D. dsmod user unserDN -disable yes

    70-640 TS Objective 4.2: Maintain Active Directory accounts

136. When user accounts are provisioned before being used, they should be disabled to avoid any security risks. When the accounts are needed they can be activated with the dsmod command. Which one of the following dsmod commands would be used to enable an account?

    A. dsmod user unserDN -enable

    B. dsmod user unserDN -disabled

    C. dsmod user unserDN -disabled no

    D. dsmod user unserDN -enable no

    70-640 TS Objective 4.2: Maintain Active Directory accounts

137. It is an important decision as to whether an unused account should be deleted or disabled. Which of the following is true about deleting a user account?

    A. A user account is deleted completely from the directory as soon as it is disabled

    B. A user account is deleted from the directory 30 days after it is deleted

    C. A user account is never completely deleted from the directory

    D. A user account cannot be re-created by simply creating a new account with the same name

    70-640 TS Objective 4.2: Maintain Active Directory accounts

138. When choosing to delete an account, which of the following statements correctly describes what happens to a deleted user account in Active Directory?

    A. A user account is deleted completely from the directory as soon as it is disabled

    B. A subset of the user's account is tombstoned for 60 days

    C. A user account is deleted from the directory 30 days after it is deleted

    D. A subset of the user's account remains in the directory

    70-640 TS Objective 4.2: Maintain Active Directory accounts

139. You need to move an account in Active Directory using the AD Users and Computers snap-in. Select the best choice concerning moving a user account in the Active Directory Users and Computers snap-in.

    A. You can drag and drop it

    B. You can select the account and select Move from the Action menu

    C. The best practice is to right-click the user and select the Move command

    D. You cannot move a user from within the snap-in

    70-640 TS Objective 4.2: Maintain Active Directory accounts

140. You need to move an account in Active Directory using a DS command. To move an account with the DS command, you would use which of the following syntax examples?

    A. `move username targetOUDN`

    B. `DNname -newparent TargetOu`

    C. `dsmove UserDN`

    D. `dsmove UserDN -newparent TargetOUDN`

    70-640 TS Objective 4.2: Maintain Active Directory accounts

141. Groups can be re-created if it is done so before the tombstone date. What is the default tombstone interval?

    A. 30 days

    B. 60 days

    C. 120 days

    D. 35 days

    70-640 TS Objective 4.2: Maintain Active Directory accounts

142. Groups can be protected from accidental deletion in Windows Server 2008 with several steps. Place the following list in the correct order by entering numbers 1 through 4 in the left column.

	Open the AD Users and Computers snap-in.
	Open Group Properties.
	Select the Object tab and select Protect Object from Accidental Deletion.
	Click View and turn on the Advanced Features.

70-640 TS Objective 4.2: Maintain Active Directory accounts

143. You want to delegate the management of a group. You have opened the Properties box and the Managed By tab is open. How can you give Write Member permission to a named user? To answer the question, draw a check mark where you would click on the figure.

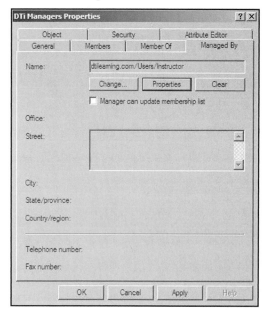

70-640 TS Objective 4.2: Maintain Active Directory accounts

144. When inserting a group into the Managed By tab of another group, you choose Change, Select User, Contact, or Group. What do you need to do next to avoid receiving an error when you attempt to add a group name to the dialog box? Circle the button on the Select User, Contact, or Group dialog box to indicate the correct next action.

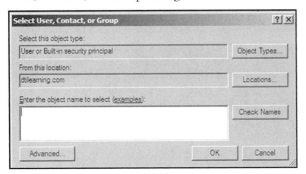

70-640 TS Objective 4.2: Maintain Active Directory accounts

145. You have an OU called DTILearning and you want to give all users in the OU access to a folder. To accomplish your goal, you press Ctrl+A to select all the users in the OU and then right-click a selected user and choose Add to Group to give access to the folder. Which choice identifies the object you have created?

A. Shadow Copy Group

B. Group Access Policy

C. Shadow Group

D. A group within an OU

70-640 TS Objective 4.2: Maintain Active Directory accounts

146. There are a number of groups created automatically on a server running Windows Server 2008. In addition to the default local groups, what additional groups are created in a domain? (Choose all that apply.)

A. Domain Admins

B. Backup Operators

C. Remote Desktop Users

D. Enterprise Admins

E. Schema Admin

F. Administrator

70-640 TS Objective 4.2: Maintain Active Directory accounts

147. There are a number of groups created automatically on a server running Windows Server 2008. Which of the following are the default local groups? (Choose all that apply.)

   A. Domain Admins

   B. Backup Operators

   C. Remote Desktop Users

   D. Enterprise Admins

   E. Schema Admin

   F. Administrator

   70-640 TS Objective 4.2: Maintain Active Directory accounts

148. The Anonymous Logon, Authenticated Users, Everyone, Interactive, and Network groups are support groups controlled by the operating system. These groups are known as which of the following?

   A. Special attributes

   B. Special privilege

   C. Special authority

   D. Special identities

   70-640 TS Objective 4.2: Maintain Active Directory accounts

149. Which of the following is true concerning the Computer container?

   A. You must create the container when you add the first computers to the domain

   B. The Computer container can be linked to Group Policy

   C. The Computer container is an object class container

   D. The Computer container can be subdivided with an OU

   70-640 TS Objective 4.2: Maintain Active Directory accounts

150. You are creating computer accounts using the New Object Computer dialog box. You enter a computer name and select the user who will be allowed to join the computer with the domain. What process have you just completed?

   A. Prestaging the account

   B. Staging the account

   C. Staging the computer

   D. User prep

   70-640 TS Objective 4.2: Maintain Active Directory accounts

151. You have created computer accounts for all computers in your domain before joining them to the domain. What is the advantage of this procedure? Select the best answer.

   A. It allows a computer to be joined to the domain quicker

   B. You can join groups of computers at the same time

   C. The computer is in the correct OU and can be within the scope of a GPO

   D. It allows for automatic enrollment of computers

   70-640 TS Objective 4.2: Maintain Active Directory accounts

152. Which of the computer properties can be configured with the dsmod command?

    A. Dial-in properties

    B. Group memberships

    C. Description and location

    D. Operating system

    70-640 TS Objective 4.2: Maintain Active Directory accounts

153. Which tab on this prestaged computer account will be read-only until the computer joins the domain? Circle the correct tab to answer the question.

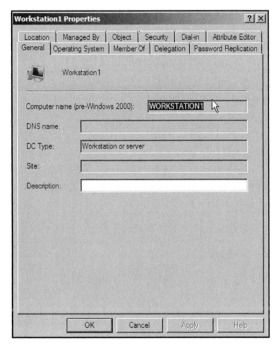

70-640 TS Objective 4.2: Maintain Active Directory accounts

154. When you create a computer object to prestage its location in an OU it should be linked to the user object of the user to whom the computer is assigned. Click on the Workstations Properties dialog box to select the correct tab to link Workstation1 to a user.

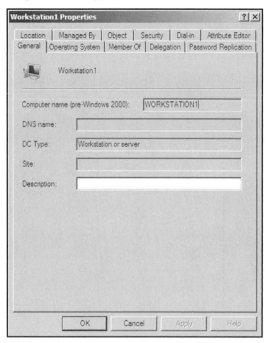

70-640 TS Objective 4.2: Maintain Active Directory accounts

155. Every computer on a domain has a computer account with a username and password. This password is changed every 30 days. How is the computer account password stored?

A. Local SAM

B. On the domain controller

C. Local Security authority (LSA) secret

D. In the Computer object container

70-640 TS Objective 4.2: Maintain Active Directory accounts

156. Every computer on a domain has a computer account with a username and password. This password is changed every _____ days. Select the correct answer.

A. 7

B. 14

C. 30

D. 60

70-640 TS Objective 4.2: Maintain Active Directory accounts

157. When the secure channel communications fails, the computer may have to be reset. Place the steps to reset a computer account in the correct order by writing the numbers 1 through 5 in the correct order in the left column.

	Right-click the computer.
	Open the Active Directory Users and Computers Snap-in.
	Click Yes.
	Select Reset.
	Reboot.

70-640 TS Objective 4.2: Maintain Active Directory accounts

158. Why does this computer account appear with a down-arrow icon?

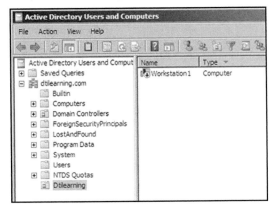

A. It has become out of synch

B. The LSA is compromised

C. The account is missing in AD

D. The Computer account has been disabled

70-640 TS Objective 4.2: Maintain Active Directory accounts

159. You have a computer that will be offline for a long period of time and you want to disable it for security reasons. How do you disable a computer account?

A. Go to Manage and select Disable

B. Right-click on the Computer account and select Remove

C. Right-click on the Computer account and select Disable Account

D. Open the system's properties and select Computer Name > Rename > Remove from Domain

70-640 TS Objective 4.2: Maintain Active Directory accounts

6

160. When a computer is going to be replaced with upgraded hardware what would you do with the computer account?

A. Rename it

B. Delete the account and create a new computer object

C. Reset the computer account

D. Export the SID and permissions

70-640 TS Objective 4.2: Maintain Active Directory accounts

161. Group Policy is a Windows feature that allows you to manage change and configurations for uses and computers. The most granular component of the Group Policy is the individual policy setting. A policy setting is also known as which of the following?

A. Policy

B. GPO

C. ACE

D. MSI

70-640 TS Objective 4.3: Create and apply Group Policy objects (GPOs)

162. Group Policy settings are defined and exist within which of the following?

A. Resultant set of policy

B. MMC

C. GPMC

D. GPO

70-640 TS Objective 4.3: Create and apply Group Policy objects (GPOs)

163. Which of the following is used to edit or modify GPO settings?

A. GPME

B. GPO edit

C. User configuration

D. Computer configuration

70-640 TS Objective 4.3: Create and apply Group Policy objects (GPOs)

164. How many policy settings are typically available in a GPO in the computer and user nodes?

A. 100s

B. 1,000s

C. 10,000s

D. Millions

70-640 TS Objective 4.3: Create and apply Group Policy objects (GPOs)

165. Which of the following is NOT a policy setting state?

A. Not Configured

B. Not Applied

C. Enabled

D. Disabled

70-640 TS Objective 4.3: Create and apply Group Policy objects (GPOs)

166. When configuration changes are made in a GPO they do not affect any computers or users until you have specified which computers or users the GPO applies to. This is referred to as which of the following terms?

A. Specifying

B. Scoping

C. Selecting

D. Securing

70-640 TS Objective 4.3: Create and apply Group Policy objects (GPOs)

167. The Group Policy refresh is applied after the first configuration, start up, and login. Within what time interval does the refresh take place?

A. 60-120 minutes

B. 90-120 minutes

C. 120-160 minutes

D. 160-210 minutes

70-640 TS Objective 4.3: Create and apply Group Policy objects (GPOs)

168. Group Policy uses client-side extensions to interpret the GPO on the client software. Group policy technology is best described by which of the following terms?

A. A push technology

B. A push-pull technology

C. A round-robin technology

D. A pull technology

70-640 TS Objective 4.3: Create and apply Group Policy objects (GPOs)

169. Group Policy client software can determine if a connection is considered a slow link and forgo policy processing. Which of the choices provided is considered a slow link?

A. Less than 768 Kbps

B. Less than 500 Kbps

C. More than 500 Kbps

D. Less than 1.2 Mbps

70-640 TS Objective 4.3: Create and apply Group Policy objects (GPOs)

170. All Windows computers running 2000, XP, and Server 2003 have one local GPO that manages the configuration of that system. Where is that GPO stored?

A. %systemroot%\GroupPolicy

B. %systemroot%\Windows

C. %systemroot%\system32

D. %systemroot%\system32\GroupPolicy

70-640 TS Objective 4.3: Create and apply Group Policy objects (GPOs)

171. Domain-based GPOs are created with Active Directory and are stored on the domain controllers. Which of the following are the default GPO(s)?

A. Default DC policy and Domain Policy

B. Default Domain Policy and User Policy

C. Default Domain and default DC Policy

D. Default Domain Controllers Policy

70-640 TS Objective 4.3: Create and apply Group Policy objects (GPOs)

172. A GPO is a group of settings that appears in the AD user tools as a GPO. What is a Group Policy actually composed of?

A. Group Policy Container

B. AD GUID

C. Group Policy Container and Group Policy Template

D. GPO and GPO GUID

70-640 TS Objective 4.3: Create and apply Group Policy objects (GPOs)

173. Group Policies are only updated when changes are made. When GPO refreshes occur the CSE needs to know if any changes have been made in the policy. The Group Policy Client identifies changes by checking which of the following?

A. Time and date stamps

B. GUID

C. Sequence number

D. Version number

70-640 TS Objective 4.3: Create and apply Group Policy objects (GPOs)

174. You have an organization that utilizes only Windows Server 2008 DCs. Which of the following methods is the best way to replicate the GPT in SYSVOL?

A. FRS

B. FRS or DFR-S

C. SMTP

D. DFS-R

70-640 TS Objective 4.3: Create and apply Group Policy objects (GPOs)

175. In the Windows Setting node, both the Computer and User node policies contain a setting that allows scripts to run. What is the default time allotted for processing scripts?

A. 1 minute

B. 3 minutes

C. 5 minutes

D. 10 minutes

70-640 TS Objective 4.3: Create and apply Group Policy objects (GPOs)

176. In both Computer and User nodes, there is a Windows Setting node that contains a policy-based QoS node. What does QoS define?

    A. Network security

    B. Network throughput

    C. Polices for managing network traffic

    D. Network mapping

    70-640 TS Objective 4.3: Create and apply Group Policy objects (GPOs)

177. Policies in the Administrative Template node of the Computer Configuration node will modify Registry values on client computers. Which of the following Registry values will be updated by policies in the Administrative Templates node?

    A. HKEY_LOCAL_MACHINE

    B. HKEY_CURRENT_USER

    C. HKEY_LOCAL_MACHINE\Software

    D. HKEY_CURRENT_USER\Software

    70-640 TS Objective 4.4: Configure GPO templates

178. In Windows Vista and Windows Server 2008, the administrative template has been changed from previous versions of Windows. Which of the following is correct when considering the changes made to the administrative template in Windows Vista and Server 2008?

    A. The Administrative template has an ADM file extension

    B. The Administrative template is one file

    C. The Administrative template is an XML file

    D. The Administrative template is an ADMX and ADML file

    70-640 TS Objective 4.3: Create and apply Group Policy objects (GPOs)

179. When considering the Central Store used to hold ADMX and ADML files in larger organizations, which one of the following statements is true?

    A. The Central Store was first available with Windows Server 2000

    B. The Central Store was first available with Windows Server 2003

    C. The Central Store was first available with Windows Server 2008

    D. The Central Store is an optional Windows Server 2003 component

    70-640 TS Objective 4.3: Create and apply Group Policy objects (GPOs)

180. New to Windows Server 2008, the GPME has the ability to display specific policy settings in the Administrative template. What is the new feature in the GPME referred to as?

    A. Sort

    B. Select

    C. Filter

    D. Exclude

    70-640 TS Objective 4.4: Configure GPO templates

181. When Registry policy settings have been applied by a GPO to a computer and the computer reverts to its original state automatically when the computer falls out of the GPO scope, this is referred to as which of the following?

    A. Implemented

    B. Unimplemented

    C. Unmanaged

    D. Managed

    70-640 TS Objective 4.4: Configure GPO templates

182. Policy settings from GPOs linked to domains can conflict with one another. What determines which policy setting the client applies?

    A. Pre-determanence

    B. Precedence

    C. Priority

    D. Inheritance

    70-640 TS Objective 4.4: Configure GPO templates

183. Preferences have a mechanism that allows Windows Server 2008 to set specific settings within the same GPO. There are over a dozen different criteria available. What is this mechanism called?

    A. Targeting preferences

    B. Item-level targeting

    C. Item-level preferences

    D. Item-level criteria

    70-640 TS Objective 4.3: Create and apply Group Policy objects (GPOs)

184. In what order are configurations defined by GPOs applied?

    A. Domain, site, OU

    B. OU, domain, site

    C. Site, OU, domain

    D. Site, domain, OU

    70-640 TS Objective 4.4: Configure GPO templates

185. Windows Server 2008 RSoP provides three tools for performing analysis, evaluation, and troubleshooting the application of Group Policy. Which of the following is NOT one of the tools included in RSoP?

    A. Group Policy Results wizard

    B. Group Policy Active Policy wizard

    C. Group Policy Modeling wizard

    D. Gpresult.exe

    70-640 TS Objective 4.4: Configure GPO templates

186. The Windows Installer package is a file that is used to install, maintain, and remove software. The Windows Installer package has which one of the following file extensions?

    A. .exe

    B. .csv

    C. .msi

    D. .wsi

    70-640 TS Objective 4.4: Configure GPO templates

187. When assigning an application with GPSI, which of the following would NOT be true of the assigned application?

    A. The application appears on the Start menu or desktop

    B. The application follows the users to any computer where they log on

    C. The application is installed the first time the user selects the application

    D. The application appears in Add/Remove Programs

    70-640 TS Objective 4.4: Configure GPO templates

188. The domain password policy is configured by a GPO scoped to the domain. Where within the GPO is the password policy setting?

    A. Computer Configuration\Policies\Windows Settings\Security Settings\Local Policies\Password Policies

    B. Computer Configuration\Policies\Windows Settings\Security Settings\Account Policies\Password Policy

    C. Computer Configuration\Policies\Windows Settings\Security Settings\Password Policies

    D. User Configuration\Policies\Windows Settings\Security Settings\Password Policies

    70-640 TS Objective 4.6: Configure account policies

189. New to Windows Server 2008 is the ability to implement more stringent password requirements for administrators. This feature is referred to as which one of the following?

    A. Granular password policy

    B. Fine-tuned password policy

    C. Enhanced password policy

    D. Fine-grained password policy

    70-640 TS Objective 4.6: Configure account policies

190. You have accessed the Advanced Security Setting dialog box and are going to enable Auditing. After clicking the Add button, what are your auditing options? Select the best answer from the choices.

    A. Success

    B. Success or denial

    C. Success and failure

    D. None of the above are valid options

    70-640 TS Objective 4.7: Configure audit policy by using GPOs

6

191. When a user connects to a folder on a server on the DTILearning domain, the server authorizes the user with which of the following? Select the best answer from the choices.

    A. Logon event

    B. Account logon event on the DC

    C. Account logon event on the computer

    D. Network logon

    70-640 TS Objective 4.7: Configure audit policy by using GPOs

192. Account logon and logon events are audited by configuring a GPO in which node?

    A. Computer configuration\Policies\Windows Settings\Local Policies\Audit Policy

    B. Computer configuration\Policies\Windows Settings\Security Settings\Local Policies

    C. Computer configuration\Policies\Windows Settings\Security Settings\Audit Policy

    D. Computer configuration\Policies\Windows Settings\Security Settings\Local Policies\Audit Policy

    70-640 TS Objective 4.7: Configure audit policy by using GPOs

7

MAINTAINING THE ACTIVE DIRECTORY ENVIRONMENT

This chapter contains 104 questions that all fall under Microsoft's fifth main exam objective for the 70-640 exam, "Maintaining the Active Directory Environment." This main objective consists of the following three sub-objectives:

- Configure backup and recovery
- Perform offline maintenance
- Monitor Active Directory

TEST PREPARATION QUESTIONS

1. What does the phrase "perform proactive performance management" refer to in terms of computer systems?

   A. Changing and upgrading hardware

   B. Performing preventive maintenance

   C. Disaster recovery

   D. Forewarning of problematic events

   70-640 TS Objective 5.1: Configure backup and recovery

2. Windows Server 2008 includes tools to identify performance issues and establish baselines for performance monitoring. Match the following tools with their correct descriptions.

List of Tools		Tool	Description
Performance Monitor			Displays current system resources
Reliability Monitor			Logs events and system performance
Event Viewer			Tracks changes
WSRM			Collects data and identifies issues
Task Manager			Contains profile-specific applications

   70-640 TS Objective 5.1: Configure backup and recovery

3. If you wanted to access information regarding physical and kernel memory from the Task Manager, which tab would you use?

   A. Applications

   B. Processes

   C. Services

   D. Performance

   70-640 TS Objective 5.1: Configure backup and recovery

4. On the Task Manager shown in the following image, which tab and options would provide access to the Resource Manager tool?

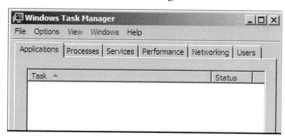

   70-640 TS Objective 5.1: Configure backup and recovery

5. Select the four system resources that are displayed in the Resource Monitor graphs.

   A. CPU

   B. Running Application

   C. Disk

   D. Processes

   E. Memory

   F. Network

   70-640 TS Objective 5.1: Configure backup and recovery

6. Event Viewer is a good indicator of the condition of your system. In a Domain Controller there are several additional logs. In which Event Viewer folder will you find the additional DC logs?

   A. Application and Services logs

   B. Application

   C. Security

   D. System

   70-640 TS Objective 5.1: Configure backup and recovery

7. One of the new features in Windows Server 2008 gives you Event Viewer information as it relates to specific roles in Windows Server 2008. Look at the figure and select the name of the program from the list.

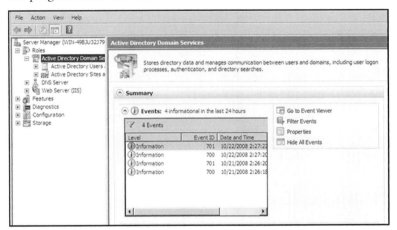

A. Event Viewer

B. Reliability Monitor

C. Server Manager

D. Performance Monitor

70-640 TS Objective 5.1: Configure backup and recovery

8. Event Viewer logs list three types of events. Which of the following is NOT a valid Event Viewer log type?

A. Failure

B. Error

C. Warning

D. Information

70-640 TS Objective 5.1: Configure backup and recovery

9. The tool shown in this figure is used to track changes made to a system. Where is it found?

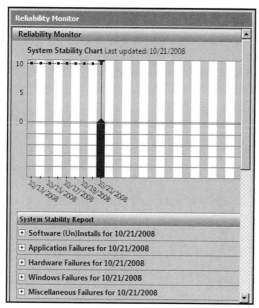

A. Task Manager > Resource Manager

B. Server Manager > Diagnostic > Reliability and Performance > Monitoring Tools

C. Performance Monitor > Reliability Monitor

D. Event log

70-640 TS Objective 5.1: Configure backup and recovery

10. When an issue appears that may be related to a recent system change, where is the first place you should check?

A. Device Manager

B. Task Manager

C. Reliability Monitor

D. Event Viewer

70-640 TS Objective 5.1: Configure backup and recovery

11. The following dialog box is used to configure which tool in Windows Server 2008?

A. Reliability Monitor

B. Network Monitor

C. Event Viewer

D. Performance Monitor

70-640 TS Objective 5.1: Configure backup and recovery

12. When a system is first installed, you should create baselines of peak and non-peak times. How long should you run a performance baseline to take a good sample of counter values?

A. 10-15 minutes

B. 20-30 minutes

C. 30-45 minutes

D. 1-2 hours

70-640 TS Objective 5.1: Configure backup and recovery

13. There are three steps to creating a baseline. Which of the following is NOT a step for creating a performance baseline?

A. ID the resources to track

B. Capture data over time

C. Capture data at specific times

D. Store the capture for future use

70-640 TS Objective 5.1: Configure backup and recovery

14. Business continuity is a very important part of planning and maintenance. What percentage of small to medium-sized organizations that face a disaster without a business plan will not survive the event?

    A. 20%

    B. 40%

    C. 55%

    D. 50%

    70-640 TS Objective 5.2: Perform offline maintenance

15. The sharing of administrative responsibilities among members of the organization is based on data and service management. Match the groups to the AD DS activities they perform.

List of Groups
Help Desk
System administrators
Users
Security and distribution group managers

Group	Activity
	Search AD for account records
	Manage group content
	Password reset
	AD and DNS contents

70-640 TS Objective 5.2: Perform offline maintenance

16. AD administration has 12 major administrative and management activities. Each task focuses on data or content management, or both. For each item listed, mark the correct answer for Data or Content Management.

Task	Content Management	Data
User and Group Administration	☐	☐
Endpoint Device Administration	☐	☐
Network Service Administration	☐	☐
GPO Management	☐	☐
DNS Administration	☐	☐
AD Topology and Replication	☐	☐
AD Configuration	☐	☐
AD Schema Management	☐	☐
Information Management	☐	☐
Security Management	☐	☐
Database Management	☐	☐
AD Reporting	☐	☐

70-640 TS Objective 5.2: Perform offline maintenance

17. To assist in offline maintenance and managing user accounts, you can add the Additional Account Info tab to the User Objects Properties page. Which of the following locations contain the necessary files for adding the tab?

A. None, it's already there

B. Windows Server Updates

C. Microsoft Website for Server Management

D. Windows Server 2003 Resource Kit

70-640 TS Objective 5.2: Perform offline maintenance

18. To assist in offline maintenance and managing user accounts, you can add the Additional Account Info tab to the User Objects Properties page. How can you add the tab?

A. Register the AcctInfo.dll

B. It's already there

C. Install Windows Server Updates

D. Download Windows Server 2003 Resource Kit

70-640 TS Objective 5.2: Perform offline maintenance

19. Specops, Special Operations Software, is a third-party add-on tool that allows AD Users and Computers to remotely manage objects in the directory. What is the name of the tool that Specops creates?

    A. Gpedit

    B. Gpremote

    C. Gpupdate

    D. Gprestart

    70-640 TS Objective 5.2: Perform offline maintenance

20. Listed are some common Active Directory tools that are used for service administration of AD and DNS. Match the correct location where each tool can be found.

Locations
Administrative tools
MMC
Command line
Start menu, Search

Tool	Location
AD Domains and Trusts	
AD Schema snap-in	
AD Sites and Services	
AD Users and Computers	
ADSI Edit	
CSVDE.exe	
DCDiag.exe	
Dcpromo.exe	
DFSRadmin.exe	

70-640 TS Objective 5.2: Perform offline maintenance

21. Listed are some common Active Directory tools that are used for service administration of AD and DNS. Match the correct location where each tool can be found.

Locations
Administrative tools
Download Microsoft.com
Start menu, Search
Command line

Tool	Location
Event Viewer	
GPfixup.exe	
Group Policy Diagnostic Best Practices Analyzer	
Group Policy Management Console	
Lpd.exe	
Netdom.exe	

70-640 TS Objective 5.2: Perform offline maintenance

22. Listed are some common Active Directory tools that are used for service administration of AD and DNS. Match the correct location to each tool.

Locations
Command line
Administrative tools
Server Manager
Download from Microsoft.com

Tool	Location
Nslookup	
Ntdsutil	
Server Manager	
System Monitor	
Ultrasound	
W32tm.exe	
Windows Server Backup	

70-640 TS Objective 5.2: Perform offline maintenance

23. Knowing how databases work is an important part of performing database maintenance. When a record is deleted, which of the following is true?

   A. The space to store the information is reclaimed

   B. The space from the deleted record is not recovered

   C. The record remains in the space, just unavailable

   D. None of the above represents a true statement

   70-640 TS Objective 5.2: Perform offline maintenance

24. Which of the following is true about AD DS?

   A. To perform maintenance, you must restart in Directory Services Repair Mode

   B. Maintenance can be performed remotely from another DC

   C. You can stop the AD DS service with only one DC

   D. The AD DS service can be stopped and started like all Windows Server services

   70-640 TS Objective 5.2: Perform offline maintenance

25. Protecting AD DS objects can be assigned explicitly on which tab of the object's properties?

   A. Advanced

   B. COM+

   C. Object

   D. None of the above is correct

   70-640 TS Objective 5.2: Perform offline maintenance

26. Windows Server 2008 audits directory changes in AD DS. When an object is modified, which of the following occurs?

   A. The new value is logged as an event

   B. Two events are logged; the first lists the old value and the second lists the new value

   C. The new and old values are logged together

   D. The second most recent value is noted with an event number

   70-640 TS Objective 5.2: Perform offline maintenance

27. Which of the following is a true statement about restoring a tombstoned AD object?

   A. Tombstoned objects require special utility software to restore

   B. Tombstoned objects are actually deleted and not available for access

   C. Tombstoned objects are restorable by using AD Users and Computers

   D. Tombstoned objects remain available in a special container until removed

   70-640 TS Objective 5.2: Perform offline maintenance

28. Which of the following is a true statement about restoring a tombstoned AD object?

    A. Tombstoned objects are restorable by using AD Users and Computers

    B. Tombstoned objects remain available in a special container until removed

    C. Tombstoned objects require a Microsoft utility downloaded from Microsoft

    D. Tombstoned objects are restored with a utility from Quest Software

    70-640 TS Objective 5.2: Perform offline maintenance

29. When you restore deleted objects by accessing the tombstoned data, which of the following is true about the object?

    A. It will retain all the attributes from before it was deleted

    B. It will have to be renamed to bring back its original state

    C. Objects restored from tombstoned containers do not include all their previous attributes

    D. None of the above statements represents a true statement

    70-640 TS Objective 5.2: Perform offline maintenance

30. What is the new Windows Server 2008 Backup tool that allows you to see data contained in a backup set?

    A. AD DS Object Restore

    B. AD DS Database Viewer

    C. AD DS Mounting tool

    D. AD DS Database Mounting tool

    70-640 TS Objective 5.2: Perform offline maintenance

31. When restoring a server, which of the following explains what performing an Install From Media, IFM, does?

    A. Creates another server from a complete copy of the server

    B. Uses a copy of the Ntds.dit file from another DC in the domain

    C. Uses a copy of the system state data from the original server

    D. Uses a copy of the system state data from another server in the domain

    70-640 TS Objective 5.2: Perform offline maintenance

32. Which of the following is a true statement about Windows Server 2008 Backup and represents the best answer?

    A. To perform backups with Windows Server Backup and Wbadmin.exe, they must be installed

    B. Performing Windows Server backups has not changed from Server 2003

    C. Backups can be performed with the built-in tool Wbadmin.exe tool

    D. Backups can be performed with the new built-in tool Windows Server Backup

    70-640 TS Objective 5.2: Perform offline maintenance

33. Windows Server 2008 Backup copies critical volumes. Select the following volumes that are considered critical on a DC.

☐	System volume
☐	User profiles
☐	Boot volume
☐	SYSVOL
☐	Data
☐	AD DS database
☐	AD DS logs
☐	Application data

70-640 TS Objective 5.2: Perform offline maintenance

34. Select the media that Windows Server 2008 Backup can be performed with. (Choose all that apply.)

A. Tape drives

B. DVD/CD

C. Network Drives

D. Removable HDD configured as dynamic disks

E. Removable HDD configured as basic volumes

F. Dynamic volumes

70-640 TS Objective 5.2: Perform offline maintenance

35. To restore a server that is down, you use the Windows Recovery Environment. WinRE is found in which of the following locations?

A. System 32 folder

B. SYSvol

C. Windows Server 2008 installation DVD

D. Admin Resource Kit

70-640 TS Objective 5.2: Perform offline maintenance

36. When using the Windows Recovery Environment on a Hyper-V server, it is recommended that you move the WinRE into an ISO file and install it on each DC you create. What additional step is needed to use the ISO of the WinRE on the Hyper-V server?

A. WAIT Kit

B. WALK Kit

C. Windows Automation Kit

D. WAIK

70-640 TS Objective 5.2: Perform offline maintenance

37. Windows Server Backup supports three restore modes. Which of the following is NOT a Windows Server Backup restore mode?

    A. Full server restore

    B. System restore

    C. System state only restore

    D. Individual file or folder restore

    70-640 TS Objective 5.2: Perform offline maintenance

38. Windows Server 2008 Backup allows backups to be created in three restore modes. Each mode allows you to recover files from backups made by Windows Server Backup. Where are files located in a particular backup?

    A. Each file is in a separate backup

    B. In the file content index

    C. Each backup is in a separate file

    D. Backups are stored in the catalog file

    70-640 TS Objective 5.2: Perform offline maintenance

39. Which of the choices is true about backups generated with Windows Server 2008 Backup?

    A. A new backup file is created with each backup and new files are added as backups continue

    B. The old file is deleted and replaced with the new backup

    C. Windows Server backs up the data to the same file and adds content as data changes

    D. Backup uses the same file and removes the old data

    70-640 TS Objective 5.2: Perform offline maintenance

40. When creating Domain Controllers in a large enterprise network, rather than utilizing local network bandwidth to replicate directory information, which of the following would be a reasonable option?

    A. Use IFM

    B. Use the Ntdsutil.exe command

    C. Use the WAIK

    D. Use WinRE

    70-640 TS Objective 5.2: Perform offline maintenance

41. To perform a full system backup with Windows Server Backup, which option do you choose from the Custom Option screen?

    A. Backup Once

    B. Enable System Recovery

    C. Different Options

    D. System recovery

    70-640 TS Objective 5.2: Perform offline maintenance

7

42. After you select the backup options from the Windows Server Backup wizard, you are then asked to choose the location for the backup. What are your destination options for Windows Server Backup?

    A. Network drives

    B. Tape drives

    C. DVD/CD

    D. Removable HDD configured as dynamic disks

    E. Dynamic volumes

    F. Removable HDD configured as basic volumes

    70-640 TS Objective 5.2: Perform offline maintenance

43. You are configuring a full server backup for the first time with Windows Server Backup. You have chosen the destination for the backup file on the Specify Advanced Option page. Which of the following should you select if you are using Windows Server Backup as your only backup tool?

    A. Enable System Recovery

    B. Use Windows Server Backup

    C. VSS Full Backup

    D. VSS Copy Backup

    70-640 TS Objective 5.2: Perform offline maintenance

44. You are configuring a full server backup for the first time with Windows Server Backup. You have chosen the destination for the backup file on the Specify Advanced Option page. You should select which of the following if you are using another backup tool?

    A. Enable System Recovery

    B. Use Windows Server Backup

    C. VSS Copy Backup

    D. VSS Full Backup

    70-640 TS Objective 5.2: Perform offline maintenance

45. Backups on Server Core installations use the Wbadmin.exe tool. To specify a full backup, you use which of the following command syntax?

    A. wbadmin start backup -all -backup:*location*

    B. wbadmin start backup -critical -backup:*location*

    C. wbadmin start backup -allcritical -backuptarget:*location*

    D. wbadmin start backup -backup:*location* -allcritical

    70-640 TS Objective 5.2: Perform offline maintenance

46. Which of the following statements is true concerning scheduling a full server backup with Windows Server Backup?

A. You can only use mapped network drives with Windows Server Backup when scheduling backup tasks

B. You cannot use mapped network drives with Windows Server Backup when scheduling backup tasks

C. You cannot use rewritable media

D. You cannot use virtual hard drives as a target for backups

70-640 TS Objective 5.2: Perform offline maintenance

47. Which of the following statements is true when setting a schedule for a full system backup and selecting a destination for the backup with Windows Server Backup?

A. You can only use mapped network drives with Windows Server Backup when scheduling backup tasks

B. You cannot use rewritable media

C. You cannot use virtual hard drives as a target for backup

D. You can only use addressable rewritable media

70-640 TS Objective 5.2: Perform offline maintenance

48. To restore data to a DC the DC must be running in Directory Services Restore mode. One method of restarting a DC into a DSRM is by changing the boot order. How do you change the boot order in Windows Server 2008?

A. Using the Bcdedit.exe command

B. Editing the boot.ini file

C. Pressing F6 when booting Windows

D. Pressing DEL when booting Windows

70-640 TS Objective 5.2: Perform offline maintenance

49. To restore data to a DC, the DC must be running in Directory Services Restore mode. One method of restarting a DC into DSRM is by changing the boot order. In Windows Server 2008, how do you change the boot order?

A. bcdedit /set safeboot dsrepair

B. bcdedit /set safeboot

C. bcdedit / deletevalue safeboot

D. bcdedit / dsrepair

70-640 TS Objective 5.2: Perform offline maintenance

50. To restore data to a DC, the DC must be running in Directory Services Restore mode. One method of restarting a DC into a DSRM is by changing the boot order. In Windows Server 2008 how do you change the boot order back to start the server normally?

A. bcdedit /set safeboot dsrepair

B. bcdedit /set safeboot

C. bcdedit / deletevalue safeboot

D. bcdedit / dsrepair

70-640 TS Objective 5.2: Perform offline maintenance

51. Prior to Windows Server 2008, you could not view the data in a backup set. In Windows Server 2008, you can use which of the following tools to view the contents of a data set?

    A. AD DS Database Viewer

    B. AD DS Database Backup tool

    C. AD DS Database Mounting tool

    D. Windows Server 2008 Backup tool

    70-640 TS Objective 5.2: Perform offline maintenance

52. When restoring a DC you can perform nonauthoritative and authoritative restores. What is the difference between the nonauthoritative and authoritative restores?

    A. The nonauthoritative restore updates the USN for the data

    B. The nonauthoritative restore is used when no data was lost; and the authoritative restore updates the Update Sequence Number and is used when data was lost

    C. The authoritative restore is used when no data has been lost

    D. The nonauthoritative restore updates the USN and the authoritative restore is used when no data has been lost

    70-640 TS Objective 5.2: Perform offline maintenance

53. You need to repair your server; you have restarted the server in DSRM and entered your DSRM account and password. You have launched an elevated command prompt. What do you need to type to get the list of available backups on drive E?

    A. `wbadmin -backuptarget:E`

    B. `wbadmin get -backup drive:e`

    C. `wbadmin get versions -backuptarget:e`

    D. `wbadmin get -versions -backuptarget:e`

    70-640 TS Objective 5.2: Perform offline maintenance

54. Following a recovery from a backup, if you are performing an authoritative restore, you need to mark the data as authoritative. Which of the following steps will you use?

    A. Ntdsutil > Authoritative Restore > Restore Database > Quit

    B. Wbadmin > Authoritative Restore

    C. Wbadmin > Authoritative Restore > Restore Database

    D. Ntdsutil > Authoritative Restore

    70-640 TS Objective 5.2: Perform offline maintenance

55. You have a DC that is down and needs to be completely rebuilt. You have a full server backup you would like to use to perform a Graphical Full Server Recovery. You have started the computer with the Windows Installation Media DVD and have cleared the operating system in the System Recovery Options dialog box. After clicking Next, what is your next step in the complete backup restore process?

    A. Select the PC restore

    B. Select Choose a Recovery Tool

    C. Select Choose a Recovery Tool and select the backup to restore

    D. Select the Choose a Recovery Tool option and select Windows Complete PC Restore

    70-640 TS Objective 5.2: Perform offline maintenance

56. You have a DC that is down and needs to be completely rebuilt. You have a full server backup you would like to use to perform a Command-Line Full Server Recovery. You have started the computer with the Windows Installation Media DVD and have cleared the operating system in the System Recovery Options dialog box. After clicking Next, what is your next step to complete the backup restore process from the command line?

A. From the Choose a Recovery Tool option, you select diskpart

B. From the Choose a Recovery Tool option, you select list vol

C. From the Choose a Recovery Tool option, you select Command Prompt

D. None of the above presents a correct solution

70-640 TS Objective 5.2: Perform offline maintenance

57. When a server is created on a virtual machine such as Microsoft Virtual Server R2 or Hyper-V, it is actually which of the following?

A. A folder

B. A directory

C. A network drive

D. A set of files

70-640 TS Objective 5.2: Perform offline maintenance

58. When a DC is running as a virtual machine and suffers a full system failure, what would you do to restore the DC? Select the best answer.

A. Restore from a full system restore with Windows Complete Restore

B. Restore from a server backup

C. Choose Ntdsutil > Authoritative Restore > Restore Database > Quit

D. Reload the image from the ISO

70-640 TS Objective 5.2: Perform offline maintenance

59. When hosting virtual machines, what is the single most important protection feature available in Windows Server 2008?

A. Volume copy

B. Shadow copy

C. Windows Server Backup

D. Volume shadow copy service

70-640 TS Objective 5.2: Perform offline maintenance

60. One of your virtual machine DCs has gone down and you want to restore an older version of the file. How do you select the correct version of the file to replace?

A. Open the VSS console and select the file

B. Right-click the file

C. Select the Previous tab in the Properties dialog box of the folder

D. Select the Backup tab in the Properties dialog box of the folder

70-640 TS Objective 5.2: Perform offline maintenance

7

61. To enable VSS on a server, you need to have the proper disk setup. Which of the following is true considering VSS disk requirements?

    A. VSS requires a minimum of five disk drives

    B. VSS requires a minimum of four disk drives

    C. VSS requires a minimum of three disk drives

    D. VSS has no minimum disk requirements

    70-640 TS Objective 5.2: Perform offline maintenance

62. When VSS is enabled on a server with the proper disk structure how should the drives be assigned for a server with the minimum three disk drives? (Choose three.)

    A. Drive C is the system drive

    B. Drive C is the boot drive

    C. Drive C is both the system and boot drive

    D. Drive D is host to the virtual machines

    E. Drive D is the VSS images drive

    F. Drive E is the host drive for the virtual machines

    G. Drive E is the VSS snapshot drive

    70-640 TS Objective 5.2: Perform offline maintenance

63. You are setting up a host system running Hyper-V for a DC virtual machine. You are in the process of enabling VSS and want to set drive D as the drive that should be copied. Which statement correctly describes how to enable drive D copies?

    A. Select VSS settings

    B. On the shadow copies tab of Drive D's properties select Enable from the Select Volume list

    C. Right-click Volume D and select Previous Versions

    D. On the Setting dialog box, set the limit for D to two copies

    70-640 TS Objective 5.2: Perform offline maintenance

64. When you are enabling VSS from the command line on a Core Server installation, which of the following commands will be used to set up copies?

    A. vssadmin add

    B. vssadmin shadow

    C. vssadmin add shadowcopies

    D. vssadmin add shadowstorage

    70-640 TS Objective 5.2: Perform offline maintenance

65. Using the Group Policy setting for computers and users can result in multiple GPOs, inheritance filters, and exceptions being applied, so that determining the correct policy setting can be difficult. Which of the following is the group of policy tools used to evaluate Group Policy settings?

A. RSoP

B. Group Policy Results wizard

C. Group Policy Modeling

D. Gpresult

70-640 TS Objective 5.3: Monitor Active Directory

66. Windows Server 2008 RSoP provides three tools for monitoring and troubleshooting the application of Group Policy. Which of the following is NOT one of the tools included in RSoP?

A. Group Policy Results wizard

B. Group Policy Active Policy wizard

C. Group Policy Modeling wizard

D. Gpresult.exe

70-640 TS Objective 5.3: Monitor Active Directory

67. To assist in analyzing GPOs and settings on a user or computers you can use the Group Policy Results wizard. Which console includes the Group Policy Results wizard?

A. Group Policy console

B. Group management console

C. Group Policy Management console

D. GPO Management console

70-640 TS Objective 5.3: Monitor Active Directory

68. The Group Policy Results wizard can report on everything about Group Policy settings applied to local or remote computers. This works with Windows Vista, XP, Server 2003, and Server 2008. How does it connect to the remote computer to gather the policy settings?

A. AD

B. Ndis

C. Remote desktop

D. WMI

70-640 TS Objective 5.3: Monitor Active Directory

7

69. Using the Group Policy Results wizard, you can view reports on Group Policy settings applied to the local or a remote computer. Which operating systems are supported by the Group Policy Results wizard? Select all that apply.

    A. Windows NT 4.0

    B. Windows ME

    C. Windows 98

    D. Windows 2000

    E. Windows XP

    F. Windows Vista

    G. Windows NT Server

    H. Windows Server 2003

    I. Windows Server 2008

    70-640 TS Objective 5.3: Monitor Active Directory

70. The Group Policy Results wizard can report on everything about Group Policy settings applied to local or remote computers. How does is connect to the remote computer to gather the policy settings?

    A. Port 53

    B. Port 449

    C. Port 135

    D. Port 4469

    E. Port 445

    F. Port 446

    70-640 TS Objective 5.3: Monitor Active Directory

71. Using the Group Policy Results wizard you can view reports on Group Policy settings applied to the local or a remote computer. Which operating systems are NOT supported by the Group Policy Results wizard?

    A. Windows 2000

    B. Windows XP

    C. Windows Vista

    D. Windows Server 2003

    E. Windows Server 2008

    70-640 TS Objective 5.3: Monitor Active Directory

72. What type of credentials are required to run the Group Policy Results wizard on a remote computer that is running Windows XP or later?

    A. Local User

    B. Authenticated User

    C. Administrative

    D. Domain Admin

    70-640 TS Objective 5.3: Monitor Active Directory

73. You are attempting to troubleshoot a user's policy setting on a remote computer. You have connected to the computer and the user's name is not in the list of users to select for analysis. Which of the following is most likely the problem?

    A. The firewall is preventing remote administration

    B. The user has never logged on to the computer

    C. The WNI service is not running

    D. You are not an administrator on the computer

    70-640 TS Objective 5.3: Monitor Active Directory

74. You are the network administrator for DTILearing.com. You have just run an RSoP analysis of a workstation where users have reported having problems performing their regularly assigned duties. You need to check for problems with Group Policy settings. In which format will your RSoP report be displayed?

    A. .txt file format

    B. .docx file format

    C. .bmp file format

    D. Dynamic HTML

    70-640 TS Objective 5.3: Monitor Active Directory

75. The Group Policy Results wizard creates a detailed RSoP report. The report has three tabs that display the report. Select the correct tabs.

    A. Summary

    B. Computer Configuration

    C. Settings

    D. User Configuration

    E. Events

    F. Policy Events

    70-640 TS Objective 5.3: Monitor Active Directory

76. The results of a Group Policy Results wizard display the resultant set of policy settings that are applied to the user or computer. The Setting tab shows the effect the Group Policy setting has on the user or computer examined in the report. Select the settings you will find on the Settings tab under Security Settings. (Choose all that apply.)

    A. IPSec

    B. Password Policy

    C. User rights

    D. Wireless Settings

    E. Security Options

    70-640 TS Objective 5.3: Monitor Active Directory

7

77. The result of the Group Policy Results wizard displays the resultant set of policy settings that are applied to the user or computer. Which of the following settings are NOT on the Settings tab?

A. Wireless settings

B. Password policy

C. User rights

D. IPSec

E. Security options

F. Windows settings

70-640 TS Objective 5.3: Monitor Active Directory

78. You have generated an RSoP report with the Group Policy Results wizard and want to save a copy as an HTML file that maintains the dynamic content. Which of the following should you do?

A. Select Print from the Action menu

B. Right-click the Group Policy Results wizard in the GPMC

C. Right-click the report and choose Save Report

D. Select File Save As

70-640 TS Objective 5.3: Monitor Active Directory

79. You have generated an RSoP report with the Group Policy Results wizard and want to rerun the query. Which of the following should you do?

A. Select Rerun Query from the Action menu

B. Right-click the report and choose Rerun Query

C. Right-click the Group Policy Results wizard in the GPMC

D. Select File and then click Rerun Query

70-640 TS Objective 5.3: Monitor Active Directory

80. You have generated an RSoP report with the Group Policy Results wizard and want to print a copy. Which of the following should you do?

A. Right-click the report and then select Print

B. Select Print from the Action menu

C. Right-click the Group Policy Results wizard in the GPMC

D. Select File > Print

70-640 TS Objective 5.3: Monitor Active Directory

81. Which of the following operating systems supports Gpresult.exe, but will NOT run the Group Policy Results wizard?

A. Widows NT

B. Windows 2000

C. Windows XP

D. Windows Vista

E. Windows Server 2003

70-640 TS Objective 5.3: Monitor Active Directory

82. When you are using the Gpresult.exe command to examine group policies on a computer, which one of the following options would you use to specify an analysis for just computer settings on the target computer?

    A. /-user

    B. /scope no computer

    C. /scope user only

    D. /scope [computer]

    70-640 TS Objective 5.3: Monitor Active Directory

83. When you are using the Gpresult.exe command to examine group policies on a computer, which one of the following options would you use to specify an analysis with super verbose data that includes details of all policy settings?

    A. /v

    B. /z

    C. /s

    D. /all

    70-640 TS Objective 5.3: Monitor Active Directory

84. When you're moving computers or users between groups or OUs, the domain or site changes in the group membership may affect the RSoP. Prior to making any such changes, you can evaluate them in RSoP by using which of the following tools? Select the best answer.

    A. Gpresult.exe

    B. Group Policy Management console

    C. Group Policy Modeling wizard

    D. Group Policy Results wizard

    70-640 TS Objective 5.3: Monitor Active Directory

85. Windows Vista and Windows Server 2008 have a new log created to log errors created by the Group Policy client that cannot connect to a DC. What is the name of this new log?

    A. Group Policy log

    B. Group Policy Operational log

    C. Group Policy Connection log

    D. Group Policy Error log

    70-640 TS Objective 5.3: Monitor Active Directory

86. Windows Server 2008 and Windows Vista have a new log to track Group Policy events. The log is found by using the Event Viewer snap-in or console. Which node is the Group Policy Operational log found in?

    A. Applications and Services logs

    B. Subscriptions

    C. Custom views

    D. Windows logs

    70-640 TS Objective 5.3: Monitor Active Directory

87. Which choice best completes this statement? While monitoring Active Directory replication a Domain Controller replicates changes from another Domain Controller because of AD DC _____.

   A. Topology

   B. Objects

   C. Connector objects

   D. Replication

   70-640 TS Objective 5.3: Monitor Active Directory

88. Connection objects in Active Directory are one way and they represent inbound-only replication. Which of the following is true concerning connector objects?

   A. Replication in AD is always push technology

   B. Replication in AD is usually push technology

   C. Replication in AD is always pull technology

   D. Replication in AD is push-pull technology

   70-640 TS Objective 5.3: Monitor Active Directory

89. Replication paths between Domain Controllers in Active Directory are created by connection objects that create the replication topology. Which of the following statements are true about monitoring replication topology?

   A. You have to create the replication topology manually

   B. Automatic topology created by Active Directory will not be very efficient

   C. You do not have to create the replication topology manually

   D. If one Domain Controller fails, replication will stop

   70-640 TS Objective 5.3: Monitor Active Directory

90. When monitoring an Active Directory Domain Controller, which component helps to optimize replication between Domain Controllers?

   A. Knowledge Consistency Checker

   B. Replication Checker

   C. Consistency Checker

   D. Knowledge Checker

   70-640 TS Objective 5.3: Monitor Active Directory

91. The KCC helps to generate and optimize replication automatically between Domain Controllers. If the Domain Controller becomes unresponsive, what will happen? Select the best answer.

   A. The KCC will submit an alert notifying the administrator

   B. The KCC will rearrange the topology temporarily without deleting or adding any connector objects

   C. The KCC will rearrange the topology by adding or deleting connector objects as needed

   D. The KCC will wait until the Domain Controller comes back online

   70-640 TS Objective 5.3: Monitor Active Directory

92. Windows provides tools for monitoring replication. Which of the tools will report on the status of replication on a DC?

    A. Dcdiag

    B. Repmon

    C. Repadmin

    D. VerifyRep

    70-640 TS Objective 5.3: Monitor Active Directory

93. Windows provides tools for monitoring replication. Which of the tools performs tests and reports on replication and security of AD DS?

    A. FrsEvent

    B. Dcdiag

    C. Repadmin

    D. VerifyRep

    70-640 TS Objective 5.3: Monitor Active Directory

94. The Directory Service Diagnosis tool, dcdiag.exe, includes reports that monitor replication. Match the correct description in the following list to the name of the report.

Report Description
Checks for timely replication between DCs
Reports on operation errors in the file replication system
Checks for failures that would prevent or delay inter-site replication
Identifies errors in the knowledge consistency checker

Report Description	Report
	Inter-site
	KCCEvents
	Replications
	FrsEvent

    70-640 TS Objective 5.3: Monitor Active Directory

95. To manage user accounts you use the Additional Account Info. Which of the following is true about adding the Additional Account Info tab?

    A. It's already present; no action is necessary

    B. Windows Server Updates downloads the accinfo.dll

    C. Windows Server 2003 Resource Kit contains the accinfo.dll

    D. Use the Microsoft Web Site for Server management to add the tab to the User Objects Properties page

    70-640 TS Objective 5.3: Monitor Active Directory

96. For monitoring and managing user accounts, you add the Additional Account Info tab to the user objects properties page. How is the Additional Account Info tab added?

A. It's already present; no action is necessary

B. Register the AcctInfo.dll

C. Windows Server Updates

D. Windows Server 2003 Resource Kit

70-640 TS Objective 5.3: Monitor Active Directory

97. Which of the following is the Windows Server 2008 Backup tool that allows you to monitor data contained in a backup set?

A. AD DA Object Restore

B. AD DA Database Viewer

C. AD DA Mounting tool

D. AD DA Database Mounting tool

70-640 TS Objective 5.3: Monitor Active Directory

98. You are using Wbadmin.exe to monitor the backups for a Windows Server 2008 core installation. Which of the following command options will return a list of disks attached to the installation?

A. `wbadmin get id`

B. `wbadmin get disks`

C. `wbadmin get disks > Diskidentifiers.txt`

D. `wbadmin.exe`

70-640 TS Objective 5.3: Monitor Active Directory

99. In a previous version of Windows, the boot.ini file controlled the boot process to allow you to specify different boot files. In Windows Server 2008 how do you change the boot order?

A. Edit the boot.ini file

B. Use the bcdedit.exe command

C. Press F6 when booting Windows

D. Press DEL when booting Windows

70-640 TS Objective 5.3: Monitor Active Directory

100. Part of why you use Volume Shadow Copy Service or VSS is to make sure that the default schedule for backups is adequate for your needs. What determines the schedule for VSS?

A. The Calendar

B. The Task Scheduler

C. The schedule is determined by the amount of data

D. It's checked daily

70-640 TS Objective 5.3: Monitor Active Directory

101. Previous versions of Windows Server had no way of viewing data in backup data sets. In Windows Server 2008 you can use which of the following tools to monitor the contents of a data set?

A. AD DS Database Viewer

B. AD DS Database Mounting tool

C. AD DS Database Backup tool

D. Windows Server 2008 Backup tool

70-640 TS Objective 5.3: Monitor Active Directory

102. You have scheduled a backup with Wbadmin.exe using the Enable Backup option. Where can you monitor the result of the backup schedule? Select the best answer.

A. Task Scheduler

B. Task Scheduler under Windows\Backup

C. Task Scheduler under Microsoft\Backup

D. Task Scheduler under Microsoft\Windows\Backup

70-640 TS Objective 5.3: Monitor Active Directory

103. You have scheduled a backup with Wbadmin.exe using the Enable Backup option. You have monitored the schedule and you need to modify it from a daily to a weekly schedule. What do you need to do to modify the scheduled task?

A. Modify the task in Task Scheduler

B. Remove the task and use wbadmin to recreate it

C. Use wbadmin

D. None of the above represents a true statement; the task cannot be moved after you've created it with wbadmin

70-640 TS Objective 5.3: Monitor Active Directory

104. You have scheduled a backup with Wbadmin.exe with the Enable Backup option. You have monitored the schedule and you want to make some adjustments to the schedule. How do you modify the scheduled task?

A. Remove the task and use wbadmin to recreate it

B. Use wbadmin

C. Modify the task in Task Scheduler

D. None of the above represents a true statement; the task cannot be moved after you've created it with wbadmin

70-640 TS Objective 5.3: Monitor Active Directory

8

CONFIGURING ACTIVE DIRECTORY CERTIFICATE SERVICES

This chapter contains 104 questions that all fall under Microsoft's sixth and last main exam objective for the 70-640 exam, "Configuring Active Directory Certificate Services." This main objective consists of the following five sub-objectives:

- Install Active Directory Certificate Services
- Configure CA server settings
- Manage certificate templates
- Manage enrollments
- Manage certificate revocations

8

TEST PREPARATION QUESTIONS

1. The distribution, organization, and control of public key certificates are referred to as which of the following?

   A. SSL

   B. Certificate Services

   C. PKI

   D. Public Key management

   70-640 TS Objective 6.1: Install Active Directory Certificate Services

2. Which Microsoft product is used to create and manage a PKI infrastructure in Windows Server 2008?

   A. Certificate Services

   B. Federated Services

   C. Active Directory Certificate Services

   D. Secure Sockets Layer

   70-640 TS Objective 6.1: Install Active Directory Certificate Services

3. The AD DS infrastructure provides each person in your enterprise with which of the following?

A. Identity

B. Tools

C. Keys

D. Certificates

70-640 TS Objective 6.1: Install Active Directory Certificate Services

4. Active Directory Domain Services along with AD CS are primarily targeted at providing authentication and authorization in which of the following environments?

A. Extranet

B. Within a corporate network

C. Internally

D. On the web

70-640 TS Objective 6.1: Install Active Directory Certificate Services

5. Because Active Directory Domain Services is a network operating system that, along with AD CS, is primarily targeted at providing authentication and authorization within a corporate environment, it can be extended beyond the corporate boundary. Which of the following would be the best when considering using Microsoft PKI infrastructure outside of the corporate environment?

A. Certificate Services

B. HTTPS

C. Third-party commercial authority

D. This question presents an untrue situation

70-640 TS Objective 6.1: Install Active Directory Certificate Services

6. When you visit a website that is using Secure Hypertext Transfer Protocol, that site will contain which of the following to identify what website you are on?

A. SSL certificate

B. Web Key

C. Hash

D. It's signed by the web host

70-640 TS Objective 6.1: Install Active Directory Certificate Services

7. The following image shows the Certificates Manager in Firefox's browser. Where did the list of trusted commercial CSs come from?

A. The list is imported by the users as needed

B. The list is obtained from the websites the user visited

C. The list is included with the browser from Firefox

D. The list is supplied by Microsoft

70-640 TS Objective 6.1: Install Active Directory Certificate Services

8. The following image shows the Certificates in Internet Explorer. Where did the list of trusted root certificate authorities come from?

A. The list is imported by the users as needed

B. The list is obtained from the websites the user visited

C. The list is included with the browser from Microsoft

D. The list is supplied from updates

70-640 TS Objective 6.1: Install Active Directory Certificate Services

9. Certificates work with your Internet browser because the trusted commercial CAs are included with the browser by the software developer. How is the list of CAs updated?

A. Manually by the user as needed

B. Automatically by the websites visited

C. It cannot be updated

D. By the operating system

70-640 TS Objective 6.1: Install Active Directory Certificate Services

10. Certificates work with your Internet browser because the trusted commercial CAs are included with the browser by the software developer and are updated with regular updates from Microsoft update services. In Windows Vista and Server 2008 how is this accomplished?

A. Automatically

B. Nightly at 3AM

C. Through a Group Policy setting that it turned on by default

D. Through the Control Panel

70-640 TS Objective 6.1: Install Active Directory Certificate Services

11. Certificates work with your Internet browser because the trusted commercial CAs are included with the browser by the software developer and are updated with regular updates from Microsoft update services. Prior to Windows Vista and Server 2008, how was this done?

A. Through the Control Panel

B. Through user intervention

C. Nightly at 3AM

D. Through a Group Policy setting that it turned on by default

70-640 TS Objective 6.1: Install Active Directory Certificate Services

12. You are planning to set up a PKI infrastructure in your enterprise. You will be issuing your own certificates to users. Which additional step do you need to take so the users can use the certificates you issue?

A. Sign them

B. Compare their hash values to authenticate them

C. Add your organization to the trusted CAs on the users' computers

D. Nothing; the users will automatically be enrolled

70-640 TS Objective 6.1: Install Active Directory Certificate Services

13. You are planning to set up a PKI infrastructure in your enterprise. You will be issuing your own certificates to some users outside of your area of control. Which of the following will you need to do?

A. Ask the users outside of your area of control to trust your certificate

B. You cannot issue certificates to users outside of your area of control

C. Link your certificates to a root authority

D. Nothing; your certificates will be trusted automatically

70-640 TS Objective 6.1: Install Active Directory Certificate Services

14. The trusted root CA is the ultimate authority in the certificate hierarchy. How do CAs control whom they give master certificates to? Select the best answer.

    A. Organizations that can afford the fees

    B. Stringent validation program

    C. Questionnaires

    D. Technical capability

    70-640 TS Objective 6.1: Install Active Directory Certificate Services

15. What are the three layers of the trusted certificate plan called?

    A. CA, Root, User

    B. Root, CA, User

    C. Root, Intermediary, Computer

    D. Root, Intermediary, Customer

    70-640 TS Objective 6.1: Install Active Directory Certificate Services

16. Microsoft Exchange Server 2007 uses self-signed certificates to validate and secure connections between internal users. Which of the following will require replacing the self-signing certificate with a trusted root certificate?

    A. OWA

    B. Client access

    C. Hub transport over TCP/IP

    D. Mailboxes

    70-640 TS Objective 6.1: Install Active Directory Certificate Services

17. Microsoft Exchange Server 2007 uses self-signed certificates to validate and secure connections between internal users. You want to enable users to connect securely to the Exchange server with OWA. Which of the following will you need to do?

    A. Create a root certificate server on the local domain

    B. Use the self-signed certificate for the external users to connect

    C. Replace the self-signed certificate with a purchased certificate

    D. Nothing; the OWA will work over any connection

    70-640 TS Objective 6.1: Install Active Directory Certificate Services

18. How are PKI architectures built? Select the best answer from the choices.

    A. All members of the PKI are chained together in a hierarchy that ends with the topmost CA

    B. All members of the PKI receive certificates directly from the root

    C. The root of a PKI that is exposed to the Internet is a self-signed certificate

    D. All members must be directly connected to the root with no intermediacy certificates

    70-640 TS Objective 6.1: Install Active Directory Certificate Services

8

19. When planning an internal-only PKI infrastructure, which of the following considerations will make it more difficult to implement?

    A. Using an Exchange server

    B. Using an intranet web server

    C. Using e-commerce

    D. Using VPN connections

    70-640 TS Objective 6.1: Install Active Directory Certificate Services

20. What does an internal PKI implementation accomplish?

    A. Identifies your organization to the outside world

    B. Establishes a web presence

    C. Enables external authentication and authorization for all your users

    D. Proves who you are to yourself

    70-640 TS Objective 6.1: Install Active Directory Certificate Services

21. What does obtaining a master certificate from a trusted certificate authority accomplish for your organization's PKI infrastructure?

    A. Identifies your organization to the outside world

    B. Establishes a web presence

    C. Provides each of your users with a certificate

    D. Proves who you are to yourself

    70-640 TS Objective 6.1: Install Active Directory Certificate Services

22. The ability to encrypt data is a product of using certificates. Which of the following requires certificates to lock and unlock data?

    A. EFS

    B. VSS

    C. File lock

    D. BitLocker

    70-640 TS Objective 6.1: Install Active Directory Certificate Services

23. Which of the following technologies used in Windows Server 2008 will provide encrypted remote communications and rely on certificates for authentication?

    A. SMTP

    B. SNNP

    C. SSTP and IPSec

    D. PPTP

    70-640 TS Objective 6.1: Install Active Directory Certificate Services

24. Which of the following technologies used in Windows Server 2008 will provide encrypted email and rely on certificates for authentication?

    A. S/MIME

    B. SSTP and IPSec

    C. SNNP

    D. PPTP

    70-640 TS Objective 6.1: Install Active Directory Certificate Services

25. Which of the following technologies used in Windows Server 2008 will provide secure logons and relies on certificates for authentication?

    A. S/MIME

    B. SSTP and IPSec

    C. Smart Cards

    D. PPTP

    70-640 TS Objective 6.1: Install Active Directory Certificate Services

26. Which of the following technologies used in Windows Server 2008 will secure all communications to your websites?

    A. S/MIME

    B. SSTP and IPSec

    C. Smart Cards

    D. IIS 7.0

    70-640 TS Objective 6.1: Install Active Directory Certificate Services

27. Which of the following technologies used in Windows Server 2008 will secure all server logons and relies on certificates for authentication?

    A. S/MIME

    B. NAP

    C. Smart Cards

    D. PPTP

    70-640 TS Objective 6.1: Install Active Directory Certificate Services

28. Which of the following Windows Server 2008 technologies will protect all your documents and information from tampering and misuse?

    A. AD CS

    B. AD DS

    C. SSL

    D. AD RMS

    70-640 TS Objective 6.1: Install Active Directory Certificate Services

29. Which model is the PKI infrastructure built upon?

    A. Standalone trust model

    B. WAN trust

    C. Trusted CA model

    D. Local trust model

    70-640 TS Objective 6.1: Install Active Directory Certificate Services

30. Which of the following components are part of the Active Directory Certificate Services? Select all that apply.

    A. Online responder

    B. CA Web Enrollment

    C. NAT

    D. Certificate authorities

    E. PKI

    F. NDES

    70-640 TS Objective 6.1: Install Active Directory Certificate Services

31. Certificate Authorities or CAs are servers used to issue and manage certificates. Which of the following are NOT types of certificates?

    A. Root

    B. Hybrid

    C. Subordinate

    D. Child

    70-640 TS Objective 6.1: Install Active Directory Certificate Services

32. In the PKI structure, which of the following will have the longest certificate duration?

    A. Root

    B. Subordinate

    C. Root and Subordinate

    D. Child

    70-640 TS Objective 6.1: Install Active Directory Certificate Services

33. Which of the following is true concerning the issuance of certificates by AD CS?

    A. Subordinate CAs issue certificates only when their own certificates are valid

    B. Subordinate CAs can issue certificates locally anytime

    C. Subordinate CAs do not issue their own certificates

    D. Subordinate CAs only issue certificates to child CAs

    70-640 TS Objective 6.1: Install Active Directory Certificate Services

34. Which of the following is true concerning the issuance of certificates by subordinate CAs?

    A. Certificates issued to users have longer durations that subordinate CAs

    B. Subordinate CAs certificates have longer durations than user certificates

    C. Subordinate CAs do not issue their own certificates

    D. Subordinate CAs only issue certificates to computers

    70-640 TS Objective 6.1: Install Active Directory Certificate Services

35. Which of the following functions does the CA Web Enrollment perform in the PKI infrastructure in Windows Server 2008?

    A. Issues certificates to users requesting web access

    B. Issues certificates to websites

    C. Connects users to the CA through a web browser to request certificates

    D. Uses the online certificate status protocol (OSCP)

    70-640 TS Objective 6.1: Install Active Directory Certificate Services

36. What does a CRL provide for your public key infrastructure?

    A. A list of valid certificates

    B. All the certificates that are due to expire

    C. A list of certificates that have been invalidated and revoked

    D. A certificate checklist

    70-640 TS Objective 6.1: Install Active Directory Certificate Services

37. How do PKI systems utilize certificate revocation lists?

    A. As a certificate validation

    B. As a check of users and computers for revocation each time a certificate is presented

    C. As a one-time reference to check validity

    D. As a place to put a certificate that is suspect

    70-640 TS Objective 6.1: Install Active Directory Certificate Services

38. Which of the following PKI components utilize the Online Certificate Status Protocol?

    A. Certificate Authorities

    B. CA Web Enrollment

    C. Online responder

    D. Network Device Enrollment Service

    70-640 TS Objective 6.1: Install Active Directory Certificate Services

39. What does an online responder system do for the PKI infrastructure?

    A. Uses OCSP

    B. Submits valid certificates

    C. Revokes certificates

    D. Submits validation requests for specific certificates

    70-640 TS Objective 6.1: Install Active Directory Certificate Services

40. Which of the following is the best reason for using an online responder in your PKI?
    A. Safer than using CRL
    B. OCSP is encrypted
    C. Eliminates the need for large CRL lists
    D. Faster and more efficient than CRLs
    70-640 TS Objective 6.1: Install Active Directory Certificate Services

41. When thinking about online responder, which of the following is true?
    A. Online responder was first available with Windows Server 2003
    B. Online responder is a new feature in Windows Server 2008
    C. Online responder is a third-party service
    D. Online responder has replaced the CRL
    70-640 TS Objective 6.1: Install Active Directory Certificate Services

42. You have several routers that use Cisco's SCEP. Which of the Windows AD CS components will you use?
    A. CA Web
    B. CA
    C. OR
    D. NDES
    70-640 TS Objective 6.1: Install Active Directory Certificate Services

43. Devices that do not have an account in AD DS cannot normally participate in the PKI hierarchy. Which of the following protocols will allow routers to receive certificates?
    A. NDES
    B. S/MIME
    C. IPSec
    D. SCEP
    70-640 TS Objective 6.1: Install Active Directory Certificate Services

44. Which of the following types of Certificate Authorities can Windows Server 2008 support? (Choose all that apply.)
    A. Root
    B. Commercial
    C. Enterprise
    D. Standalone
    E. Workgroup
    F. Internal
    70-640 TS Objective 6.1: Install Active Directory Certificate Services

45. Which of the following is true concerning standalone CAs?

    A. Standalone CAs are integrated automatically into AD DS

    B. Standalone CAs are CAs running on DCs

    C. Standalone CAs run on member or standalone servers

    D. Standalone CAs are never taken offline

    70-640 TS Objective 6.1: Install Active Directory Certificate Services

46. Which of the following is true concerning standalone CAs?

    A. Standalone CAs are integrated automatically into AD DS

    B. Standalone CAs are taken offline for security reasons

    C. Standalone CAs are CAs running on DCs

    D. Standalone CAs remain online for security reasons

    70-640 TS Objective 6.1: Install Active Directory Certificate Services

47. Which of the following is true concerning standalone CAs?

    A. Standalone CAs are often used as the internal root CA

    B. Standalone CAs are CAs running on DCs

    C. Standalone CAs cannot run on member or standalone servers

    D. Standalone CAs are never taken offline

    70-640 TS Objective 6.1: Install Active Directory Certificate Services

48. Which of the following operating systems can run standalone CAs?

    A. Windows Server 2008 Standard Edition

    B. Windows Server 2008 Enterprise Edition

    C. Windows Server 2008 Datacenter Edition

    D. Windows Server 2008, all editions

    70-640 TS Objective 6.1: Install Active Directory Certificate Services

49. In a standalone CA running on a member server acting as an internal root CA, which of the following will be true?

    A. Certificate issuing is performed manually

    B. Certificates are issued automatically

    C. Standalone CAs are based on custom certificates

    D. All of the above are true about a standalone CA in this environment

    70-640 TS Objective 6.1: Install Active Directory Certificate Services

50. Enterprise CAs are integrated into AD DS and act as issuing CAs. Which of the following describes issuing CAs?

    A. CAs that issue certificates to standalone CAs

    B. CAs that issue certificates to intermediate CAs

    C. CAs that issue certificates to end users

    D. CAs that issue certificates to internal root servers

    70-640 TS Objective 6.1: Install Active Directory Certificate Services

8

51. Which of the following is true concerning issuing CAs?
    A. Issuing CAs are offline except when issuing certificates
    B. Issuing CAs are available at all times
    C. Issuing CAs provide certificates to root CAs
    D. None of the above represents true statements
    70-640 TS Objective 6.1: Install Active Directory Certificate Services

52. Enterprise CAs can be run on which of the following Windows Server 2008 editions? Select the best answer.
    A. Windows Server 2008 Standard
    B. Windows Server 2008 Core
    C. Windows Server Enterprise
    D. Windows Server Enterprise and Datacenter
    70-640 TS Objective 6.1: Install Active Directory Certificate Services

53. Which of the following statements concerning Enterprise CAs is true?
    A. AD DS membership is not required
    B. Certificates issued by Enterprise CAs use advanced templates which can be edited
    C. Enterprise CAs are often used for root certificates
    D. Certificates issued by Enterprise CAs use standard templates which cannot be modified
    70-640 TS Objective 6.1: Install Active Directory Certificate Services

54. Which of the following statements concerning Enterprise CAs is true?
    A. Enterprise CAs are often used for root certificates
    B. Certificates issued by Enterprise CAs use standard templates which cannot be modified
    C. Enterprise CAs are used to issue certificates to end users
    D. Enterprise CAs are often used as the internal root authority
    70-640 TS Objective 6.1: Install Active Directory Certificate Services

55. Which of the following is a true statement when considering the use of standalone CAs in an enterprise?
    A. Standalone CAs are best for delivering specific services
    B. Standalone CAs are general-purpose servers
    C. Standalone CAs are fully automated
    D. Standalone CAs are not a good choice for use as a root server
    70-640 TS Objective 6.1: Install Active Directory Certificate Services

56. Which of the following is a true statement when considering the use of standalone CAs in an enterprise?
    A. Standalone CAs are general-purpose servers
    B. Standalone CAs are fully automated
    C. Standalone CAs are a good choice for use as internal root servers
    D. Standalone CAs are not a good choice for use as root servers
    70-640 TS Objective 6.1: Install Active Directory Certificate Services

57. Which of the following is a true statement when considering the use of Enterprise CAs in an enterprise?

A. Enterprise CAs should be considered as root CAs

B. Enterprise CAs should be considered mostly as issuing CAs

C. Enterprise CAs cannot be automated

D. Enterprise CAs should not be used to issue certificates to end users

70-640 TS Objective 6.1: Install Active Directory Certificate Services

58. Which of the following is a true statement when considering the use of Enterprise CAs in an enterprise?

A. Enterprise CAs should be considered as root CAs

B. Enterprise CAs should not be used to issue certificates to end users

C. Enterprise CAs are automatic

D. Enterprise CAs cannot be automated

70-640 TS Objective 6.1: Install Active Directory Certificate Services

59. Which of the following statements correctly describes how an Enterprise CA can be deployed in your enterprise network?

A. As a standalone server

B. As a standalone server or member server

C. As a Domain Controller

D. As a DC or member server

70-640 TS Objective 6.1: Install Active Directory Certificate Services

60. Which of the following statements correctly describes how a standalone CA can be deployed in your enterprise network? Select the best answer.

A. As a standalone server

B. As a standalone server or member server

C. As a standalone server, member server, or Domain Controller

D. As a DC or member server

70-640 TS Objective 6.1: Install Active Directory Certificate Services

61. Which of the following certificate servers can use the Certificate Microsoft Management Console for certificate requests and validation?

A. Standalone

B. Enterprise

C. Standard and Enterprise

D. Standard when integrated with AD DS

70-640 TS Objective 6.1: Install Active Directory Certificate Services

8

62. The security of the root CA in the CA hierarchy is of highest priority. Which of the following is the best way to make the root CA as secure as possible?

    A. Firewall it

    B. Place the root CA in a DMZ

    C. Place the root CA in its own subnet

    D. Take the root CA offline

    70-640 TS Objective 6.1: Install Active Directory Certificate Services

63. When creating the CA hierarchy, when should a single-tiered hierarchy with a single root CA be utilized?

    A. Most of the time

    B. When you think the root may not be secure

    C. Only when you're sure the root cannot be compromised

    D. Never

    70-640 TS Objective 6.1: Install Active Directory Certificate Services

64. You would create a two-tiered hierarchy with a root and issuing CAs to address which of the following concerns?

    A. You need to protect your root CA by taking it offline if your organization is too small to support a three-tiered approach

    B. You have a large organization and need to protect your root CA

    C. You have a small organization

    D. You have a complex organization

    70-640 TS Objective 6.1: Install Active Directory Certificate Services

65. What are the three types of CAs you would find in a typical three-tiered AD CS hierarchy? Select the best single answer.

    A. Root, intermediate, final

    B. Root, level two, and final

    C. Root, intermediate, and user

    D. Root, intermediate, and issuing

    70-640 TS Objective 6.1: Install Active Directory Certificate Services

66. You have created a three-tiered AD CS hierarchy. Which if any of the CAs would you take offline to protect the security of the root?

    A. Root

    B. Intermediate

    C. Root and intermediate

    D. None; the three-tiered hierarchy protects the root CA

    70-640 TS Objective 6.1: Install Active Directory Certificate Services

67. Here are three AD CS CA models for deployment. List them in the correct CA server that would be selected in each model for the root CA.

Root Server Type
Standalone CA
Enterprise CA
Intermediate CA

Root Server Type	Tier Model
	One tier
	Two tier
	Three tier

70-640 TS Objective 6.1: Install Active Directory Certificate Services

68. When creating a three-tiered AD CS hierarchical model, what type of CA would you use for the intermediate CA? Select the best single answer.

A. Root CA

B. Root or intermediate CA

C. Enterprise CA

D. Standalone CA offline

70-640 TS Objective 6.1: Install Active Directory Certificate Services

69. If you were creating a three-tiered AD CS hierarchical model, what type of CA would you use for the issuing CA?

A. Root CA

B. Root or intermediate CA

C. Enterprise CA

D. Standalone CA offline

70-640 TS Objective 6.1: Install Active Directory Certificate Services

70. Which of the following are NOT suggested practices for AD CS deployments?

A. Use Windows Server 2008 Hyper-V for root CAs

B. Use Windows Server 2008 Hyper-V for intermediate CAs

C. It is not necessary to store the VM files for security purposes

D. Remove the VM files from the server when the CA is taken offline

70-640 TS Objective 6.1: Install Active Directory Certificate Services

71. Which of the following are NOT suggested practices for AD CS deployments?

A. You can change a CA from standalone to enterprise if necessary

B. Use Windows Server 2008 Hyper-V for root and intermediate CAs

C. Store the VM files for security purposes in a vault

D. Remove the VM files from the server when the CA is taken offline

70-640 TS Objective 6.1: Install Active Directory Certificate Services

8

72. Which of the following are NOT suggested practices for AD CS deployments?
    A. You can change a server name after the AD CS service is installed if necessary
    B. Use Windows Server 2008 Hyper-V for root and intermediate CAs
    C. Store the VM files for security purposes in a vault
    D. Remove the VM files from the server when the CA is taken offline
    70-640 TS Objective 6.1: Install Active Directory Certificate Services

73. Which of the following are NOT suggested practices for AD CS deployments?
    A. You cannot change a server name after the AD CS service is installed
    B. It is not necessary to secure access to the physical server
    C. Use Windows Server 2008 Hyper-V for root and intermediate CAs
    D. Remove the VM files from the server when the CA is taken offline
    70-640 TS Objective 6.1: Install Active Directory Certificate Services

74. Which of the following are NOT suggested practices for AD CS deployments?
    A. You cannot change a server name after the AD CS service is installed
    B. Use Windows Server 2008 Hyper-V for root and intermediate CAs
    C. You should install AD CS on a DC
    D. Remove the VM files from the server when the CA is taken offline
    70-640 TS Objective 6.1: Install Active Directory Certificate Services

75. Which one of the following is true concerning servers hosting AD CS?
    A. Use separate disks for data, OS, and log files
    B. Multiple processors do not accelerate the certificate allocation process
    C. RAM should be at the maximum amount supported
    D. Key lengths have no impact on CPU and disk usage
    70-640 TS Objective 6.1: Install Active Directory Certificate Services

76. Which one of the following is true concerning servers hosting AD CS?
    A. Multiple processors do not accelerate the certificate allocation process
    B. RAM should be at the maximum amount supported
    C. Key lengths have no impact on CPU and disk usage
    D. RAID is used in physical servers that are balanced between reliability and improved performance
    70-640 TS Objective 6.1: Install Active Directory Certificate Services

77. Which one of the following is true concerning servers hosting AD CS?
    A. Multiple processors do not accelerate the certificate allocation process
    B. Long keys require more CPU usage and lower disk usage
    C. RAM should be at the maximum amount supported
    D. Key lengths have no impact on CPU and disk usage
    70-640 TS Objective 6.1: Install Active Directory Certificate Services

78. Which of the following is NOT a step in finalizing the configuration of an issuing CA?
    A. Create a certificate revocation configuration
    B. Configure and personalize certificate templates
    C. Configure the CRL
    D. Configure enrollment and issuance options
    70-640 TS Objective 6.2: Configure CA server settings

79. Which of the following is NOT a step in creating a revocation configuration for a CA?
    A. Configure enrollment and issuance options
    B. Specify CRL distribution points
    C. Schedule the publication of the CRLs
    D. Configure the CRL
    70-640 TS Objective 6.2: Configure CA server settings

80. Which of the following is NOT a step in configuring and personalizing certificate templates?
    A. Configure each template
    B. Deploy the templates to the CAs
    C. Configure the CRL
    D. Identify which templates to use
    70-640 TS Objective 6.2: Configure CA server settings

81. If you plan to use EFS with your certificate templates, you need to create which of the following?
    A. An EFS Recovery Agent template
    B. A basic EFS profile
    C. A basic WS08 template
    D. Any of the above
    70-640 TS Objective 6.3: Manage certificate templates

82. To create an EFS template, which of the following should you do first?
    A. Publish the recovery agent
    B. Publish the recovery agent certificate in AD
    C. Select the basic EFS template and copy it
    D. None of the choices is a true answer
    70-640 TS Objective 6.3: Manage certificate templates

8

83. If your network will be using a wireless connection, you will need to create a Network Policy Server (NPS) template for use with your AD CS system. Which of the following will you use as the NPS template?

    A. NPS template

    B. RAS and IAS server templates

    C. RAS template

    D. IAS server template

    70-640 TS Objective 6.3: Manage certificate templates

84. When users will be using a Smart Card to log on to their computers, you will need to create a Smart Card template for use with your system. Which of the following will you use as the Smart Card template?

    A. Smart Card template

    B. Smart Card user template

    C. Smart Card logon and Smartcard user templates

    D. Smart Card logon template

    70-640 TS Objective 6.3: Manage certificate templates

85. To make administrative accounts more secure, you can use Smart Card logons. You will need to create a Smart Card template for use with your system. Which of the following will you use as the Smart Card template?

    A. Smart Card logon and Smart Card user templates

    B. Smart Card template

    C. Smart Card user template

    D. Smart Card logon template

    70-640 TS Objective 6.3: Manage certificate templates

86. Which of the following would NOT use auto-enrollment?

    A. Wireless

    B. Smart Cards

    C. EFS

    D. Web servers

    70-640 TS Objective 6.3: Manage certificate templates

87. To customize templates for web servers, which of the following would you do?

    A. Create duplicates of the DC template

    B. Create duplicates of the web server authentication template

    C. Create duplicates of the Domain Controller authentication template

    D. Create duplicates of the web server and DC authentication templates

    70-640 TS Objective 6.3: Manage certificate templates

88. After certificate templates are created they must be issued. From where do you issue certificate templates?

    A. Service Manager/Active Directory Certificate Services/Templates/Issuing CA Name/Certificate Templates

    B. Server Manager/ AD Certificate Services

    C. Server Manage/Active Directory Certificate Services/Templates

    D. Service Manager /Active Directory Certificate Services /Templates/Issue

    70-640 TS Objective 6.4: Manage enrollments

89. When issuing certificates from the Enable Certificates Templates dialog box, how do you select multiple templates?

    A. You have to select templates individually

    B. Use the Select button

    C. Use Ctrl-click

    D. Use Ctrl+Shift

    70-640 TS Objective 6.4: Manage enrollments

90. How is certificate enrollment done in Windows Server 2008?

    A. Using the Windows settings

    B. Using Group Policies

    C. From the user settings

    D. Using auto-enrollment

    70-640 TS Objective 6.4: Manage enrollments

91. To configure enrollment manually, which Group Policy is the best choice?

    A. You should create a new GP

    B. You can use any existing GP that is not assigned to all domain members

    C. You should use the default Domain Policy

    D. Any of the above

    70-640 TS Objective 6.4: Manage enrollments

92. To configure auto-enrollment, which Group Policy is the best choice?

    A. Create a new GP with GPMC and assign it to all members

    B. Use any existing GP that is not assigned to all domain members

    C. Use a copy of the default template

    D. Any of the above

    70-640 TS Objective 6.4: Manage enrollments

93. To enable auto-enrollments where would you find the correct policy to enable?

    A. Computer Configuration\ Policies\Windows Settings\Security Settings\Public Key Policies

    B. User configuration Policies\Windows Settings\Security Settings\Public Key Policies

    C. Computer Configuration\Public key Policies\Security

    D. User configuration\Public key Policies\Security

    70-640 TS Objective 6.4: Manage enrollments

94. Which of the following check boxes in the Certificate Services Client Auto Enrollment policy would you select to re-enroll any certificates that have been issued manually?

    A. Renew Expired Certificates

    B. Update Pending Certificates

    C. Remove Revoked Certificates

    D. Update Certificates that Use Certificate Templates

    70-640 TS Objective 6.4: Manage enrollments

95. You are setting up an online responder and are starting the configuration of your issuing CA server. Where is the template you will use for the online responder configuration located?

    A. Service Manager Roles\AD Certificate Services\Certificate Templates\ AIA extension

    B. Service Manager Roles\AD Certificate Services\Certificate Templates\OCSP Response Signing

    C. Service Manager Roles\AD Certificate Services\Certificate Templates\ Response

    D. Service Manager Roles\AD Certificate Services\Certificate Templates\ Response Signing

    70-640 TS Objective 6.4: Manage enrollments

96. You have completed the OCSP Response Signing certificate. What is the next step to finalizing your online responder?

    A. It is ready

    B. You need to duplicate the certificate

    C. You need to configure the Authority Information Access Port

    D. You need to configure the Authority Information Access Extension

    70-640 TS Objective 6.4: Manage enrollments

97. Where do you find the AIA to support the Online Response?

    A. Open Server Manager\Active Directory Certificate Services\Issuing CA Name, select the Action menu option, and then choose Properties

    B. Open Server Manager\Active Directory\DC

    C. Open Server Manager\Active Directory Certificate Services\Issuing CA Name

    D. Open Server Manager\Active Directory Certificate Services\Issuing CA Name, and select the Action menu option for Extensions

    70-640 TS Objective 6.4: Manage enrollments

98. You are finalizing the configuration of an online responder, and you have created an OCSP Response Signing Template, published the template to Active Directory, and configured the Authority Information Access Extension. What is the next step?

    A. Nothing

    B. Assign the template to the server

    C. Reboot the server to assign the template to the server

    D. None of the above is a true statement

    70-640 TS Objective 6.4: Manage enrollments

99. You need to verify that the OCSP certificate has been assigned to the server. Which of the following should you do?

    A. Use the built-in Certificates snap-in

    B. Choose Computer Manager, Certificates

    C. Create a new Certificates snap-in console

    D. Any of the above

    70-640 TS Objective 6.4: Manage enrollments

100. You have created a new Certificates snap-in console to verify that the OCSP certificate has been assigned to your CA server. Where in the snap-in will the OCSP certificate be found?

    A. Certificates\Personal\Certificates

    B. Certificates\Computer\OCSP

    C. Certificates\User

    D. Personal\Certificates\OCSP

    70-640 TS Objective 6.5: Manage certificate revocations

101. Where in Server Manager do you add the Revocation Configuration?

    A. Server Manager\Roles\Revocation

    B. Server Manager\Active Directory\Revocation

    C. Server Manager\Roles\AD Certificates Services\Online Responder\Revocation Configuration

    D. Server Manager\Roles\Active Directory Certificates Services\Revocation Configuration

    70-640 TS Objective 6.5: Manage certificate revocations

102. What does each Revocation Configuration ask for on the welcome page?

    A. Assign the server

    B. Name the Revocation Configuration

    C. User name

    D. CAs name

    70-640 TS Objective 6.5: Manage certificate revocations

103. There are three choices offered from the Select a Signing Certificate page of the online responder's response to clients. Which of the following is NOT one of the choices?

   A. Automatic

   B. Manually

   C. CA Certificate

   D. Root Certificate

   70-640 TS Objective 6.2: Configure CA server settings

104. When configuring a revocation configuration for an online responder, you choose Automatically Select a Signing Certificate and select Auto-Enroll for an OCSP signing certificate. The wizard then selects the revocation provider. In the event that the revocation provider cannot be located, you must manually add the provider. To add a revocation provider, you manually enter which of the following?

   A. `//localhost`

   B. `http://localhost/ca.crl`

   C. `//ca.crl`

   D. `http://ca.crl`

   70-640 TS Objective 6.5: Manage certificate revocations

Part III

ANSWERS TO
PRACTICE TESTS

3

CONFIGURING DOMAIN NAME SYSTEM (DNS) FOR ACTIVE DIRECTORY

Note that the interactive questions of the "list and reorder" type do not have a simple A/B/C answer and are therefore grouped at the end of the following grid.

Question	Answer	Explanation
1	B	Using the same DNS name for your internal domain structure and your external Internet name is referred to as a split-brain DNS service.
2	C	The process of booting a computer on a domain starts with locating the SRV record in DNS in order to locate the closest domain controller.
3	C	Both traditional IPv4 and the new 128-bit IPv6 are built into Windows Server 2008.
4	B	IPv6 is the new 128-bit addressing scheme build into Windows Server 2008.
5	C	DNS translates IP addresses into common terms or domain names that are easier to relate to than just numbers.
6	A	The DNS service is linked to the AD DS to authenticate member computers.
7	B	DNS always uses TCP/IP port 53 to communicate with clients and servers.
8	C	DNS always uses TCP/IP port 53 to communicate with clients and servers.
9	A	DNS always uses TCP/IP port 53 to communicate with clients and servers.
10	C	The naming structure used by the Domain Naming System is hierarchical.
11	C	Common root names are registered on the Internet and include names such as .com, .net, and.org.
12	B	In the DNS naming structure, the root is the first level, and the first name added to the root becomes the second level.

3A

Question	Answer	Explanation
13	C	In the DNS naming structure the root is the first level and each name after is another level.
14	C	IPv6 addresses use eight 16-bit address pieces from a 128-bit address.
15	B	IPv6 uses hexadecimal format to display the 128-bit addresses.
16	C	IPv6 unspecified addresses or :: indicates the absence of an address. The IPv4 equivalent addresses would be 0.0.0.0.
17	B	Experimental address class is the only one that's not part of IPv4.
18	C	IPv6 provides 340 billion billion billion billion, or 2^{128}, addresses.
19	C; D; A; B	See below for more information.
20	B; A; C	See below for more information.
21	E; B; C; A; D	See below for more information.
22	C	The Peer Name Resolution Protocol is fully supported in Windows Server 2008 when using IPv6.
23	D	Peer Name Resolution Protocol is a distributed naming system and does not rely on a centralized server to locate objects.
24	A	Peer Name Resolution can support billions of names.
25	C	Peer Name Resolution is a distributed service and does not require administrative intervention as does DNS.
26	D	The use of digital signatures protects the names so they cannot be spoofed or replaced with counterfeit names.
27	D	To provide resolution PNRP relies on the concept of a cloud. Up to two clouds may exist—a global cloud and a link-local cloud.
28	B	The move to IPv6 will allow PNRP to become commonly used.
29	B	The three Windows Server 2008 DNS roles are DDNS, read-write DNS, and read-only DNS.
30	B	Primary DNS servers are deployed in perimeter networks and are not intergraded with AD DS.
31	A	Read-only DNS servers contain a read-only copy of the DNS data.
32	C	Firewalls protect your network by blocking the internal network's TCP ports from outside the world.
33	C	FQDN is a fully qualified domain name and is used to name directory forests and the domains they contain.
34	C	Using the same DNS name for your internal domain structure and your external Internet name is referred to as using a split-brain DNS service.
35	D	It is not true that non-Windows–based DNS servers will not work with Windows DNS clients.

Question	Answer	Explanation
36	C	When mixing DBS technologies, the use of a whole-brain approach is the best.
37	N/A	Whole-brain is on the right and split-brain is on the left of the image.
38	D	Devices running older Windows operating systems like Windows NT do not register their own names with DNS.
39	B	Devices that do not support DDNS can use the DHCP server to register their DNS names.
40	C; A; D; B; E; F	See below for more information.
41	D; E; A; C; B	See below for more information.
42	D	The Global Name Zone in DNS replaces single-level names and replaces the WINS Server in Windows Server 2008.
43	B; C; A	See below for more information.
44	A; C; B; E; D	See below for more information.
45	C; B; D; A; E	See below for more information.
46	C	By default, Windows Server 2008 creates two application directory partitions named ForestDnsZones and DomainDnsZones.
47	D	By using background loading, Windows Server 2008 can respond to requests more quickly. It continues to load zone data in the background after the computer is started and logon is initiated.
48	A	Using a RODC in unprotected servers ensures that the records cannot be spoofed by unauthorized access to the server.
49	A	The Global Names Zone provides support for single-level names in Windows Server 2008 DNS.
50	D	In organizations with older applications that use single-level names the use of WINS is still recommended.
51	A	Web Proxy Automatic Discovery Protocol is used by clients for web browser configuration.
52	B	ISTAP is a transition protocol that allows IPv4 and IPv6 networks to work together.
53	C	Global query block lists contain specific blocked address ranges, which helps to reduce the potential of routing packets to malicious servers.
54	B	When no DHCPv6 servers are present on the network, IPv6 will automatically assign link-local addresses that allow local browsing only.
55	C	PNRP can scale to millions of names, but DNS is limited in the scope.

3A

Question	Answer	Explanation
56	C	The first step in the logon process is to locate the SRV record for the closest domain controller.
57	D	dcpromo.exe is used to add and remove the DC role from a server.
58	C	The correct format for an FQDN is object.namespace.rootname.
59	D	DNS uses a hierarchical naming structure.
60	B	Windows Server 2008 is installed by default with an IPv6 link-local address.
61	B; A; C	See below for more information.
62	C	Windows clients running Windows 2000 and later can register and update DNS records dynamically.
63	C	A Denial of Service attack is an attack that floods the DNS server with more requests than the server can respond to.
64	D	Footprinting the network is an attack whereby an attacker obtains all the data within the DNS.
65	D	Each record in DNS is assigned a TTL value that specifies how long a record will remain before being removed.
66	C	Scavenging cleans all active zones on the server.
67	C	To set scavenging for a server you must add the setting through the server's action menu.
68	C	The No-Refresh Interval is the time between the most recent refresh of a record stamp and the moment when the system allows the timestamp to be refreshed.
69	B	The Refresh Interval setting is the earliest moment when a record may be updated or scavenged if no updates are applied.
70	N/A	You click Action in the menu bar to find the Clear Cache option.
71	A	If you have Windows 2000 Server DCs in your network, you must use the Use the All Domain Controllers in This Domain for Windows 2000 Compatibility option because Windows 2000 Server does not support application directory partitions.
72	C	On the Forward Lookup properties tab, assign WINS if you are not using GNZ and have deployed WINS.
73	N/A	See below for more information.
74	B	A cell phone is not required for creation of a Responsible Person (RP).
75	C	Reverse Lookup Zones (RLZs) are not typically required with networks of fewer than 500 computers.

Question	Answer	Explanation
76	B	Custom records are created as the last step in the DNS server configuration. Custom records are created manually and are provided to support a variety of services. Three reasons you may want to use custom records are MX records, an alias, and SRV zones. An FLZ zone is not a service that could be supported by custom records.
77	N/A	Uncheck the "Use Root Hints if No Forwarders Are Available" option to prevent internal DNS servers from communicating directly with the Internet.
78	C	Conditional forwards are used when specific conditions are met.
79	B; E; C; D; A	See below for more information.
80	B	Use `dnscmd /config/ enableglobalnamessupport 1` to modify the Registry and allow GNZ creation through Service Manager.
81	D	GNZ name records are known as aliases.
82	D	GNZ names have the same requirement as NetBIOS and computer names.
83	D	The three parts of the name needed are the DNS server name, single global name, and the DNS name.
84	A	`dnsservername / recordadd globalnames singlelabelname cname corre-spondingdnsname` is the correct syntax to use for the `dnscmd` command.
85	B	WINS servers should be installed with a minimum of two servers.
86	C	When configuring your Windows Server 2008 to provide WINS, the server should be set up for push-pull synchronization.
87	B	DHCP server should have options for 044 WINDS/NBNS and 046 WINS/NBT when you are using WINS on the network.
88	C	DNS and WINS together will give you both FQDN and single-label name resolution.
89	C	Microsoft made all of its DNS clients compatible with dynamic DNS, starting with Windows 2000.
90	C	When integrating DNS with AD, you should add the name-resolution service and 006 DNS server value to the DHCP scope.
91	C	`dnsservername` and `partitionfqdn` are needed to create a custom application directory with `dnscmd`.
92	C	To create an application directory, you need to be a member of the Enterprise Administrator group.
93	D	After deciding to use a Custom Application Directory Partition, you need to create the partition, enlist DNS servers, and assign zones for replication.

3A

Question	Answer	Explanation
94	C	The dnscmd enlistdirectorypartition will enlist DNS servers into a custom application directory.
95	D	/startscavenging initiates a scavenging operation.
96	C	dnscmd /exportsettings will create a backup of your DNS server setting.
97	D	/clearcache will clear the cache in the DNS server.
98	B	ipconfig is NOT normally used to manage DNS server maintenance or administration but instead is used for the IP configuration of a client computer.
99	A; B; D; C	See below for more information.
100	D	DNS manager is located in both the Administrative Tools program group and in Server Manager.
101	D	flushdns is used with ipconfig to clear the client DNS cache.
102	C	dnscmd uses the /config option to modify server configuration parameters.
103	C	dnslint /d is used to request domain name resolution tests.
104	C	ipconfig/renew6 is used to renew an IPv6 address on a TCP/IP host.
105	C	ipconfig/renew6 is used to release an IPv6 address on a TCP/IP host.
106	A	dnslint / ad is used to verify records specifically related to Active Directory.
107	D	ipconfig/registerdns will force the registration of a dynamic DNC client with the DNS server.
108	B	Windows DNS uses root hints for name resolution.
109	B	When you install a DNS server, it creates two application directory partitions: one for the forest data and one for the domain data.
110	D	By default, in a Windows Server 2008, domain name resolution between two child domains will pass through the forest root domain.
111	B	To allow name resolution in the remote site, you simply need to make sure that all DCs are running the DNS Server role.
112	B	Network administrator would traditionally provide two central DNS servers in the server options of the DHCP setting.
113	E; C; B; A; D	End of grid chart shows the common IPv6 address type and the corresponding IPv4 addresses.
114	D	The SOA, Start of Authority, record should contain the contact information of the person responsible for the DNS information.
115	C	To provide high availability, multiple records are created for the same resource, each with a different IP address. When the name is queried the DNS server will respond with the first IP address, then the second, third, and so on.

Question	Answer	Explanation
116	C	DNS servers that do not support Dynamic DNS are referred to as legacy DNS servers.
117	C; D; A; B	End of grid chart shows the correct DNS term paired with its meaning.
118	C	Windows Server 2008 uses root hints to locate authoritative Internet root servers. These are updated regularly through Microsoft Windows Updates.
119	C	If you require single-label name resolution, use GNZ if you have a limited number of names, and use WINS if a multitude of names is needed.
120	D	To create and configure a GNZ in Windows Server 2008, you start in Server Manager and select the Forward Lookup Zones in the DNS role. Then, select the Primary Zones.
121	D	The Debug option for trace logging of the DNS server to a text file is an option for Event Viewer.
122	E; C; D; A; B	See below for more information.
123	B; A; C	See below for more information.
124	N/A	Uncheck the "Store the Zone in Active Directory" option to store the zone file as a text file.
125	D	Windows Server DNS creates application directory partitions to host DNS data into ForestDnsZone and DomainDnsZone.
126	A	Older devices that did not support dynamic DNS updates had their name records in the DNS server updated by the DHCP server when they logged onto the network.
127	C; A; B	See below for more information.
128	D	DNC always uses TCP/IP port 53 to communicate with clients and servers.

3A

Question 19

Unspecified	C. ::
Loopback	D. ::1
Link-local	A. FE80::
Site-local	B. FEC0::

Question 20

Link-local	B. Assigned by default when no DHCP is available
Site-local	A. Private IP addresses, routed locally only
Global unicast	C. Internet addresses

Question 21

Address Type	Description
Unspecified	E. Indicates absence of an address
Loopback	B. Comparable to 127.0.0.1
Link-local	C. Comparable to 169.254.9.9/16
Site-local	A. Internal addresses comparable to 10.0.0.0/8, 172.16.0.0/12 and 192.168.0.0/16
Global unicast	D. Unique addresses for specific interfaces

Question 40

The name-resolution process goes in this order:

C. A request is sent to the local DNS server
A. The DNS server sends a referral request to the .com name server
D. The request is sent to the authoritative DNS server for dtilearning.com
B. The DNS server for dtilearning.com sends the IP address to the client
E. The client name resolver uses the IP address to request the web page
F. The web page is sent to the user

Question 41

Domain DNS zone	D. The zone that contains the records for a particular domain
Forest DNS zone	E. The zone that contains the records for the entire forest
Forward lookup zone	A. The DNS containers for name resolution
Primary zones	C. Zones that contain the read-write information
Stub zone	B. Records other DNS servers

Question 43

AXFR	B. Asynchronous full transfer
IXFR	C. Incremental zone transfer
Secure	A. AD DS multimaster replication

Question 44

Alias	A. CNAME
Host	C. AAAA
Mail	B. MX
Pointer	E. PTR
Service	D. SRV

Question 45

Alias	C. Alternate record for a name specified in another record type
Host	B. Computer objects used to resolve IP addresses to devices
Mail	D. Routes email to a namespace
Pointer	A. Reverse lookups within the namespace
Service	E. Location of specific TCP/IP service

Question 61

Primary	B. Read-write zones that support name resolution
Secondary	A. Read-only copies
Stub	C. Pointers to other DNS servers

Question 73

Serial number	Assigned to the zone when it is created
Primary server	The master server for the zone
Responsible person	The name of the operator of the server
SOA	Intervals and time-based setting for the record
TTL	The Time to Live for this record

3A

Question 79

The five steps in the basic process of creating a GNZ on each DC with a DNS service are as follows:

B. Create the GlobalNames FLZ
E. Set its replication scope of all DNS servers in the forest
C. Do not enable dynamic updates for this zone
D. Enable GNZ support on each DNS server in the forest
A. Add single-label names to the DNS zone

Question 99

dnscmd	A. Manages aspects of DNS
dnslint	B. Diagnoses name resolution issues
nslookup	D. Performs query testing
ipconfig	C. IP configuration information

Question 113

Unspecified ::	E. 0.0.0.0
Loopback ::1	C. 127.0.0.1
Link-local FE80::	B. APIPA
Site-local FEC0::	A. 10.0.0.0, 172.16.0.0, 192.168.0.0
Global unicast	D. Public addresses

Question 117

Term	Description
Name recursion	C. Contacts a name server for name lookup.
Iterative	D. Query in which a name server contacts a second name server to perform a name lookup.
Recursive	A. Resolver contacts a name server to perform a name lookup, and the name server either returns a result or an error.
Reverse lookup	B. Provides an IP address to obtain an FQDN.

Question 122

A DNS server should be set up in the following order:

E. Add DNS Security
C. Set the scavenging configuration
D. Finalize the FLZs
A. Create RLZs
B. Add custom records to FLZ as needed

Question 123

Primary zone	B. Is authoritative for the namespace it contains
Secondary zone	A. Copy of the authoritative server for a namespace
Stub zone	C. Pointer to other authoritative servers for the namespace

Question 127

C. The computer boots
A. The identification of the SRV by DNS to find the closest DC
B. The computer authenticates to the DC

4

CONFIGURING THE ACTIVE DIRECTORY INFRASTRUCTURE

Note that the interactive questions of the "list and reorder" type do not have a simple A/B/C answer and are therefore grouped at the end of the following grid.

Question	Answer	Explanation
1	C	The directory that holds the AD DS is a file named ntds.dit.
2	See below	Active Directory Domain Services Identity, AD Lightweight Directory Services, Applications, AD Certificates Services, Trust, AD Rights Management, Integrity and AD Federation Services, Partnership represents the five technologies that comprise the complete Windows IDA solution.
3	E	The leaf is not one of the Active Directory Infrastructure components.
4	C	A site creates a boundary of replication and service in a portion of the network where connectivity is good.
5	A	There are three domain functional levels: Windows 2000 native, Windows Server 2003, and Windows Server 2008.
6	C	OUs can have object calls linked to them through GPOs that will automatically manage settings to users and computers within the OU.
7	D	The Kerberos Key Distribution Center service is run by the Domain Controller that performs the AD DS role.
8	D	The forest is the collection of all the domains in the AD DS; the first domain installed is called the forest root domain.
9	D	The Access Control List on a resource reflects the security permissions that have been applied to a particular resource.
10	B	Microsoft has combined into Windows Server 2008 five technologies—AD DA, AD LDS, AD CS, AD RMS, and AD FS—to provide a complete identity and access (IDA) solution.
11	B	To validate identity, users must provide secrets known only to them. This information is compared to the information stored in the identity store and is called authentication.

4A

Question	Answer	Explanation
12	C	In an Active Directory domain, Kerberos is used to authenticate identities.
13	C	When Kerberos identifies a user or computer it generates a package of information that is used to identify the authenticated user or computer, called a TGT.
14	A	DCs are considered critical to authentication in the AD DS, so a minimum of two DCs are recommended in each domain forest.
15	C	The correct command-line entry to add or remove a Domain Controller is `dcpromo.exe`.
16	B	Instructions to automate the installation of a DC are contained in an answer file. The answer file is a text file that has a section heading `[INSTALL]`, followed by options and various values used during the installation of the DC.
17	A	Options can be provided at the command line during DC installation by using `dcpromo / unattendedOption:value`.
18	C	The correct syntax for the answer file option is `/unattend:"path to the answer file"`.
19	C	When you're adding a Windows 2008 server to an existing forest or domain that contains Windows 2000 or 2003 servers, you must update the schema with the `adprep/forestprep` command.
20	B; D; A; C	To prep the forest schema for Windows Server 2008, you must complete the steps in this order before creating the first Windows Server 2008 Domain Controller.
21	D	To install a Windows Server 2008 domain into an existing Windows 2000 or 2003 domain, you need to prepare the domains by running `adprep/domainprep/gppreq`.
22	D	Use the Install from Media option when you're in Advanced mode during the installation of a Domain Controller. You now have an option that will allow you to install a new DC from replicated data created by existing Domain Controllers. This option is especially useful when installing over slow network links.
23	B	When you want to create a new child domain from an existing domain you need to prepare AD before creating the Windows Server 2008 Domain Controller by running `adprep/forest`.
24	A	The creation of an RODC requires an account, a name, an AD site, and optionally a user or group that will complete the installation.
25	D	To create the prestaged account for an RODC, you use Active Directory User and Computer snap-in. Right-click on the DC OU and choose Pre-Create Read-Only Domain Controller Account.

Question	Answer	Explanation
26	C	After creating an account for the RODC and prestaging it, you attach the account to a server by using the command dcpromo/useexistingaccount:attach.
27	D	The IFM installation media is created by using the ntdsutil.exe command followed by activate instance ntds.
28	C; A; D; B	To create IFM media for the installation of a new DC in an existing forest use the ntdsutil.exe command. Type activate instance ntds and, at the IFM command line, enter the command to select the type of installation media you want to create.
29	B	You can remove a DC with either the AD Domain Services Installation Wizard or from the command prompt with dcpromo.exe.
30	D	If a Domain Controller must be demoted and is not connected to the network you can use the dcpromo/forceremoval.
31	B; E	AD DC contains five single operation masters. Of the five two are performed for the entire forest; these are Domain naming and Schema master.
32	A; B; E	AD DC contains five single operation masters. Of the five, three are performed for the entire domain—RID, Infrastructure, and PDC Emulator.
33	D	When you have a multidomain infrastructure and a member is moved or renamed, the infrastructure master is responsible for updating the member attribute.
34	C	The RID master for the domain allocates unique RIDs to each DC in the domain.
35	D	Timestamps are used by AD, Kerberos, FRS, and DFS-R, whereas the PDC Emulator synchronizes the time across all the systems.
36	A	To identify the PDC role, you use the Active Directory User and Computer snap-in.
37	D	To identify the RID master role, you use the Active Directory User and Computer snap-in.
38	C	To identify the Infrastructure master role, you use the Active Directory User and Computer snap-in.
39	B	To identify the Domain Naming master role, you use the AD Domains and Trusts snap-in.
40	B	To identify the Domain Schema master role, you use the AD Domains and Trusts snap-in.
41	A; E	The PDC emulator and infrastructure master are the only operations master roles that can be transferred back to the original master DC after the DC is brought back online.

4A

Question	Answer	Explanation
42	B	Windows Server 2008 supports only three domain functional levels—Windows Server 2000, 2003, and 2008. NT is no longer supported in Windows Server 2008.
43	A	If you have Windows Server 2000 and 2003 DCs, you should use the lowest functional level, which is the Windows 2000 Native functional level.
44	D	Domain functional levels add features as the level rises. Fine-grained password policies enable you to specify different password policies for users and groups in the domain and is a feature of Windows Server 2008.
45	C	Domain functional levels add features as the level rises. Last interactive logon information is a feature of Windows Server 2008 and updates the time and workstation that a user logs onto.
46	B	Domain functional levels add features as the level rises. Advanced Encryption Services increases the authentication AES support for Kerberos and is a feature of Windows Server 2008.
47	D	Domain functional levels add features as the level rises. DFS-R of SYSVOL is Distributed File System Replication and replaces File Replication Services to provide a more detailed replication of SYSVOL data. It is a feature of Windows Server 2008.
48	A	For Windows Server 2008, the default forest functional level is set at Windows 2000 Native.
49	C	The original recommendation was to create a dedicated forest root domain. It is now recommended to create a forest with a single domain.
50	C	The domain model should be designed around the characteristics of the domain itself.
51	A	Domains are characterized by a single domain partition, a single Kerberos policy, and a single DNS namespace.
52	B	Domains running functional levels under Server 2008 will not support multiple password policies. Windows Server 2008 functional level will support fine-grained password policies.
53	A	Adding domains in a forest will increase all aspects of administrative and equipment costs.
54	See below	A single-tree forest consists of a contiguous DNS namespace arranged as a single tree forest.
55	See below	The correct answer is to create a multiple tree forest due to the noncontiguous namespace used by the two domain names.
56	See below	Inter-forest domain restructuring copies the existing sources' domains and copies the accounts into a target domain. Intra-forest migration moves the accounts between domains in the same forest.

Question	Answer	Explanation
57		A describes inter-forest migration. It copies domain accounts into a target domain in separate forests. B describes intra-forest migration, which moves domain objects between domains in the same forest.
58	D	The Active Directory Migration tool is used to migrate objects between a source and a target domain. The ADMT is used for both intra-forest and inter-forest migrations.
59	D	The discretionary ACL, or DACL, describes resource access permissions.
60	B; E; A; D; C; F	SIDs are domain unique values assigned to accounts of all security principles. Security Descriptors (SD) describe the permissions, ownership, rights, and the auditing of the resource. System ACL (SACL) describes auditing. DACL describes resource access permissions. ACEs link a specific permissions with the SID of the security principle, and LSASS compares the SIDs in the user token to the SID in the ACE.
61	D	During migration sIDHistory is used to maintain access to accounts. After the migration is completed, security translation is performed with a tool like the ASMT.
62	C; A; B	In an inter-forest migration, you must first migrate global groups to the target domain, and then migrate the users. Use ADMT to evaluate group membership and add the new account to the same group in the target domain. In an intra-forest migration, you create a universal group that can contain users from both the source and target domains during the migration. Resource access is maintained because the sIDHistory in the universal group is the same as the source global group. After the migration is completed, you change the scope of the universal group to global.
63	C	During the migration process of moving objects, including users and computers, from one domain or forest to another, there are a number of concerns and issues including the ones listed in the question.
64	A	There are two domains in a trust relationship—the trusting domain and the trusted domain. The user is authenticated by the trusted domain, which holds the identity store and provides authentication for the user in the trusting domain.
65		Domain A trusts Domain B, which means Domain A is the trusting domain and Domain B is the trusted domain.
66	F; E; B; C; D; A	When a user logs on to a client the authentication request is forwarded to a DC so the KDC can give the authenticated user a TGT. When the user requests access to a resource on a computer the user needs to obtain a valid session ticket. The tickets are provided by the KDC and are used to preset to the KDC when the user requests access to a service. When users with a TGT request access to a service, they receive a session ticket for the service from the KDC.

4A

Question	Answer	Explanation
67	See below	The root domain of each tree in a domain trusts the forest root domain with an automatic default, two-way, transitive trust.
68	D	Shortcut, external, realm, and forest trusts are all created manually. Tree-root trusts are created automatically between all trees in a forest.
69	C	To create a trust, open the Active Directory Domains and Trusts snap-in, right-click the domain that you want to create the trust for, select the Trust tab on the Properties page, and then select New Trust. The wizard starts.
70	See below	A shortcut one-way trust optimizes authentication between domains in a multi-domain forest. The answer is the bold single arrow.
71	B	To connect between your domain and another Windows domain that is NOT in your forest, you must create an external trust.
72	C	Realm trusts are used when cross-platform interoperability is needed for authentication using Kerberos v5.
73	C	When you need to establish a trust relationship between two separate forests, you use a forest trust.
74	B	Shortcut trusts will optimize authentication between domains and reduce the time required to traverse the trust path.
75	D	External trusts are used to create relationships between domains that are in different Windows-based forests.
76	C	When authentication in a non-Windows Kerberos domain is used to authenticate Windows clients in a Windows domain, a realm trust is used to provide cross-platform interoperability with the security services based on the Kerberos v5 implementation.
77	F; E; G; H; A; C; B; D	To validate a trust relationship, you complete the following steps: Open AD Domains and Trusts and right-click the domain that you want to validate. Click Properties and then click the Trust tab. Select the trust you want to validate and click Properties. Click Validate and then confirm by clicking Yes.
78	F; D; A; E; G; B; C	To remove a trust manually, perform the following steps: Open AD Domains and Trusts and right-click the domain that contains the trust you want removed. Click the Trusts tab and select the trust to be removed. Click remove and confirm by clicking Yes. Enter authorized credentials for a member of the Domain Admins or Enterprise Admins Group in the reciprocal domain.
79	D	It is after creating a trust relationship that creating the trust will result in access to domain resources by virtue of the fact that many resources are secured with ACLs that give permissions to the Authenticated Users Group.
80	See below	Mark the Allowed to Authenticate ALLOW permission.

Question	Answer	Explanation
81	D	AD uses sites to manage AD replication and service localization.
82	D	Replication is the transfer of changes between Domain Controllers; changes must be communicated to all the Domain Controllers in the domain.
83	D	AD sees two types of networks within your infrastructure—the highly connected and less highly connected. AD should replicate changes immediately to other DCs in the highly connected network and will replicate as managed over the less highly connected network.
84	A	The Active Directory site represents a highly connected segment of your network where changes are replicated almost immediately.
85	C	An AD site is a highly connected portion of your enterprise. When you define a site, the DCs within the site replicate changes almost instantly.
86	B	Active Directory is distributed across the network when you want to encourage clients to authenticate with the DC in their site (called service localization).
87	D	Active Directory sites are used to control replication and to enable service locations.
88	C	Service placement, connection speed, and user population are all factors that should be considered in determining which AD sites are necessary.
89	D	The default site created when you set up a forest with the first DC is named Default-First-Site-Name.
90	D	If users in a remote location need access to a central data center, a site and local DC will not help if the link goes down.
91	D	To define an AD site you create a site object, the container that manages the replication, and one or more subnet objects to define a range of IP addresses.
92	See below	Draw a check mark where you would right-click on the Site node under Active Directory Sites and Services.
93	B	After creating the site, you rename it using the New Object-Site dialog box shown in the illustration.
94	D	This is the New Object-Subnet dialog box used for defining a range of addresses used by the site.
95	C	The correct prefix notation for the subnet 10.0.6.1 to 10.0.6.254 with a 16-bit subnet mask would be 10.0.6.0 / 24.
96	D	A subnet can be associated with only one site.
97	D	To change the site to which a subnet is linked, open the properties of the subnet and use the Properties dialog box for the subnet.

4A

Question	Answer	Explanation
98	See below	The first Domain Controller is automatically placed under the site object called Default-First-Site when you create your Active Directory forest.
99	C	The Server container should only show Domain Controllers.
100	D	To move a Domain Controller to a site after installation, right-click the server in the Active Directory Sites and Services snap-in and select Move to open the Move Server Dialog box.
101	D	If a site does not contain a Domain Controller, clients will still be able to log on by using Domain Controllers in an adjacent site or using other Domain Controllers in the domain.
102	See below	To remove a Domain Controller object, select Servers to open the Servers container and right-click on the server that will be removed. Then select Delete.
103	D	Domain Controllers advertise their services by using Service Locator records or SRV records in DNS.
104	A; B; C; D	SRV records in Windows Server 2008 include the port associated with the services that are available and include LDAP port 389, Kerberos port 88, Kerberos Password protocol port 464, and GC services port 3268.
105	I; H; G; D; F; E; C; B; A	When a client first joins a domain it receives an IP address from DHCP. The client queries the _tcp folder for a Domain Controller. This will have all the Domain Controllers in the domain. The client will attempt to contact all of the listed DCs. The first DC to respond to the client will look at the IP address of the client and cross-reference that with subnet objects to find the correct site to which the client belongs. The client will store this site information and then query the site-specific _tcp folder for the DCs in the site. The client will authenticate with the first DC 2.0 that responds from the site.
106	B	When a site has no DC for authenticating clients a process called site coverage will register in the SRV record a DC nearby that will authenticate clients.
107	See below	The three major naming contexts or directory partitions are Domain, Configuration, and Schema.
108	D	Each Domain Controller maintains a copy of the domain NC, configuration, and schema.
109	D	Read-only Domain Controllers became available with Server 2008.
110	D	Generally certain attributes are not replicated to an RODC such as user passwords, unless the password policy of the RODC allows it.
111	C	The GC is also called the partial attribute set or PAS and is used to optimize searching of forest objects by containing a subset of attributes that are useful for searching across domains.

Question	Answer	Explanation
112	C	Another term used to describe the GC, which also describes what the GC does, is partial attribute set or PAS.
113	A	Any time an application specifies port 3268, it is searching the Global Catalog to perform directory queries.
114	D	The first GC is created when you create the first domain in the forest.
115	See below	Right-click the NTDS Setting node to open the NTDS Site Setting Properties box.
116	D	To remove the GC role from a DC, you would right-click the NTDS Setting node and select Properties. In the General tab, remove the check in GC.
117	A	To create a global catalog server from a DC you open the Active Directory Sites and Services, expand the Site and the Servers container, right-click the NTDS setting, and check the Global Catalog box.
118	D	To specify which GC a DC will use to enable Universal Group Membership Caching Open Active Directory Sites and Services, select the site, in the Details pane right-click the NTDS Site Setting, and choose Properties. Then, check Enable UGMC.
119	B	When you have Universal Group Membership Caching enabled on a DC it is updated every eight hours from the designated Global Catalog Server.
120	D	To enable Universal Group Membership Caching Open Active Directory Sites and Services, select the site. In the Details pane right-click the NTDS Site Setting and choose Properties to display the NTDS Site Setting Properties.
121	N/A	The Domain, Configuration, and Schema (A, B, and C) partitions of the directory are replicated to all DCs in a domain and the Configuration and Schema partitions (B and C) are replicated to all DCs in the forest.
122	B	Application directory partitions are not by default replicated to all DCs but to targeted Domain Controllers.
123	D	To view the application directory partitions in your forest, you use ADSI Edit.
124	B	Enterprise Admins can create application directory partitions manually with the ntdsutil.exe database tool.
125	B	You can use the tools ldp.exe and ntdsutil.exe to manage application directory partitions directly.
126	D	If you want to view the application directory partition in your forest, use ADSI Edit and choose Connect To. From the Select a Well Known Naming Context option, select Configuration. Expand the Configuration and the folder representing the configuration partition and select CN=Partitions in the console tree. The partitions in your AD DS data store are displayed in the Details pane.

4A

Question	Answer	Explanation
127	See below	To view the application directory partitions in a forest, you use ADSI Edit. Open ADSI Edit, and then click More Actions or right-click the root and choose Connect To.
128	C; D; A; B	The high-level steps to install an RODC are as follows: Set the forest functional level to Windows Server 2003 or higher, run adprep/rodcprep on any DCs running Windows Server 2003, make sure one writable DC is a Windows 2008 server, and then install the RODC.
129	D	Authentication occurs when users first log in and service tickets are requested whenever a user connects to a service like Print or File Servers. All of these activities require access to the DC at the hub site, so they will all generate activity over the WAN link to the hub site.
130	D	The main concerns with placing a DC in a remote or branch office location are security, AD security, and administration. Unreliable performance would not be a concern if the DC were placed at the remote branch office.
131	D	RODCs replicate changes from DCs in the hub site. Replication is one-way from a writable Domain Controller to an RODC. No changes to the RODC are replicated to any other DC.
132	C	To upgrade an existing forest to include a Windows Server 2008 DC, run adprep/rodcprep from the DC that is acting as the schema master to update the permissions on all the DNS application directory partitions in the forest. This allows them to be replicated successfully by all RODCs that are also DNS servers.
133	C	To run adprep, copy the contents of the \sources\adprep folder on the Windows Server 2008 installation DVD to the schema master.
134	A; C; E; F	An RODC must replicate updates from a writable Windows Server 2008 DC. The replication should be to the closest site. RODC can perform DNS functions only if the replication connection is with a DC acting as a DNS server that hosts the DNS domain zone. RODC can only run on Windows Server 2008 in either the full or core installations.
135	D	Password Replication Policy allows user and computer credentials to be cached on an RODC. If users and computer credentials are cached then authentication and service ticket activities can be processed by the RODC and not referred to a writable DC.
136	D	The two attributes of an RODC that allow caching of user and computer credentials are the Allowed RODC Password Replication Group and Denied RODC Password Replication Group.
137	C; D	The Policy Usage tab of the Password Replication Policy tab allows you to select two reports to find the accounts that are stored on the RODC and the accounts that have been authenticated by the RODC.

Question	Answer	Explanation
138	D	You use the Advanced tab of the Password Replication Policy tab of the RODC properties computer account in the Domain Controllers OU.
139	D	At Windows Server 2008 functional level, you can use DFS-R to replicate SYSVOL.
140	B; A; D; C	Migration of SYSVOL from FRS to DFS-R is done in four stages. First you use FRS to make a copy of SYSVOL and add it to a replication set where DFS-R begins to replicate but the original SYSVOL FRS continues. You change the SYSVOL share to SYSCOL_DFSR\sysvol so clients can use it to obtain logon scripts and GP templates. Finally, you stop the old SYSVOL.
141	B	To move a Domain Controller through the four stages of migration, use the dfsrmig.exe command.
142	See below	AD balances accuracy (integrity) and consistency (convergence) with performance to keep replication traffic to a reasonable amount.
143	C	Connector objects appear in the Administrative tools in AD Sites and Services. The DC replicates changes from one DC to another because of the AD DC connector object.
144	C	Replication in Active Directory is always a pull technology.
145	D	Active Directory will create a topology that ensures replication automatically.
146	C	Replication topology is two-way to ensure replication even in the event of a Domain Controller failure.
147	D	The topology created by Active Directory ensures that there are no more than three hops between any two DCs.
148	D	The Knowledge Consistency Checker or KCC helps to generate and optimize replication automatically between DCs within a site.
149	B	If a Domain Controller goes off-line, the KCC will dynamically rebuild the two-way three-hop replication.
150	C	One situation that will require creating a connection object is in the event that an operations master role must be transferred.
151	D	Notification is the process of informing downstream partners that changes are available. The delays between notifications are referred to as initial notification delay, a three-second delay, and subsequent notification delay and are staggered to help with network traffic.
152	B	Notification is the process of informing downstream partners that changes are available. The delays between notifications are referred to as initial notification delay, a three-second delay, and subsequent notification delay and are staggered to help with network traffic.
153	D	Once the downstream partner requests the changes from the upstream partner, the Directory Replication Agent or DRA performs the transfer.

4A

Question	Answer	Explanation
154	C	After a replication partner receives a change it waits 15 seconds to notify its downstream partner that it has changes.
155	A	Active Directory replication topology will ensure that there are no more than three hops between all Domain Controllers in a site. If each partner waits approximately 15 seconds between changes all changes will have fully replicated the site within one minute.
156	B	Polling is when the downstream partner contacts the upstream partner with a query to see if changes are available for replication.
157	A	The default interval for polling a partner for intra-site partners is once per hour.
158	C	In the event that an upstream partner fails to respond to repeated polling requests, that partner will launch the KCC to check the replication topology.
159	D	The inter-site topology generator or ISTG is a component of the KCC that builds connections objects between servers in sites to enable replication between sites.
160	C	The ISTG builds connections between servers to enable replication between sites that are called Site Link objects.
161	D	When a forest is created, one site link is created called DEFAULTIPSITELINK.
162	A	A site link tells Active Directory that it can be replicated between those sites and the ISTG will create the connection objects to set the replication path.
163	C	The container in the AD Sites and Services snap-in is a container, Inter-Site Transport. Within Inter-Site Transport is the IP container that holds the site links.
164	C	Directory Service Remote Procedure Call (DS-RPC) is the default, preferred protocol used for inter-site replication.
165	D	Inter-site messaging-SMTP protocol requires the use of a certificate authority to secure the replication.
166	A	Inter-Site Messaging-SMTP does not support domain name context, so sites using SMTP to replicate must be in different domains.
167	C	When ISTG creates a replication topology between sites one Domain Controller is responsible for all replication into and out of the site for a partition. This server is called the bridgehead server.
168	C	The bridgehead server is responsible for replicating changes to partitions from one site to another.
169	A	A manually selected bridgehead server is referred to as a preferred bridgehead server.

Question	Answer	Explanation
170	D	A manually selected bridgehead server is referred to as a preferred bridgehead server.
171	A	Consider three sites, Atlantic, Pacific and Headquarters, whereby Atlantic and Headquarters sites are linked. The Pacific and Headquarters sites are also linked, so the link between Atlantic and Pacific would be referred to as being transitive. That means that the Pacific and Atlantic sites are also linked.
172	C	Site link transitivity can be disabled by going to the Inter-site Transport container, clicking on the IP folder properties, and deselecting the Bridge All Site Links.
173	D	Site link bridges are necessary only when you disable site link transitivity by deselecting the Bridge All Site Links.
174	D	Site link costs are used to manage replication by configuring a cost to the site link. Higher costs are used for slow links.
175	D	Site link costs are used to manage replication by configuring a cost to the site link and lower costs are used for fast links.
176	C	Site link costs are used to manage replication by configuring a cost to the site link and by default all site links are set at a value of 100.
177	C	The default polling interval is three hours.
178	C	The minimum polling interval is 15 minutes.
179	C	The default setting is for replication to occur 24 hours a day unless link scheduling is selected.
180	B; A	Repadmin.exe is a tool that reports on the status of replication on a Domain Controller. Dcdiag.exe is a tool that performs tests and reports on the status of replication and security on AD DS.
181	D; A; C; B	Dcdiag.exe tests parameters and their functions.
182	A; E	The Domain Naming master role and the Schema master role must be performed by only one Domain Controller in the entire forest.
183	C	The PDC Emulator binds to the Group Policy Management Editor when changes are made to GPOs.
184	D	The PDC Emulator emulates a primary Domain Controller for backward compatibility.
185	B	User password resets or changes are replicated immediately to the PFC Emulator to ensure that the Domain Controllers know about the password as quickly as possible.
186	B	The PDC emulator acts as the domain master browser and holds the browse lists created by the Browser service.

4A

Question	Answer	Explanation
187	A	The PDC emulator acts as the domain master browser and holds the browse lists created by the Browser service that display the computer, workgroups, and domain in the network.
188	D	The Schema Master and the Domain Naming Master roles should be placed on a single Domain Controller. This Domain Controller should also be a GC server.
189	D	The RID and PDV Emulator roles should be placed on a single Domain Controller.
190	C	The infrastructure master should, as best practice, not be placed on a Domain Controller that is a GC server but should be physically well connected to a GC server.
191	C	The Infrastructure master can be placed on the same Domain Controller that performs the RID master and RDC emulator roles.
192	C	When you first create the forest root domain with the first Domain Controller all five operations master roles are performed by the DC.
193	D	The PDC Emulator is the operations master that would have an immediate impact on users if it were to become unavailable.
194	B	The infrastructure master is responsible for updating the names of group members from other domains.
195	C	The RID master is responsible for creating new SIDs and will prevent you from creating new user and computer accounts.
196	C	The RID master is responsible for creating new SIDs and will prevent you from creating new user and computer accounts.
197	B	The failure of the Schemas master would not make a significant impact on normal network operations until a change in the schema were needed to install an Active Directory integrated application that requires a change in the schema.
198	C	The domain naming master role is only needed to add a domain to the forest or to remove an existing domain from a forest.
199	B	When you establish your forest all five roles are performed by the first Domain Controller you install—Domain Naming master, Schema master, RID master, Infrastructure master, and PDC Emulator.
200	A	When you add the first domain to a forest, all three domain roles are performed by the first Domain Controller in the domain—RID master, Infrastructure master, and PDC Emulator.

Question 2

Identity	Active Directory Domain Services
Applications	AD Lightweight Directory Services
Trust	AD Certificates Services
Integrity	AD Rights Management
Partnership	AD Federation Services

Question 28

Command	Description
create sysvol full	C. IFM with SYSVOL for a writable DC
create full	A. IFM without SYSVOL for a writable DC or an AD LS
create sysvol rodc	D. IFM with SYSVOL for an RODC
create RODC	B. IFM without SYSVOL for a read-only DC

Question 54

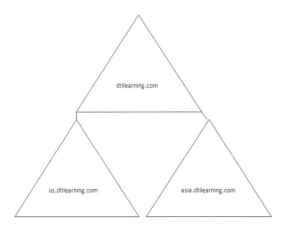

Question 55

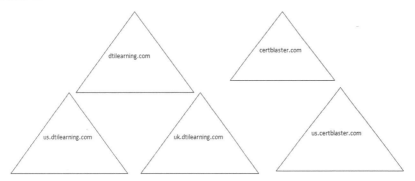

Question 56

Inter-Forest Migration	Intra-Forest Migration
A. Preserves existing accounts	D. Moves objects
E. Nondestructive	B. Consolidates domains
F. Separate forest	C. Same forest

Question 60

Term	Description
SIDs	B. Domain unique values assigned to accounts of all security principle
SD	E. Describes the permissions, ownership, rights, and auditing procedure for the resource
SACL	A. Describes auditing
DACL	D. Describes resource access permissions
ACE	C. Link a specific permissions with the SID of the security principle
LSASS	F. Compares the SIDs in the user token to the SID in the ACE

Question 62

Inter-Forest	Intra-Forest
Migrate global groups	C. Create universal groups and change to global after migration
Migrate users	A. Populate universal groups with sIDHistory
Use ADMT to add new accounts	B. Change universal to global after migration to target groups

Question 67

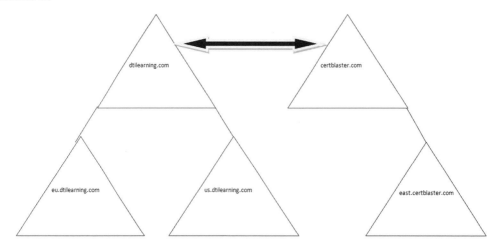

Question 70

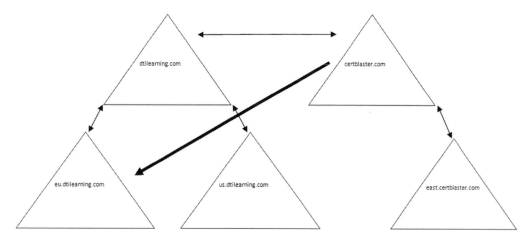

Question 80

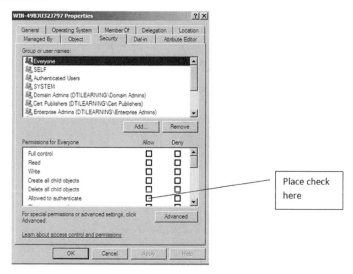

4A

Question 92

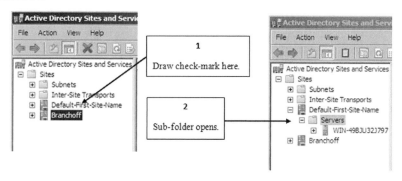

Question 98

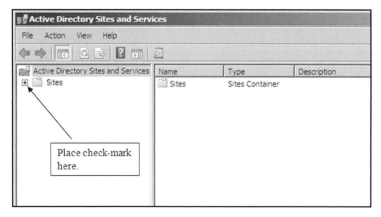

Question 102

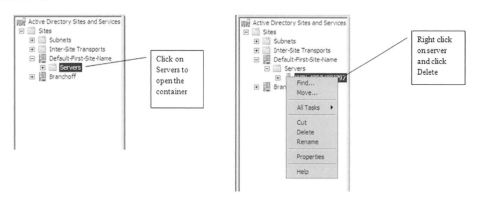

Question 104

Port	Service Name
389	A. LDAP
88	B. Kerberos
464	C. Kerberos Password protocol
3268	D. GC Services

Question 107

Naming Conventions	Definitions
A. Domain	NC contains all the objects stored in a domain and GPCs
B. Configuration	Objects that represent the logical structure of the forest, includes sites, subnets, and services
C. Schema	Defines the object classes and their attributes for the directory

Question 115

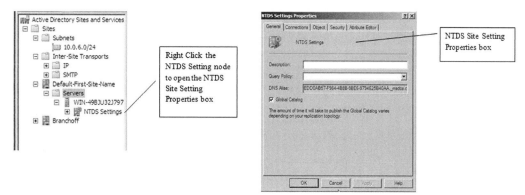

Question 127

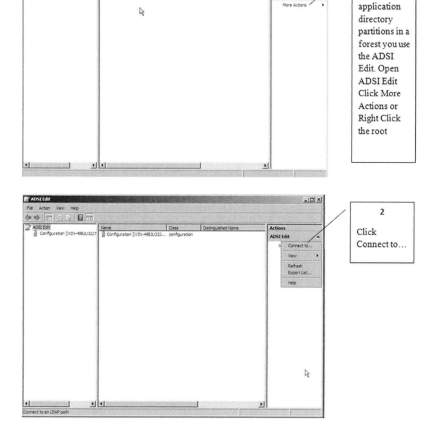

4A

Question 142

Term	Meaning
Integrity	Accuracy
Convergence	Consistency
Performance	Keeping traffic levels reasonable

Question 181

Inter-site	D. Checks for failures that would prevent or delay inter-site replication.
KCCEvent	A. IDs errors in the knowledge consistency checker.
Replications	C. Checks for timely replication between DCs.
FrsEvent	B. Reports on operation errors in the file replication system.

5

CONFIGURING ADDITIONAL ACTIVE DIRECTORY SERVER ROLES

Note that the interactive questions of the "list and reorder" type do not have a simple A/B/C answer and are therefore grouped at the end of the following grid.

Question	Answer	Explanation
1	See below	
2	C	AD LDS does not require a reboot and it makes no changes to the configuration of the server.
3	A	AS LDS is a subset of the code that is AD DS and is simpler to work with than AD DS.
4	A	AD LDS is based on the Lightweight Directory Access Protocol, which is a hierarchical database service.
5	D	AD LDS directory partitions can rely on X.500 naming conventions.
6	D	AD LDS will run on Windows Vista and server platforms.
7	D	AD LDS cannot include security principles to access a Windows Server Network.
8	C	AD LDS creates the ADAM folder on the system root.
9	D	The AD LDS directory store is named adamntds.dit.
10	C	When AD LDS is installed on a server core, fewer files are installed than in an installation on a Windows Server 2008 full installation.
11	See below	
12	See below	
13	See below	
14	A; B; C	To prepare for the creation of an AD LDS instance, you first create a data drive on your server for the directory stores, name the instance, and then identify the ports you will be using. Do not use the default AS DS ports 389 or 636.
15	C	The default port used by LDAP to communicate over the network is 389.
16	D	The secure LDAP port is 636.

5A

Question	Answer	Explanation
17	A	AD DS uses two ports to communicate with Global Catalog servers— 3268 and 3269 for Secure LDAP.
18	D	Secure LDAP uses communication port 3269 to access the Global Catalog.
19	D	The AD LDS Setup wizard will propose 50,000 and 50,001 for each instance of the AD LDS.
20	D	The AD LDS Setup wizard will propose 50,000 and 50,001 for each instance of AD LDS and suggest additional ports in the 50,0000+ range.
21	B	There are three ways to create an application partition for AD LDS: when you create the instance, when you install the application, and when you create the partition manually through the LDP.exe tool.
22	D	According to service account guidelines you should name the service account used by the instance the same as the instance.
23	B	Service account guidelines state that you should use a domain account when you are in a domain.
24	See below	
25	See below	
26	See below	
27	C	adamInstall.exe is the command used to perform unattended instance setups.
28	B	adamInstall.exe is the command used to perform unattended instance setups.
29	C	Use caution with the answer file because it contains passwords that are displayed in clear text. Passwords are removed after the file is used by the AD LDS creation tool.
30	C	The instance answer file is saved in the %systemroot%\ ADAM folder and named using the instance you are creating.
31	A	To run the adaminstall.exe, you need local administrator rights.
32	D	To perform an unattended AD LDS instance creation at a command prompt, enter adaminstall /answer:*filename.txt* where *filename* is the name of the answer file.
33	B	Use the LDIFDE.exe command to export contents from legacy instances to AD LDS.
34	D	To perform an export or upgrade to an instance you must have local administrative rights and administrative rights to the instance.
35	C	To import passwords from legacy instance, you use the -h switch with ldifde.

Question	Answer	Explanation
36	B	When passwords are imported from a legacy instance using the -h switch, all passwords are encrypted using simple authentication and security layer (SASL).
37	D	AD LDS creates two log files in the %systemroot%\Debug folder called ADAMSetup.log and ADAMSetup_loader.log.
38	B	The Rights Management Services tool has been replaced with AD Rights Management Services (AD RMS).
39	B; C; A	Organizations can choose to implement AD RMS in stages, which include implementing access rights for documents, content sharing with partners, and finally distributing materials outside the network border. The correct order is 1) Implementing access rights for documents produced in house 2) Content sharing with partners 3) Distribution of materials outside network perimeter
40	See below	
41	A	When you install AD RMS you create an AD RMS root cluster. One root cluster per AD DS can exist in the forest.
42	B	As documents are created, the user rights are embedded directly into the document.
43	C	AD RMS servers are self-enrolled when they are created, which creates a Server Licensor Certificate without access to the Microsoft Enrollment Center through the Internet.
44	B	Processor and RAM requirements for the AD RMS installation system are one Pentium, 4.3 GHz, with 512MB RAM.
45	D	The hardware requirements are two Pentiums, 4.3 GHz, and 1024MB RAM.
46	C	The hard disk space recommendation is 80GB.
47	B	The minimum required hard disk space is 40GB.
48	D	Authentication occurs when users first log in, and service tickets are requested whenever a user connects to a service like print or file servers. All of these activities require access to the DC at the hub site, so they will all generate activity over the WAN link to the hub site.
49	D	The main reasons for placing an RODC in a remote or branch office location are security, AD security, and administration. Unreliable performance would not be a concern if the RODC were placed at the remote branch office.

5A

Question	Answer	Explanation
50	D; C; A; B	The correct order is as follows: 1. Set the Forest Functional Level to Windows Server 2003 or higher 2. Run `adprep/rodcprep` on any DCs running Windows Server 2003 3. Ensure that one writable DC is a Windows 2008 server 4. Install the RODC
51	D	RODCs replicate changes from DCs in the hub site. Replication is one way from a writable domain controller to an RODC. No changes to the RODC are replicated to any other DC.
52	D	The Password Replication Policy allows user and computer credentials to be cached on an RODC. If user and computer credentials are cached then authentication and service ticket activities can be processed by the RODC and not referred to a writable DC. This maximizes user responses and saves on network traffic.
53	D	There are two attributes of the RODC that allow caching of user and computer credentials—the Allowed RODC Password Replication Group and the Denied RODC Password Replication Group.
54	B	The typical perimeter network will have two layers of protection.
55	See below	
56	D	AD FS is an AD technology that extends a service similar to the Forest trust through common HTTP ports.
57	C	AD DS extends the functionality of the Forest trust to networks outside your internal network with HTTP port 443.
58	C	AD FS can be used when implementing a partnership with other organizations that have AD DS with AD FS deployed.
59	C	AD FS uses the original authentication the client performed in its own network and passes that to all web applications that are using AD FS.
60	See below	There are two categories of business relationships with AD FS—resource organizations and the account organizations.
61	C; A; B	AD FS uses three designs that support different business needs—Federated Web SSO, Federated Web SSO with Forest trusts, and Web SSO. See below for more information.
62	C	Claims are the basis of authorization and are obtained in three ways—the FS server queries the internal directory store for claims, the account organization provides the claims to the resource federation server, and the federation service queries the AD DS for the claims.
63	B	Cookies are used during the Web sessions that are authenticated through AD FS. There are three types of cookies used by AD DS—Authentication cookies, Account Partner cookies, and sign-out cookies.

Question	Answer	Explanation
64	See below	Federation servers must have both a server authentication and token-signing certificate. Federation service proxies need a server authentication certificate. AD FS Web agents also need a server authentication certificate.
65	A; B; C	See below for more information.
66	See below	
67	See below	
68	See below	
69	See below	
70	See below	
71	See below	
72	A	The processor and memory requirements for AD FS deployment are a modest 133 MHz processor with X86-based computers and 512MB of RAM.

Question 1

LDAP Directory	Relational Database
Fast read and search	Fast writes
Hierarchical	Structured
Schema structure	Non-schema
Decentralized	Centrally located data

5A

Question 11

Tool	Description
AC Schema snap-in	Modify schema for AD LDS instances
AD Sites and Services	Configure and manage replication scopes
AD LDS Setup	Create AD LDS instances
ADSI Edit	Manage AD LDS content

Question 12

Tool	Use
CSVE	Import data into AD LDS
DSACLS	Control access control lists on AD LDS objects
DSAMain	Mount AD Store backups
DSDBUtil	Perform db maintenance

Question 13

Tool	Use
Dcdiag	Diagnose AD LDS instances
DSMgmt	Support application partition and policy management
LDIFDE	Import data into AD LDS instances
LDP	Modify content and AD LDS instances through LDAP

Question 24

Filename	Purpose
MS–ADAM–Upgrade–1	Upgrade the AD LDS schema
MS–asamschemaw2ke	Prerequisite for synchronizing an instance with AD 2k3
MS–adamschemaw2k8	Prerequisite for synchronizing an instance with AD 2k8
MS–AdamSynMetadata	Prerequisite for synchronizing data with AD DS forest and AD LDS

Question 25

Filename	Purpose
MS–AZMan	Required to support Windows Authorization Manage
MS–InetOrgPerson	Required to create inetOrgPerson
MS–User	Required to create user classes and attributes
MS–UserProxy	Required to create a simple userProxy class

Question 26

Filename	Purpose
MS–ADLDS–DisplaySpecifiers	Required for the AD Sites and Services operation
MS–UserProxyHull	Required to create a full userProxy class
MS–UserProxy	Required to create a simple userProxy class

Question 40

Function	Component
AD DS Forest	Authentication
AD RMS Root Cluster	Certification and licensing
SQL Servers	Configuration and logging
IIS Servers	Hosts AD RMS URL
AD RMS Clients	Consumption of AD RMS

Question 55

Port	Service
53	DNS traffic
80	HTTP
443	HTTP and SSL
25	SMTP

Question 60

Resource organizations	Companies that have external websites and want to simplify authentication to resources
Account organizations	Companies that enter into AD FS partnerships for resource organizations that mange the accounts

Question 61

C. Federated Web SSO	Links applications within an extranet to the internal directory stores of account organization
A. Federated Web SSO with Forest Trust	This uses two AD DS forests
B. Web SSO	All users for an extranet application are external without AD DS accounts

Question 64

Server Role	Certificates(s)
Federation Servers	Server authentication and token-signing
Federation Service proxies	Server authentication
AD FS web agents	Server authentication

Question 65

Term	Description
Account Federation Server	A. The AF server that is hosted in the account organizations internal network
AF server proxy	B. The FSP that is hosted in the account organization's perimeter network
Account partner	C. The AD DS directory that contains the accounts of the users accessing the applications

5A

Question 66

Term	Description
Federated application	ASP.NET application
Federated user	User granted claims in the account directory
Federation	Two organizations with a federation trust
Federation trust	One-way trust between a resource organization and account organization

Question 67

Term	Description
Client account discovery web page	Lists partner organizations and identifies organizations during logon
Client certificate	AD FS uses two-way authentication between federation server and proxies
Client logon page	Web page that gives feedback to users

Question 68

Term	Description
Resource account	Using Windows Integrated authentication to create resource accounts for each user
Resource federation server	Server that performs claims mappings and issues access security tokens
Resource federation service proxy	Located in the perimeter network of the resource organization
Resource Group	Located in the resource forest to map incoming claims
Resource partner/organization	Organization that hosts the federated applications

Question 69

Term	Description
Security token	Digitally signed object with the claim
Security token service	AD FS web service that issues tokens
Server authentication certificate	Enables two-way authentication between federation server and proxies
Server farm	Group of federation servers acting together

Question 70

Term	Description
SOA	Standards-based and language-agnostic architectures that rely on web services to support distributed services
SSO	Simplifies access with single logon for users
Token-signing certificate	Certificate used to sign security tokens from the resource federation server
Trust policy	How partners, certificates, claims, and account stores are identified

Question 71

Term	Description
Uniform Resource Identifier	Used by AD FS to identify partners and account stores
Verification certificate	Public key of a token-signing certificate
WS-★	Standards-based Internet service that forms part of an SOA
WS-Security	SOA specification on digitally signing and encrypting SOAP message
WS-Federation	Web server specifications for federation implementation

5A

6

CREATING AND MAINTAINING ACTIVE DIRECTORY OBJECTS

Note that the interactive questions of the "list and reorder" type do not have a simple A/B/C answer and are therefore grouped at the end of the following grid.

Question	Answer	Explanation
1	C	When a large number of users must be added to a domain, using the AD User and Computers snap-in is not the most productive method.
2	A	The user password is the only listed item that is not used in user templates.
3	D	The Copy Object User wizard creates users based on the user template and prompts you for the name, logon name, and the password settings for the new user.
4	F; D; B; C; A; E	See below.
5	B	The DS command dsadd creates objects in the directory, including user accounts.
6	A	Type DSADD USER/? for documentation on the DSADD USER parameters.
7	C	A comma-delimited file is also known as a .CSV file.
8	B	CSVD is a command-line tool that uses comma-delimited files known as .csv files.
9	See below	
10	D	The CSVDE command cannot be used to import passwords, so all accounts created will be disabled until the password is reset.
11	C	For more information about using CSVDE, use the /? parameter.
12	B	The Lightweight Directory Access Protocol Data Interchange Format is an Internet standard for file formats that can be used to perform batch operations in LDAP directories.
13	A	Each operation begins with the DN attribute of the object.

6A

Question	Answer	Explanation
14	A	For more information about using LDIFDE, use the /? parameter.
15	See below	
16	See below	
17	B	To Install PowerShell, open the Service Manager and choose the Add Features link.
18	C	Windows PowerShell is a command-line shell and scripting language that includes over 130 command-line tools.
19	See below	To install PowerShell, click on Add Features.
20	D	To open PowerShell, you use the Start menu.
21	C	You can tell when you're in PowerShell because it has a blue background and the prompt includes a PS.
22	D	PowerShell directives are single-feature commands that manipulate objects. cmdlets are verb-noun syntax directives that manipulate Microsoft .NET objects.
23	A	The Get-Service cmdlet is used to display a collection of all services.
24	C	PowerShell cmdlets use a verb-noun syntax to issue directives in the shell.
25	B	The Get-Help cmdlet followed by the service you need information about is the best way to get help using Windows PowerShell.
26	A	The format-list cmdlet was pipelined to the Get-Service cmdlet to produce the output shown in the image.
27	C; B; D; A	You connect to the container, invoke Create, populate the attributes with put, and then commit the changes using SetInfo.
28	D	Windows PowerShell can create users by importing user information from a comma-delimited text file or csv file.
29	A	VBScript can be created with Notepad and saved with a .vbs extension.
30	B	To execute a vbs file, you double-click on it and it will open with Wscript.exe.
31	See below	
32	C	The Attribute Editor displays all the system attributes.
33	B	To turn on the Attribute Editor, you choose the View menu and select the Advanced Features option.
34	A	To select several objects, hold down the Ctrl key and click the objects you want to select.
35	A; D; E; F; G	The properties that are available when you are managing attributes of multiple users are General, Account, Address, Profile, and Organization.

Question	Answer	Explanation
36	D	The sAMAccountName is the pre-Windows 2000 name and must be unique for the entire domain.
37	B	The userPrincipalName or UPN includes the logon name and a UPN suffix which is the DNS name of the domain.
38	C	The RDN or relative distinguished name must be unique within its container.
39	D	The displayName attribute appears in the exchange (GAL) global address list.
40	N/A	To limit the workstation to which a user can log on, you must use the Log On To button.
41	N/A	Click User Must Change Password at Next Logon. Best practice states that you should select the reset password at next logon option when resetting a user's password.
42	C	The correct DS command to change a user password is dsmod user UserDN -pwd NewPassword.
43	A	The DS command to change the password and force the user to change the password at first logon is dsmod user UserDN -pwd NewPassword -mustchpwd yes.
44	B	An account lockout policy specifies that when a user has too many failed logon attempts within a specified amount of time his or her account is locked out.
45	D	To unlock an account that has been locked due to too many failed logon attempts, right-click the Account, select Properties, choose the Account tab, and then uncheck the Unlock Account check box.
46	C	To disable an account with dsmod, use dsmod user unserDN -disabled yes.
47	A	To disable an account with dsmod, use dsmod user unserDN -disabled yes.
48	D	A user account cannot be re-created by simply creating a new account with the same name because the new account will have a new SID and will not have the same group memberships.
49	B	A subset of the user's accounts is tombstoned for 60 days by default after the account has been deleted.
50	B	User accounts can be recycled and retain the SID and group memberships so when the account is reactivated it will have the same group membership and user rights.
51	D	To remove a user account from Active Directory, use dsrm followed by the UserDN.

6A

Question	Answer	Explanation
52	C	You can drag and drop it in the snap-in or right-click the user and select the Move command.
53	A	To move a user account with the DS command dsmove, enter dsmove UserDN -newparent TargetOUDN.
54	C	The two names in the New Object Group dialog box are the cn name and sAMAccountName.
55	B	There are two types of groups you can create—Security and Distribution.
56	A	Distribution groups are not security enabled and thus do not have SIDs.
57	D	The Group scopes that are available from the New Object Group dialog box are Domain Local, Global, and Universal.
58	See below	N/A
59	See below	N/A
60	See below	N/A
61	B	The Select User, Computers, or Groups dialog box is used to add or remove a member from a group.
62	See below	By default, Windows searches only for users and groups. To add a computer to a group, you must click the Objects Types button and select Computers.
63	A	The best practice for nesting groups is known as AGDLA—Accounts, Global Groups, Domain Local groups, and ACLs.
64	D	The correct command to add a group is dsadd group GroupDN where GroupDN is the DN of the group.
65	C	CSVCE uses comma-separated value files (.csv) to import data and create groups in AD.
66	B	LDIFDE uses text files in the Lightweight Directory Access Protocol Data Interchange Format.
67	A	The recommended method for adding computers to a domain is to create custom OUs to hold computer objects and not use the default Computer container.
68	C	The creation of computer objects in an OU before joining them to the domain is called prestaging the account.
69	C	To join a computer to a domain after prestaging the computer object, change the workgroup setting by right-clicking Computer, selecting Properties, and in Computer Name clicking Change Settings.
70	D	Use the redircmp command on a DC to redirect the default computer container with "DN of OU for new computer objects".

Question	Answer	Explanation
71	A	The `Ms-MachineAccountQuota` attribute of the domain allows any authenticated user to join up to 10 computers with the domain without any additional permissions.
72	D	The `Ms-MachineAccountQuota` attribute of the domain allows any authenticated user to join up to 10 computers with the domain without any additional permissions.
73	B	When importing computer objects using SCVDE, you need to include the `userAccountControl` attribute and set it to 4096.
74	C	To create a computer object with `dsadd`, use the command `dsadd computer ComputerDN`, where DN is the distinguished name of the computer.
75	C; B; A; D	You connect to the container, use the Create method, populate the mandatory attributes, and then commit the changes.
76	D; A; B; C	You connect to the container, use the Create method, populate the mandatory attributes, and then commit the changes.
77	B	Lightweight Access Protocol Data Interchange Format uses text files that are specified by blocks of lines separated by a blank space. Each operation begins with the DN attribute.
78	D	To create a computer with netdom, use `Netdom add Computername / domain:DomainName`.
79	A	CSVDE is a command-line tool that can be used to import or export computer objects from a comma-delimited file, which is also known as a .csv file.
80	See below	
81	B	OUs create a collection of objects for the purpose of administration.
82	See below	N/A
83	See below	Windows Server 2008 includes a new feature: Protect Container from Accidental Deletion.
84	D	The Protect Container from Accidental Deletion adds two permissions to the OU—`Everyone::Deny::Delete` and `Everyone::Deny::Delete::Subtree`.
85	See below	To delete an OU that is protected, you need to turn on the Advanced features from the AD User and Computers snap-in, right-click the OU and select Properties, click the Object tab and clear the Protect Object from Accidental Deletion check box.
86	See below	To create a new user, you open AD Users and Computers snap-in, expand the node, and then right-click the node and select New. Following correct naming conventions, fill in the logon name, select a UPN suffix, set an initial password, and choose User Must Change Password.

6A

Question	Answer	Explanation
87	See below	To create a new group, you open the AD Users and Computers snap-in, expand the node to navigate to the container, and then right-click the container and select New. Following the correct naming conventions, choose Group Type, Select Group Scope, open Group Properties, and finally Enter the properties for group.
88	D	The computer's name in AD is simply the computer's name with a $ sign appended to it.
89	See below	To add a new computer, you open the AD Users and Computers snap-in, expand the node to navigate to the container, and then right-click the container and select New Computer. Type a computer name, specify the User or Group to join the computer to the domain, right-click and open Properties, and to finish, enter properties for the computer.
90	A	The computer description field is used to indicate who the computer is assigned to or its role and must be entered in the properties of the computer account.
91	C	To add columns to the Details pane, use the Add/Remove Columns command from the View menu in AD Users and Computers snap-in.
92	D	The figure shows the AD Users and Computers snap-in in Detail view.
93	D	To sort a column, click on the heading in the Details pane.
94	B	Windows Server 2003 introduced Saved Queries in AD Users and Computers snap-in to create rule-driven views of your objects.
95	C	To use Saved Queries, you must first open the AD Users and Computer snap-in from a custom console.
96	A	To view Saved Queries in AD Users and Computers, you must use a snap-in or custom console.
97	C	To open the New Query dialog box, right-click on Saved Queries and select New, Query.
98	See below	To create a saved query, you open AD Users and Computers from a snap-in, right-click Saved Query, Select New, and then Select Query. You need to type a name and a description. Then, click Browse, define the query, select Type AD object, and to finish select OK.
99	A	Saved Queries will be saved within the AD Users and Computer snap-in, as dsa.msc.
100	B	When you are assigning permissions, adding members to a group or a group to a user, or creating a linked property, you will use the Select Users, Contacts, Computers, or Groups dialog box. Creating a new user will NOT open the Select Users, Contacts, Computers, or Groups dialog box.
101	B	Multiple names can be added into the Enter the Object Names to Select text box if they're separated by semicolons.

Question	Answer	Explanation
102	A	The Select dialog box does not by default search for computers.
103	C	When you are using the Select User, Contacts, Computers, or Groups dialog box and specify a name on the Managed By tab, groups are not searched by default.
104	D	To search for things such as disabled accounts, non-expiring passwords, and stale accounts, you use the Advanced button on the Select dialog box.
105	C	The Find box is also called the Active Directory Query tool.
106	B	For complete control over your search, choose the Custom Search drop-down list from the Find drop-down box.
107	D	To create a shortcut on the desktop for the Find box, the target of the shortcut would be Rundll32 dsquery, OpenQueryWindow.
108	D	Typing Dsquery.exe/? will give you documentation and syntax for the dsquery command.
109	B	The delegation of administrative tasks to a help desk or to other individuals is referred to as delegation of administrative control.
110	A	The Security tab is not available if the Advanced features are not selected from the View menu of the AD User and Computers snap-in.
111	B	The Permissions tab of the Advanced Security Settings dialog box for the AD object shows the DACL of the object.
112	A	The Permissions tab of the Advanced Security Setting dialog box will show the granular ACEs of a permission entry.
113	B	If you have rights to change a password, you must know and enter the current password.
114	D	If you have rights to reset a password, you are not required to know the previous password.
115	See below	To assign the reset password permission to the Support Group, open the AD Users and Computers snap-in, select Advanced from the View menu, open the user object properties, click the Security tab, click the Advanced button, click Add, select Support Groups security principal, and click OK. Configure the Allow::Reset password and then click OK and close the dialog boxes.
116	D	Explicit permissions always override permissions that are inherited from parent objects.
117	D	To use the Delegation of Control wizard, right-click on the domain or OU that you want to delegate control and select Delegate Control.
118	See below	The procedure for using the Delegation of Control wizard is to open the AD Users and Computers snap-in, right-click the node to delegate control, select the group to grant privileges to, Add Users or Groups, specify a task to delegate, and finally apply ACEs to enable delegation.

6A

Question	Answer	Explanation
119	D	Dscals.exe can be used to set permissions, delegate, and report on directory service objects from the command line.
120	N/A	You click the Restore Defaults button. The default permissions are defined by the AD schema and are reset with the Restore Defaults button.
121	A	The command-line tool dscals provides the /s switch to reset permissions to the schema-defined defaults.
122	C	The user password is not an item used in user templates.
123	A	The Account Tab properties include logon names, passwords, and account flags.
124	B	The General tab of the User Properties dialog box contains the names, properties, and basic description and contact information.
125	A	The Address tab of the Properties dialog box contains detailed contact information.
126	C	The Profile tab is where user profile path, logon script, and home folder are configured.
127	D	The Member Of tab is used to add or remove group membership.
128	See below	N/A
129	D	Best practice states that you should select the Reset Password at Next Logon option when resetting a user's password.
130	D	When you're creating accounts in advance, they should be disabled until needed.
131	A	The correct DS command to change a user password is dsmod user UserDN -pwd NewPassword.
132	B	The DS command to change the password and force the user to change the password at first logon is dsmod user UserDN -pwd NewPassword -mustchpwd yes.
133	D	An account lockout policy specifies that when a user has too many failed logon attempts within a specified amount of time his or her account is locked out.
134	C	To unlock an account that has been locked due to too many failed logon attempts right-click the account, select Properties, select the Account tab, and uncheck the Unlock Account check box.
135	C	To disable an account with dsmod, use dsmod user unserDN -disabled yes.
136	C	To enable an account with dsmod, use dsmod user unserDN -disabled no.

Question	Answer	Explanation
137	D	A user account cannot be re-created by simply creating a new account with the same name because the new account will have a new SID and will not have the same group memberships.
138	B	A subset of the user account is tombstoned for 60 days by default after the account has been deleted.
139	C	You can drag and drop it in the snap-in, or right-click the user and select the Move command, but it is more accurate and preferable to use the Move command.
140	D	To move a user account with the DS command `dsmove`, enter `dsmove UserDN -newparent TargetOUDN`.
141	B	The default tombstone interval is 60 days.
142	See below	Open the AD Users and Computers snap-in, click the View menu, and select the Advanced Features option; then open the properties for the group. Select the Object tab and select Protect the Object from Accidental Deletion.
143	See below	The Managed By tab provides for the delegation of membership management from the Manager Can Update Membership List check box.
144	See below	Select the Objects Type button and click OK to add Groups.
145	C	Using a Shadow Group to assign permissions to members of an OU.
146	A, D, E	The default local groups are Administrator, Backup Operators, and Remote Desktop users. The additional domain groups include Domain Admins, Enterprise Admins, and Schema Admins.
147	B, C, F	The default local groups are Administrator, Backup Operators, and Remote Desktop users. The additional domain groups include Domain Admins, Enterprise Admins, and Schema Admins.
148	D	The special identities groups have membership controlled by the operating system and cannot be viewed in AD Users and Computers.
149	C	The Computer container is created by default with the domain and cannot be subdivided. It is not an OU and cannot be linked to a Group Policy object. The Computer is an object of class container.
150	A	The process of creating computer accounts before joining the computer to the domain is called prestaging the account.
151	C	The advantage of prestaging accounts is that the computer will be placed into a managed OU when it joins the domain and not in the unmanaged Computers container object.
152	C	The `dsmod` command can only modify the description and location attributes of the computer account.
153	See below	The Operating System tab will be read-only until the computer joins the domain.

6A

Question	Answer	Explanation
154		Click the Managed By tab. The Member Of tab in the computer's Properties dialog box will link to the user object of the user to whom the computer is assigned.
155	C	The computer account password is stored in the form of a Local Security authority (LSA) secret and changes its password every 30 days.
156	C	The computer account password is stored in the form of a Local Security authority (LSA) secret and changes its password every 30 days.
157	See below	To reset a computer, right-click the computer and choose Reset Account. Click Yes to confirm and reboot the computer to rejoin the domain.
158	D	The down arrow in the AD User and Computers snap-in appears when the account has been disabled.
159	C	To disable a computer account in AD, right-click on the account in the AD Users and Computers snap-in and select Disable Account from the menu.
160	C	Resetting the computer account resets the password while maintaining all the computer object's properties. After the reset the account becomes available and any computer can join the domain using that account.
161	A	The most granular component of Group Policy is the policy setting; it is also simply referred to as a policy.
162	D	Policy settings are defined and exist within the Group Policy object or GPO.
163	A	Group Policy objects are managed in AD by using the Group Policy Management console or GPME.
164	B	The GPME displays thousands of policy settings that are available in a GPO.
165	B	The three policy setting states are Not Configured, Enabled, and Disabled.
166	B	The scope of a GPO is the collection of computers and users that a Group Policy object will apply to.
167	B	Group Policy refresh is applied at 90-120 minutes after startup or logon.
168	D	Group Policy clients pull the GPOs from the domain.
169	B	By default a link is considered to be slow if it is less than 500 Kbps.
170	D	The local GPO is stored in %systemroot%\system32\GroupPolicy.
171	C	The two default GPOs created when AD DS is installed are the Default Domain Policy and the Default Domain Controllers Policy.
172	C	A GPO consists of two components—a Group Policy Container and a Group Policy Template.

Question	Answer	Explanation
173	D	Group Policy clients identify GPOs by their version numbers.
174	D	SYSVOL replication using Distributed File System Replication (DFS-R) is more efficient and robust.
175	D	The default time allotted to process scripts is 10 minutes.
176	C	The Policy Based QoS node defines how network traffic will be handled by policy.
177	A	HKEY_LOCAL_MACHINE Registry values will be updated by policies in the Administrative Templates node.
178	D	The Windows Vista and Server 2008 Administrative Template file is in two parts, one with an ADMX file extension and one with an ADML file extension.
179	C	The Central Store was first available with Windows Server 2008 and is used in large organizations to hold the ADMX/ADML files.
180	C	The GPME in Windows Server 2008 can now filter policies to choose the exact settings you need to configure.
181	D	A managed policy setting will reverse its Registry settings after the computer is no longer within the scope of the GPO.
182	B	Precedence of the GPOs determine which policy setting is applied by the client when there are multiple GPOs linked to an object.
183	B	Preference new is a built-in feature that allows multiple preference items within a single GPO in Windows Server 2008.
184	D	GPOs are applied in the order site, domain, and then OU, with OU overriding earlier settings.
185	B	The tools for performing RSoP functions in Windows Server 2008 are the Group Policy Results wizard, the Group Policy Modeling wizard, and Gpresult.exe.
186	C	Windows Installer packages have an .msi extension.
187	D	When an application is assigned it appears on the Start menu and installs on first use. When an application appears in Add/Remove Programs, it has been published.
188	B	The domain password policies are located in the Computer Configuration\Policies\Windows Settings\Security Settings\Account Policies\Password Policy node.
189	D	Fine-grained password policy in Windows Server 2008 allows you to configure a policy that applies to one or more groups or users in your domain.
190	C	You can audit objects for success, failures, or both.

6A

Question	Answer	Explanation
191	D	When a user connects to a folder on a server in the domain, a logon is authorized by the DTILearning DC and is called a network logon.
192	D	Account logon and logon events are configured by configuring the GPO in Computer configuration \Policies\Windows Settings\Security Settings\Local Policies\Audit Policy.

Question 4

Command	Description
A. dsadd	5. Creates an object in the directory
B. dsget	3. Returns specified attributes of an object
C. dsmod	4. Modifies specified attributes of an object
D. dsmove	2. Moves an object to a new container
E. dsrm	6. Removes an object
F. dsquery	1. Performs a query based on parameters

Question 9

Parameter	Function
Default	Export
-i	Import
-k	Ignore errors

Question 15

Parameter	Use
-i	Import mode
-f	Filename
-s	Domain controller to bind for query
-v	Verbose mode
-j path	Log file location

Question 16

Parameter	Use
-d RootDN	Root of the LDAP search
-r Filter	LDAP search filter
-p	Search scope
-l list	Comma-separated list of attributes
-o list	Comma-separated list of attributes

Question 19

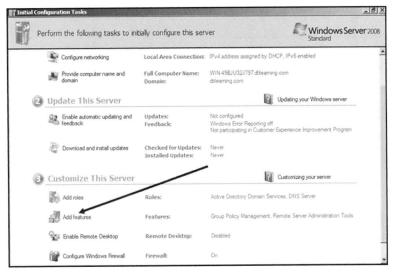

Question 31

Account Tab	Logon Names, Passwords, and Account Flags
General tab	Name properties, contact information
Addresses	Detailed contact information
Profile tab	Logon script and home folder
Member Of tab	Group membership

Question 58

Members from the Same Domain	Members from Another Domain and Same Forest	Members from a Trusted External Domain
Users	Users	Users
Computers	Computers	Computers
Global Groups	Global Groups	Global Groups
Domain Local Groups	Universal Groups	
Universal Groups		

6A

Question 59

Members from the Same Domain	Members from Another Domain and Same Forest	Members from a Trusted External Domain
Users	Users	
Computers	Computers	
Global Groups	Global Groups	
Universal Groups	Universal Groups	

Question 60

Members from the Same Domain	Members from Another Domain and Same Forest	Members from a Trusted External Domain
Users		
Computers		
Global Groups		

Question 62

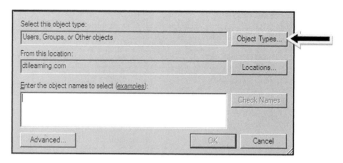

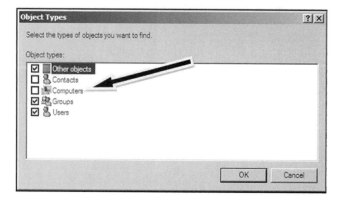

Question 80

Parameter	Function
Default	Export
-i	Import
-k	Ignore errors
-f	Filename

Question 82

1	Open the AD Users and Computers snap-in.
2	Right-click the Domain or OU where you want to add the new OU.
3	Name the OU.
4	Select Protect from Accidental Deletion.
5	Right-click and go to Properties.
6	Complete the Description and Managed by information.

Question 83

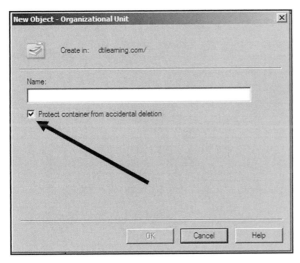

Question 85

1	Turn on Advanced Features in the AD User and Computer snap-in.
2	Select the OU Properties.
3	Select the Object tab.
4	Clear the check box.
5	Click OK.

6A

Question 86

1	Open the AD Users and Computers snap-in.
2	Expand your domain and open the target OU or container.
3	Right-click the node and select New User.
4	Follow the correct naming conventions.
5	Fill in the logon name.
6	Select a UPN suffix.
7	Set an initial password.
8	Select User Must Change Password.

Question 87

1	Open the AD Users and Computers snap-in.
2	Expand the node to navigate to the container.
3	Right-click the container and select New Group.
4	Follow the correct naming conventions.
5	Choose Group Type.
6	Select Group Scope.
7	Open Group Properties.
8	Enter properties for the group.

Question 89

1	Open the AD Users and Computers snap-in.
2	Expand the node to navigate to the container.
3	Right-click the container and select New Computer.
4	Type the Computer name.
5	Specify the User or Group to join the computer to the domain.
6	Right-click and open Properties.
7	Enter properties for the computer.

Question 98

1	Open the AD Users and Computers from a snap-in.
2	Right-click Saved Query.
3	Select New.
4	Select Query.
5	Type a name.
6	Enter a description.
7	Click Browse.
8	Define the query.
9	Select Type AD Object.
10	Select OK.

Question 115

1	Open the AD Users and Computers snap-in.
2	Select Advanced from the View menu.
3	Open the user's object properties.
4	Click the Security tab.
5	Click the Advanced button.
6	Click Add.
7	Select the Support Groups security principal.
8	Click OK.
9	Configure the Allow::Reset password.
10	Close the dialog boxes.

Question 118

1	Open the AD Users and Computers snap-in.
2	Right-click the node to delegate control.
3	Select the group to grant privileges to.
4	Add Users or Groups.
5	Specify the task to delegate.
6	Apply ACEs to enable delegation.

6A

Question 128

General	Description, Office, Phone, Fax, Web Page, and Email
Account	UPN Suffix, Logon hours, Restrictions, Account options, and Account Expiration
Address	Street, PO, City, State, ZIP, and Country
Profile	Path, Logon Script, and Home Folder
Organization	Title, Department, Company, and Manager

Question 142

1	Open the AD Users and Computers snap-in.
2	Click View and turn on Advanced Features.
3	Open Group Properties.
4	Select the Object tab and select Protect Object from Accidental Deletion.

Question 143

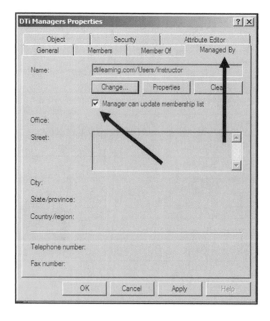

Question 144

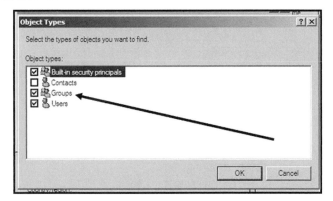

Question 153

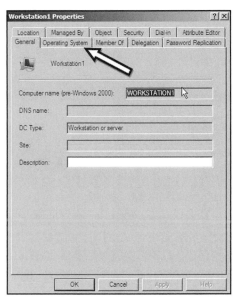 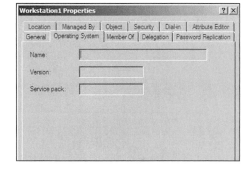

6A

Question 157

1	Open the Active Directory Users and Computers snap-in.
2	Right-click the computer.
3	Select Reset.
4	Click Yes.
5	Reboot.

7

MAINTAINING THE ACTIVE DIRECTORY ENVIRONMENT

Note that the interactive questions of the "list and reorder" type do not have a simple A/B/C answer and are therefore grouped at the end of the following grid.

Question	Answer	Explanation
1	D	Proactive performance management allows you to identify and correct problems quickly and accurately.
2	See below	N/A
3	D	The Performance tab gives you physical and kernel memory usage.
4		To open Resource Monitor, you open Task Manager, select the Performance tab, and then click the Resource Monitor button.
5	A; C; E; F	Resource Monitor gives you graphic displays of the CPU, disk, memory, and network usage.
6	A	The additional logs specifically related to a Domain Controller are located in the Application and Services Logs folder in Event Viewer.
7	C	Server Manager provides custom log views related to specific server roles.
8	A	The three types of events listed by Event Viewer are error, warning, and information.
9	B	The illustration shows the Windows Reliability Monitor, found in the Server Manager.
10	C	Reliability Monitor is the first place to check because it tracks changes and may reveal the issue that is causing the system instability.
11	D	This is the Add Counters dialog box from Performance Monitor and is used to add counters to Performance Monitor.
12	C	To create a performance baseline, you need to take samples for 30-45 minutes.
13	B	To create a performance baseline, you need to capture the data at peak and nonpeak times.

7A

Question	Answer	Explanation
14	B	Studies have shown that up to 40% of small businesses that do not have a plan for continuity and face a disaster will, in the event of a disaster, not survive it.
15	See below	N/A
16	See below	N/A
17	D	The Additional Account Info tab is added by registering the acctinfo.dll file, which is located in the Windows Server 2003 Resource Kit.
18	A	The Additional Account Info tab is added by registering the acctinfo.dll file, which is located in the Windows Server 2003 Resource Kit.
19	C	Specops Gpupdate is a tool that will add remote functionality to AD Users and Computers.
20	See below	N/A
21	See below	N/A
22	See below	N/A
23	B	As new records are added, space is allocated for them. However, as records are deleted the space is not recovered.
24	D	Starting with Windows Server 2008, the AD DS service is now manageable and can be started and stopped like all Windows Server services.
25	C	The Object tab can only be viewed when you have the Advanced Features turned on in the View menu.
26	B	When an object is changed two events are logged—the first lists the old value and the second lists the new value.
27	A	Tombstoned AD objects are moved to a special hidden container and are reinstalled with a special utility from Quest Software.
28	D	Tombstoned AD objects are moved to a special hidden container and are reinstalled with a special utility from Quest Software.
29	C	Objects restored from tombstoned containers do not include all their previous attributes.
30	D	The new Windows Server 2008 tool for restoring backup sets is AD DS Database Mounting tool.
31	B	Install From Media is a setup that uses a copy of the Ntds.dit file from another DC in the domain.
32	A	Windows Server 2008 backups use Windows Server Backup and Wbadmin.exe. These tools are not installed by default.
33	N/A	The DC Backup should contain the system, boot, and SYSVOL volumes, the AD DS database, and the volume that hosts the AD DS logs.
34	B; C; E	Backup can be performed with network drives, removable basic hard drives, DVDs, and CDs.

Question	Answer	Explanation
35	C	The Windows Recovery Environment is used to restore a server that is down and is found on the Windows Server 2008 installation media.
36	D	To use the ISO WinRE to restore a DC in Hyper-V you need the Windows Automated Installation Kit or WAIK.
37	B	System Restore is not a Windows Server Backup restore mode.
38	D	The catalog file is used to locate data for a particular backup.
39	C	Windows Server backs up the data to the same file and adds content as data changes with each backup.
40	A	To create copies of the directory contents to install DCs, use the Install From Media option, which uses a copy of the Ntds.dit.
41	B	The Enable System Recovery check box on the Custom Option screen will automatically capture all the data required to recover a full system.
42	A; C; E; F	Windows Server Backup can use local drives, DVD/CDs, network drives, and removable hard disk drives.
43	C	From the Specify Advanced Option page, you should select VSS Full Backup if you are using Windows Server Backup as your only backup tool.
44	C	From the Specify Advanced Option page, you should select VSS Copy Backup if you are using another backup tool.
45	C	The Wbadmin.exe command to run a full system backup is `wbadmin start backuptarget -allcritical -backup:`*location*.
46	B	You cannot use mapped network drives with Windows Server Backup when scheduling backup tasks.
47	D	You cannot use mapped network drives. Windows Server backup will use addressable removable media and virtual hard drives for backup.
48	A	To start Server 2008 in Directory Service Restore mode by changing the boot order, you use the command line tool Bcedit.exe or press F8 during Windows boot up. This will start the Advanced Boot Options and select Directory Services Restore mode.
49	A	To start Server 2008 in Directory Service Restore mode by changing the boot order, you use the command-line tool Bcedit.exe or press F8 during Windows boot up. This will start the Advanced Boot Options and select Directory Services Restore mode.
50	C	To start Server 2008 in Directory Service Restore mode by changing the boot order, you use the command-line tool Bcedit.exe or press F8 during Windows boot up. This will start the Advanced Boot Options and select Directory Services Restore mode.
51	C	The AD DS Database Mounting tool works by generating a database snapshot.

7A

Question	Answer	Explanation
52	B	The nonauthoritative restore is used when no data was lost, whereas the authoritative restore is used when data was lost and it therefore updates the Update Sequence Number (USN).
53	C	To list the available backups located on drive E, you type `wbadmin get versions -backuptarget:e`.
54	A	To mark a backup as authoritative from the elevated command prompt, you type `Ntdsutil > authoritative restore > restore database > quit`.
55	D	To completely restore a DC from a backup, you start the computer from the Windows Server 2008 installation media. Then, in the System Recovery Options dialog box, you clear any operating systems that are selected for repair and click Next. Then select the Choose a Recovery Tool option and select Windows Complete PC Restore.
56	C	To perform a complete computer recovery from a command prompt after clearing any operating systems for repair, you select the Command Prompt option from Choose A Recovery Tool. Then type `diskpart` and then `list vol` to indentify the volumes of the backup set and use `wbadmin` to start the backup.
57	D	When a server is created on a virtual machine it is a set of files on a disk.
58	B	Virtual machines are easier to protect in the event of full system failure. You simply go back to the latest backup and boot it up.
59	D	Volume Shadow Copy Service or VSS automatically takes snapshots of disk contacts at regular intervals. This enables the fastest restore time of all available restore methods.
60	C	To restore an older version of a file you can use the Previous tab found in the Properties dialog box.
61	C	VSS can be enabled on any Windows Server 2008 that has at least three disk drives.
62	C; D; G	The drive structure of a host system running Virtual Machines and VSS should be as follows—drive C should be the system and boot drive, drive D should be the data drive with the Virtual Machines images, and drive E should be the VSS snapshot drive.
63	B	To set drive D as the data that should be copied, select drive D in Explorer, right-click and select Properties, and then click the Shadow Copies tab. From there, you click the Setting button. Finally, select D from the Select Volume list and click Enable.
64	D	From a command line, type `vssadmin add shadowstorage` to begin the VSS setup on a Server Core installation.
65	A	The Resultant Set of Policy or RSoP is a collection of tools used to manage and troubleshoot group policy issues.

Question	Answer	Explanation
66	B	The tools for performing RSoP functions in Windows Server 2008 are the Group Policy Results wizard, the Group Policy Modeling wizard, and Gpresult.exe.
67	C	The Group Policy Management Console includes the Group Policy Results wizard.
68	D	The Group Policy Results wizard connects to policy settings through the WMI provider.
69	E; F; H; I	Computers running Windows Vista, XP, Server 2003, and Server 2008 can be monitored with the Group Policy Results wizard.
70	C; D	The Group Policy Results wizard connects to policy settings through the WMI provider on ports 135 and 445.
71	A	Computers running Windows Vista, XP, Server 2003, and Server 2008 can be monitored with the Group Policy Results wizard. The wizard cannot access Windows 2000 computers.
72	C	You must have administrative credentials on the local computer to run the Group Policy Results wizard.
73	B	To analyze a user's RSoP, the user must have logged on at least once on the computer.
74	D	The Group Policy Results wizard produces an RSoP report in dynamic HTML. You can view the dynamic content using Explorer.
75	A; C; F	The report generated by the Group Policy Results wizard has three tabs—Summary, Settings, and Policy Events.
76	A; B; E	Password Policy, Security Options, and User Rights are some of the settings found on the Settings Tab > Security Settings. IPSec and Wireless settings are not reported.
77	A; D	Password Policy, Security Options, and Windows Setting are some of the settings found on the Settings Tab. IPSec and Wireless settings are not reported.
78	C	To save or print the RSoP report, right-click on it and select Save or Print from the menu.
79	B	To rerun the RSoP query, right-click on it and select Save or Print from the menu.
80	A	To save or print the RSoP report, right-click on it and select Save or Print from the menu.
81	B	Gpresult.exe is the command-line version of the Group Policy Results wizard that will run on Windows 2000 with a limited report.
82	D	To specify RSoP analysis for the computer settings on the target computer, you use the /scope [computer] option.

7A

Question	Answer	Explanation
83	B	To specify an RSoP analysis that displays super verbose data, you use the /z option with the Gpresult.exe command.
84	C	To perform an RSoP "what-if" analysis, you can use the Group Policy Modeling wizard.
85	B	The new log called Group Policy Operational Log was created to log Group Policy events. The log it is located in is the Application and Services Logs\Microsoft\Windows\GroupPolicy\Operational.
86	A	The Group Policy Operational Log is found in the Applications and Services Logs group.
87	C	Connector objects appear in the Administrative tools in AD Sites and Services. The DC replicates changes from one DC to another because of the AD DC connector object.
88	C	Replication in Active Directory is always a pull technology.
89	C	By default Active Directory will create a topology that ensures replication automatically.
90	A	The Knowledge Consistency Checker or KCC helps to generate and optimize replication automatically between DCs within a site.
91	C	If a Domain Controller goes offline, the KCC will dynamically rebuild the two-way three-hop replication.
92	C	Repadmin.exe is a tool that reports on the status of replication on a Domain Controller. Dcdiag.exe is a tool that performs tests and reports on the status of replication and security on AD DS.
93	B	Repadmin.exe is a tool that reports on the status of replication on a domain controller. Dcdiag.exe is a tool that performs tests and reports on the status of replication and security on AD DS.
94	See below	N/A
95	C	The Additional Account Info tab is added by registering the acctinfo.dll file, which is located in the Windows Server 2003 Resource Kit.
96	B	The Additional Account Info tab is added by registering the acctinfo.dll file, which is located in the Windows Server 2003 Resource Kit.
97	D	The new Windows Server 2008 tool for restoring backup sets is the AD DS Database Mounting tool.
98	C	The command-line tool wbadmin.exe will ID the disks attached to a system and place them in the specified text file; in this instance it would be Diskidentifiers.txt.

Question	Answer	Explanation
99	B	To start Server 2008 in Directory Service Restore mode by changing the boot order, you use the command-line tool Bcedit.exe or press F8 during Windows boot up. This will start the Advanced Boot Options and select Directory Services Restore mode.
100	B	The VSS schedules for copies are scheduled tasks controlled by the Task Scheduler or the Schtasks.exe command-line tool.
101	B	The AD DS Database Mounting tool works by generating a database snapshot.
102	D	The result of a backup scheduled with wbadmin is found in the Task Scheduler under Microsoft\Windows \Backup.
103	A	To modify a task created with wbadmin, you use the Task Scheduler after the task has been created.
104	C	To modify a task created with wbadmin, you use the Task Scheduler after the task has been created.

Question 2

Tools	Description
Task Manager	Displays current system resources
Event Viewer	Logs events and system performance
Reliability Monitor	Tracks changes
Performance Monitor	Collects data and identifies issues
WSRM	Contains profile-specific applications

Question 15

Group	Activity
Users	Search AD for account records
Security and distribution group managers	Manage group content
Help Desk	Password reset
System administrators	AD and DNS contents

7A

Question 16

The table lists the 12 major activities of AD administration and shows which tasks focus on data and content management.

Task	Content Management	Data
User and Group Administration		✓
Endpoint Device Administration		✓
Network Service Administration	✓	✓
GPO Management	✓	
DNS Administration	✓	
AD Topology and Replication	✓	
AD Configuration	✓	
AD Schema Management	✓	
Information Management		✓
Security Management	✓	
Database Management	✓	
AD Reporting	✓	✓

Question 20

Tool	Location
AD Domains and Trusts	Administrative tools
AD Schema snap-in	MMC
AD Sites and Services	Administrative tools
AD Users and Computers	Administrative tools
ADSI Edit	Administrative tools
CSVDE.exe	Command line
DCDiag.exe	Command line
Dcpromo.exe	Start menu, Search
DFSRadmin.exe	Command line

Question 21

Tool	Location
Event Viewer	Administrative tools
GPfixup.exe	Command line
Group Policy Diagnostic Best Practices Analyzer	Download Microsoft.com
Group Policy Management Console	Administrative tools
Lpd.exe	Start menu, Search
Netdom.exe	Command line

Question 22

Tool	Location
Nslookup	Command line
Ntdsutil	Command line
Server Manager	Administrative tools
System Monitor	Server Manager
Ultrasound	Download from Microsoft.com
W32tm.exe	Command line
Windows Server Backup	Administrative tools

Question 33

✓	System Volume
	User Profiles
✓	Boot volume
✓	SYSVOL
	Data
✓	AD DS Database
✓	AD DS Logs
	Application Data

7A

Question 94

Report Description	Report
Checks for failures that would prevent or delay intersite replication	Intersite
Identifies errors in the Knowledge Consistency Checker	KCCEvents
Checks for timely replication between DCs	Replications
Reports on operation errors in the file replication system	FrsEvent

8

CONFIGURING ACTIVE DIRECTORY CERTIFICATE SERVICES

Note that the interactive questions of the "list and reorder" type do not have a simple A/B/C answer and are therefore grouped at the end of the following grid.

Question	Answer	Explanation
1	C	The Public Key Infrastructure is the core element for the distribution and management of public key certificates.
2	C	Microsoft Server 2008 PKI is Active Directory Certificate Services or AD CS.
3	D	The AD DS generates and maintains an infrastructure that supports the distribution of certificates to individuals to use as proof of identity.
4	B	Active Directory Domain Services along with AD CS are primarily targeted at providing authentication and authorization within a corporate environment.
5	C	A third-party commercial certificate authority (CA) is used when the PKI infrastructure is extended beyond the boundaries of the corporate environment.
6	A	When you visit a website that is using Secure Hypertext Transfer Protocol, that site contains an SSL certificate that proves to you that you are actually on the correct website.
7	C	Certificates work with your Internet browser because the trusted commercial CAs are included with the browser by the developer and are updated regularly.
8	C	Certificates work with your Internet browser because the trusted commercial CAs are included with the browser by the software developer and are updated regularly from Microsoft update services.
9	D	The trusted CAs are automatically updated through the regular operating system updates.
10	C	In Windows Vista and Server 2008 trusted CAs are updated with regular updates controlled by a Group Policy setting that is turned on by default.

8A

Question	Answer	Explanation
11	A	In Windows Vista and Server 2008 trusted CAs are updated with regular updates controlled by a Group Policy setting that is turned on by default. In earlier Windows operating systems, the Trusted Root Certificate was updated through the Control Panel.
12	C	When you issue your own certificates you need to add your organization to the trusted CAs on the computers of the users who will be using the certificates.
13	C	When certificates are issued to users who don't know you, they are being asked to trust someone they don't know. Linking your certificates to a trusted root certificate will create a chain of responsibility so that the certificate from your organization will be trusted because each user's browser already trusts the trusted root authority.
14	B	Trusted root CAs use stringent validation programs to verity the credentials of all organizations that they give master certificates to.
15	D	The trusted certification chain consists of the Root Certificate, the Intermediary Certificate, and the Customer Certificate.
16	A	Microsoft Outlook Web Access (OWA) allows users to remotely connect to an Exchange server and uses certificates to prove which users may connect to the Exchange server securely.
17	C	Microsoft Outlook Web Access (OWA) allows users to remotely connect to an Exchange server and uses certificates to prove which users may connect to the Exchange server securely. Certificates used with OWA can be purchased from valid vendors.
18	A	All members of the PKI are chained together in a hierarchy that ends at the top-most CA.
19	C	Implementing a PKI infrastructure when using e-commerce will require the use of a trusted root authority.
20	D	An internal only PKI proves who you are to yourself by authenticating and authorizing your users to network resources.
21	A	Using a trusted certificate authority for your PKI organization proves who you are to the outside world and your certificates will automatically be trusted.
22	A	Encrypted File System (EFS) uses certificates to lock and unlock encrypted files.
23	C	The use of Secure Sockets Tunneling Protocol (SSTP) and IPSec provide secure remote communication and rely on certificates to authenticate the communications.

Question	Answer	Explanation
24	A	The use of Secure Multipurpose Internet Mail Extension (S/MINE) relies on certificates to protect the messages from tampering and to prove the origin of the messages.
25	C	The use of Smart Cards relies on certificates to prove who all users are. This is especially useful to administrative-level access.
26	D	Using Internet Information Services (IIS) 7.0 and Windows Server 2008 you can secure all communications to your websites.
27	B	Use certificates assigned to servers in a Network Access Protection (NAP) infrastructure to secure your server services.
28	D	Active Directory Rights Management Services (AD RMS) will protect documents and information from tampering and misuse.
29	C	The PKI infrastructure is built on a trusted CA model.
30	A; B; D; F	Active Directory Certificate Services consists of certificate authorities, CA Web Enrollment, online responder, and Network Device Enrollment Service (NDES).
31	B	AD CS issues and manages root, subordinate, and child CAs.
32	A	The Root CA will have certificate durations that have a much longer duration than any of the subordinates.
33	A	Subordinate CAs issue certificates only when their own certificates are valid. The subordinate CA must obtain a renewal before it can issue additional certificates.
34	B	Subordinate CAs issue certificates only when their own certificates are valid. The subordinate CA must obtain a renewal before it can issue additional certificates. The certificates that the subordinate receives have a longer duration than the certificates the subordinates issue to users and computers.
35	C	CA Web Enrollment connects users to the CA through a web browser to request certificates.
36	C	The certificate revocation list (CRL) provides users with a list of revoked or invalided certificates.
37	B	PKI systems will poll the CA server for the CRLs each time a certificate is presented to see whether it has been revoked.
38	C	The online responder uses the Online Certificate Status Protocol to validate specific certificate requests.
39	D	An online responder can submit a validation request for a specific certificate so the CRL list is not needed.
40	D	Using the online responder is a faster and more efficient system for verifying the status of certificates than using CRLs.

8A

Question	Answer	Explanation
41	B	Online responder is a new feature in Windows Server 2008 included with AD CS.
42	D	Low-level devices can use Network Device Enrollment Service (NDES) to participate in the PKI with Simple Certificate Enrollment Protocol developed by Cisco Systems.
43	A	Low-level devices can use Network Device Enrollment Service (NDES) to participate in the PKI with Simple Certificate Enrollment Protocol developed by Cisco Systems.
44	C, D	AD CS can support two CA types—Standalone CA and Enterprise CA.
45	C	Standalone CAs run on standalone or member servers and are taken offline for security purposes after generating certificates for subordinate servers.
46	B	Standalone CAs run on standalone or member servers and are taken offline for security purposes after generating certificates for subordinate servers.
47	A	Standalone CAs run on standalone or member servers and are often used as the internal root CA.
48	D	Standalone CAs can run on Windows Server 2008 Standard, Enterprise, and Datacenter editions.
49	A	In a standalone CA, certificates are issued manually and certificates are based on standard templates that cannot be modified.
50	C	Enterprise CAs are often used as issuing CAs. They issue certificates to end users and act as subordinates to other CAs.
51	B	Issuing CAs are usually online at all times and are highly available.
52	D	Enterprise CAs can be run on Windows Server Enterprise and Datacenter.
53	B	Certificates issued by Enterprise CAs use advanced templates that can be edited.
54	C	Enterprise CAs are used to issue certificates to end users.
55	A	Standalone CAs are best used for providing specific services such as root servers for an internal PKI.
56	C	Standalone CAs are best used for providing specific services such as root servers for an internal PKI.
57	B	Enterprise CAs should be considered mostly as issuing CAs in internal AD DS networks.
58	C	Enterprise CAs automate certificate allocation and should be considered mostly for issuing CAs in internal AD DS networks.

Question	Answer	Explanation
59	D	An Enterprise CA can be deployed to a DC or a member server.
60	C	A standalone CA can be deployed to a DC, a member server, or a stand-alone server.
61	B	The Certificate MMC can be used with an Enterprise CA to manage certificate requests.
62	D	If a server is offline it is as secure as it can be.
63	C	Create a single-tiered hierarchy with a single root CA only in situations where the root CA cannot be compromised.
64	A	Consider creating a two-tiered AD CS hierarchy when you need to protect your root CA by taking it offline and your organization is too small to support a three-tiered approach.
65	D	With a three-tiered AD CS hierarchy, the CA will be the root CA, intermediate CAs, and issuing CAs.
66	C	In the three-tiered AD CS hierarchy model, you should take both the root and intermediate CAs offline to protect them.
67	See below	N/A
68	D	When creating a three-tiered CA hierarchy for the intermediate CA, use a standalone CA offline.
69	C	When creating a three-tiered CA hierarchy for the issuing CA, you use an Enterprise CA online.
70	C	It is necessary to store the VM files for security purposes because it is easier to remove a virtual server than a physical one.
71	A	Once AD CS is installed you cannot change a CA from standalone to enterprise.
72	A	You cannot change a server name after the AD CS service is installed.
73	B	It is necessary to secure the VM files and the server for security purposes.
74	C	As a general practice you should not install AD CS on a DC. The AD DS server role is independent of other roles.
75	A	Using separate disks for the certificate store is ideal.
76	D	Use a redundant array of inexpensive disks (RAID) with physical servers that are balanced between reliability and improved performance.
77	B	Long keys require more CPU usage and lower disk usage.
78	C	Configuring the certificate revocation list (CRL) is not part of finalizing the configuration of an issuing CA; it is part of the revocation configuration for a CA.

8A

Question	Answer	Explanation
79	A	Configuring enrollment and issuance options are not part of creating the revocation configuration for a CA.
80	C	Configuring the certificate revocation list (CRL) is not part of configuring and personalizing certificate templates.
81	A	If you plan to use EFS with your certificate templates, you need to create an EFS Recovery Agent template.
82	C	The first step in creating an EFS template is to select the basic EFS template and copy it.
83	B	To create an NPS template, use the RAS and IAS server templates as the source for the new NPS template.
84	C	Use the Smart Card logon and Smart Card user templates as the source for the new Smart Card template.
85	A	To create a new Smart Card template, you use the Smart Card logon and Smart Card user templates as the source.
86	B	Do not use auto-enrollment for these certificates because you use Smart Cards to enroll stations to distribute the Smart Cards to users.
87	D	To create web server templates, you create duplicates of the Web Server and DC Authentication templates. Do not use the Domain Controller template.
88	A	To issue the certificate templates, open Service Manager/Active Directory Certificate Services/Templates/Issuing CA Name/Certificate Templates.
89	C	To select multiple templates from the Enable Certificates Templates dialog box, use Ctrl+Click.
90	B	Use the Group Policy Management console to create or use an existing group policy to configure enrollment.
91	C	The default Domain Policy is the best choice to use for manual enrollment because it must be assigned to all members of the domain.
92	A	The default Domain Policy is the best choice to use for auto-enrollment because it must be assigned to all members of the domain. If you do not want to change the default Domain Policy, you can create a new policy and assign it to the entire domain using the GPMC.
93	A	The auto-enrollments policy is located in Computer Configuration\Policies\Windows Settings\Security Settings\Public Key Policies.
94	D	Use the Update Certificates That Use Certificate Templates check box if you have issued some certificates manually.

Question	Answer	Explanation
95	B	The template used for the online responder configuration is located in Service Manager Roles\AD Certificate Services\Certificate Templates\OCSP Response Signing.
96	D	To finalize the configuration of an online responder, you must configure and install an OSCP Response Signing certificate and configure the Authority Information Access Extension.
97	A	To find the Authority Information Access extensions, go to the Server Manager\Active Directory Certificate Services\Issuing CA Name and then select the Action menu and choose Properties.
98	C	To complete the online responder configuration, you reboot the server to assign the template to the server.
99	C	To verify that the OCSP certificate has been assigned, you must create a new Certificates snap-in console.
100	A	To verify that the OCSP certificate has been assigned, you must create a new Certificates snap-in console where the Certificates\Personal\Certificates node will contain the OCSP certificate.
101	C	To add the Revocation Configuration, you open Server Manager\Roles\AD Certificates Services\Online Responder\Revocation Configuration.
102	B	When you add a Revocation Configuration, the Name the Revocation Configuration page opens, where you assign a valid name to the configuration.
103	D	The three choices are Automatic, Manual, and use the CA certificate.
104	B	To add a revocation provider manually, you can enter the HTTP address `http://localhost/ca/crl`.

Question 67

Root Server Type	Tier Model
Enterprise CA	One tier
Standalone CA	Two tier
Standalone CA	Three tier

8A

Part IV

SUPPLEMENTARY INFORMATION

A

EXAM OBJECTIVES FOR MCITP: SERVER ADMINISTRATOR

The MCITP: Server Administrator requires that you pass three exams. You will need to pass two Microsoft Certified Technology Specialist (MCTS) exams, what Microsoft refers to as prerequisite exams, and you will also need to pass one Professional Series exam.

The three exams are as follows:

- Exam 70-640, which earns you the MCTS: Windows Server 2008, Active Directory Configuration certification
- Exam 70-642, which earns you the MCTS: Windows Server 2008, Network Infrastructure Configuration certification
- Exam 70-646, which earns you the PRO: Windows Server 2008, Server Administrator certification

SKILLS MEASURED FOR EXAM 70-640: WINDOWS SERVER 2008, ACTIVE DIRECTORY CONFIGURATION

Configuring Domain Name System (DNS) for Active Directory (16 Percent)

Configure zones. May include but is not limited to Dynamic DNS (DDNS), Non-dynamic DNS (NDDNS), and Secure Dynamic DNS (SDDNS), Time to Live (TTL), GlobalNames, primary zones, secondary zones, Active Directory Integrated zones, Stub zones, SOA, zone scavenging, forward lookup, and reverse lookup.

Configure DNS server settings. May include but is not limited to forwarding, root hints, configuring zone delegation, round robin servers, disabling recursion, debug logging, and server scavenging.

Configure zone transfers and replication. May include but is not limited to configuring replication scope (forestDNSzone and domainDNSzone), incremental zone transfers, DNS Notify, secure zone transfers, configuring name servers, and application directory partitions.

A

Configuring the Active Directory Infrastructure (25 Percent)

Configure a forest or a domain. May include but is not limited to removing a domain, performing an unattended installation, using the Active Directory Migration tool (ADMT) v3 (pruning and grafting), raising forest and domain functional levels, interoperability with previous versions of Active Directory, using the alternate user principal name (UPN) suffix, and using forestprep and domainprep.

Configure trusts. May include but is not limited to using forest trusts, selective authentication versus forest-wide authentication, using transitive trusts, external trusts, and shortcut trusts, and SID filtering.

Configure sites. May include but is not limited to creating Active Directory subnets, configuring site links, configuring site link costing, and configuring site infrastructure.

Configure Active Directory replication. May include but is not limited to using a distributed file system, one-way replication, using a bridgehead server, replication scheduling, configuring replication protocols, and forcing inter-site replication.

Configure the Global Catalog. May include but is not limited to using Universal Group Membership Caching (UGMC), using partial attribute set, and promoting files to Global Catalog.

Configure operations masters. May include but is not limited to seizing and transferring schemas, using backup operations master, using operations master placement, using Schema Master, extending the schema, and using time services.

Configuring Additional Active Directory Server Roles (9 Percent)

Configure Active Directory Lightweight Directory Service (AD LDS). May include but is not limited to migrating to AD LDS, configuring data within AD LDS, configuring an authentication server, using Server Core, and using Windows Server 2008 Hyper-V.

Configure Active Directory Rights Management Service (AD RMS). May include but is not limited to certificate request and installation, self-enrollments, delegation, Active Directory Metadirectory Services (AD MDS), and using Windows Server virtualization.

Configure the read-only domain controller (RODC). May include but is not limited to: unidirectional replication, Administrator role separation, read-only DNS, BitLocker, credential caching, password replication, syskey, and using Windows Server virtualization.

Configure Active Directory Federation Services (AD FS). May include but is not limited to installing AD FS server role, using exchange certificate with AD FS agents, configuring trust policies, configuring user and group claim mapping, and using Windows Server virtualization.

Creating and Maintaining Active Directory Objects (24 Percent)

Automate creation of Active Directory accounts. May include but is not limited to bulk importing, configuring the UPN, creating computer, user, and group accounts (scripts, import, migration), creating template accounts, contacts, and distribution lists.

Maintain Active Directory accounts. May include but is not limited to configuring group membership, account resets, delegation, AGDLP/AGGUDLP, denying domain local group, local versus domain accounts, using Protected Admin, disabling accounts versus deleting accounts, deprovisioning, creating organizational units (OUs), and delegation of control.

Create and apply Group Policy objects (GPOs). May include but is not limited to enforcing GPOs, OU hierarchy, block inheritance, and enabling user objects, Group Policy processing priority, WMI, Group Policy filtering, and Group Policy loopback.

Configure GPO templates. May include but is not limited to user rights, ADMX Central Store, administrative templates, security templates, restricted groups, security options, starter GPOs, and shell access policies.

Configure software deployment GPOs. May include but is not limited to publishing to users, assigning software to users, assigning to computers, and software removal.

Configure account policies. May include but is not limited to domain password policy, account lockout policy, and fine-grain password policies.

Configure audit policy by using GPOs. May include but is not limited to auditing logon events, auditing account logon events, auditing policy changes, auditing access privilege use, auditing directory service access, and auditing object access.

Maintaining the Active Directory Environment (13 Percent)

Configure backup and recovery. May include but is not limited to using Windows Server backup, backing up files and system state data to media, backing up and restoring data by using removable media, performing an authoritative or non-authoritative Active Directory restore, using linked value replication, using Directory Services Recovery Mode (DSRM) (reset admin password), and backing up and restoring GPOs.

Perform offline maintenance. May include but is not limited to offline defragmentation and compaction, Restartable Active Directory, and Active Directory database storage allocation.

Monitor Active Directory. May include but is not limited to Network Monitor, Task Manager, Event Viewer, ReplMon, RepAdmin, Windows System Resource Manager, Reliability and Performance Monitor, Server Performance Advisor, and RSoP.

Configuring Active Directory Certificate Services (13 Percent)

Install Active Directory Certificate Services. May include but is not limited to stand-alone versus enterprise, CA hierarchies (root versus subordinate), certificate requests, and certificate practice statement.

Configure CA server settings. May include but is not limited to key archival, certificate database backup and restore, and assigning administration roles.

Manage certificate templates. May include but is not limited to using certificate template types, securing template permissions, managing different certificate template versions, and using the key recovery agent.

Manage enrollments. May include but is not limited to using the network device enrollment service (NDES), understanding auto-enrollment, Web enrollment, and Smart Card enrollment, and creating enrollment agents.

Manage certificate revocations. May include but is not limited to configuring online responders, using a Certificate Revocation List (CRL), using a CRL Distribution Point (CDP), and using Authority Information Access (AIA).

A

Skills Measured for Exam 70-642: Windows Server 2008, Active Directory Configuration

Configuring IP Addressing and Services (24 Percent)

Configure IPv4 and IPv6 addressing. May include but is not limited to configuring IP options, subnetting, supernetting, and using alternative configurations.

Configure Dynamic Host Configuration Protocol (DHCP). May include but is not limited to using DHCP options, creating new options, using PXE boot, knowing the default user profiles, using DHCP relay agents, using exclusions, authorizing servers in Active Directory, using scopes, using Server Core, and using Windows Server Hyper-V.

Configure routing. May include but is not limited to static routing, persistent routing, using the Routing Internet Protocol (RIP), and using Open Shortest Path First (OSPF).

Configure IPsec. May include but is not limited to creating IPsec policy, using the IPsec Authentication Header (AH), and using the IPsec Encapsulating Security Payload (ESP).

Configuring Name Resolution (27 Percent)

Configure a Domain Name System (DNS) server. May include but is not limited to conditional forwarding, external forwarders, root hints, using cache-only servers, using Server Core, WINS and DNS integration, and Windows Server virtualization.

Configure DNS zones. May include but is not limited to DNS refresh and no-refresh, DNS list-serv address (NSLOOKUP), primary/secondary zones, Active Directory integration, Dynamic Domain Name System (DDNS), using GlobalNames, and using SOA refresh.

Configure DNS records. May include but is not limited to record types, hosts, pointers, MX, SRV, NS, using dynamic updates, and using Time to Live (TTL).

Configure DNS replication. May include but is not limited to using DNS secondary zones, using DNS stub zones, using the DNS scavenging interval, and using replication scope.

Configure name resolution for client computers. May include but is not limited to understanding DNS and WINS integration, configuring the HOSTS and LMHOSTS files, using the node type, using Link-Local Multicast Name Resolution (LLMNR), broadcasting, configuring resolver caches, using a DNS server list, using Suffix Search order, and managing client settings by using group policy.

Configuring Network Access (22 Percent)

Configure remote access. May include but is not limited to understanding dial-up settings, Remote Access Policy, Network Address Translation (NAT), Internet Connection Sharing (ICS), VPN, Routing and Remote Access Services (RRAS), inbound/outbound filters, configuring Remote Authentication Dial-In User Service (RADIUS) server, configuring RADIUS proxy, using remote access protocols, and using Connection Manager.

Configure Network Access Protection (NAP). May include but is not limited to network layer protection, DHCP enforcement, VPN enforcement, configuring NAP health policies, IPsec enforcement, 802.1x enforcement, and flexible host isolation.

Configure network authentication. May include but is not limited to LAN authentication by using NTLMv2 and Kerberos, WLAN authentication by using 802.1x, RAS authentication by using MS-CHAP, MS-CHAP v2, and using EAP.

Configure wireless access. May include but is not limited to setting Service Identifier (SSID), Wired Equivalent Privacy (WEP), Wi-Fi Protected Access (WPA), Wi-Fi Protected Access 2 (WPA2), understanding ad hoc versus infrastructure mode, and understanding group policy for wireless access.

Configure firewall settings. May include but is not limited to incoming and outgoing traffic filtering, Active Directory account integration, identifying ports and protocols, Microsoft Windows firewalls versus Windows firewalls with Advanced Security, configuring firewall by using group policy, and using the isolation policy.

Configuring File and Print Services (13 Percent)

Configure a file server. May include but is not limited to file share publishing, configuring offline files, sharing permissions, configuring NTFS permissions, and using the encrypting file system (EFS).

Configure Distributed File System (DFS). May include but is not limited to configuring DFS namespace, DFS configuration and application, creating and configuring targets, and DFS replication.

Configure shadow copy services. May include but is not limited to recovering previous versions, setting schedule, and setting storage locations.

Configure backup and restore. May include but is not limited to configuring backup types, configuring backup schedules, managing backups remotely, and restoring data.

Manage disk quotas. May include but is not limited to managing quota by volume or by user, using quota entries, and using quota templates.

Configure and monitor print services. May include but is not limited to configuring printer share, publishing printers to Active Directory, using printer permissions, deploying printer connections, installing printer drivers, exporting and importing print queues and printer settings, adding counters to Reliability and Performance Monitor to monitor print servers, using print pooling, and setting print priorities.

Monitoring and Managing a Network Infrastructure (14 Percent)

Configure Windows Server Update Services (WSUS) server settings. May include but is not limited to configuring update type selection, configuring client settings, using Group Policy object (GPO), configuring client targeting, configuring software updates, configuring test and approval settings, and configuring disconnected networks.

Capture performance data. May include but is not limited to using Data Collector Sets, Performance Monitor, using Reliability Monitor, and monitoring the System Stability index.

A

Monitor event logs. May include but is not limited to using custom views, using application and services logs, setting up subscriptions, and using a DNS log.

Gather network data. May include but is not limited to using Simple Network Management Protocol (SNMP), using the Baseline Security Analyzer, and using Network Monitor.

Skills Measured for Exam 70-646: Windows Server 2008, Server Administrator

Planning for Server Deployment (19 Percent)

Plan server installations and upgrades. May include but is not limited to selecting Windows Server 2008 edition, planning rollbacks, and knowing the BitLocker implementation requirements.

Plan for automated server deployment. May include but is not limited to planning for standard server images, and automating and scheduling server deployments.

Plan infrastructure services server roles. May include but is not limited to assigning addresses, using name resolution, understanding network access control, using directory services, using application services, and using certificate services.

Plan application servers and services. May include but is not limited to virtualization server planning, availability, resilience, and accessibility.

Plan file and print server roles. May include but is not limited to access permissions, storage quotas, replication, indexing, understanding file storage policy and availability, and printer publishing.

Planning for Server Management (23 Percent)

Plan server management strategies. May include but is not limited to remote administration, remote desktop, server management technologies, Server Manager and ServerManagerCMD, and delegation policies and procedures.

Plan for delegated administration. May include but is not limited to delegating authority, delegating Active Directory objects, and application management.

Plan and implement group policy strategy. May include but is not limited to GPO management, GPO backup and recovery, group policy troubleshooting, and group policy planning.

Monitoring and Maintaining Servers (20 Percent)

Implement patch management strategy. May include but is not limited to operating system patch level maintenance, Windows Server Update Services (WSUS), and application patch level maintenance.

Monitor servers for performance evaluation and optimization. May include but is not limited to server and service monitoring, optimization, event management, and trending and baseline analysis.

Monitor and maintain security and policies. May include but is not limited to remote access, monitoring and maintaining NPAS, monitoring network access, monitoring server security, understanding firewall rules and policies, understanding authentication and authorization, securing data, and auditing your servers.

Planning Application and Data Provisioning (19 Percent)

Provision applications. May include but is not limited to presentation virtualization, terminal server infrastructure, resource allocation, application virtualization alternatives, application deployment, and using System Center Configuration Manager.

Provision data. May include but is not limited to setting up shared resources and setting up offline data access.

Planning for Business Continuity and High Availability (19 Percent)

Plan storage. May include but is not limited to understanding storage solutions and storage management.

Plan high availability. May include but is not limited to service redundancy and availability.

Plan for backup and recovery. May include but is not limited to planning data recovery strategies, planning server recovery strategies, planning directory service recovery strategies, and setting up object level recovery.

A

B

EXAM OBJECTIVES FOR MCITP: ENTERPRISE ADMINISTRATOR

The MCITP: Server Administrator requires that you pass three exams. You will need to pass two Microsoft Certified Technology Specialist (MCTS) exams, what Microsoft refers to as prerequisite exams, and you will also need one Professional Series exam.

The MCITP: Enterprise Administrator requires that you pass five exams (the three required for the MCITP: Server Administrator, plus two others):

- MCTS exam 70-640, which earns you Windows Server 2008 Active Directory, Configuration certification
- MCTS exam 70-642, which earns you Windows Server 2008 Network Infrastructure, Configuration certification
- MCTS exam 70-643, which earns you Windows Server 2008 Applications Infrastructure, Configuring certification
- Either exam 70-620 MCTS: Windows Vista, Configuring or exam 70-624 MCTS: Deploying and Maintaining Windows Vista Client and 2007 Microsoft Office System Desktops
- PRO exam 70-647 Windows Server 2008, Enterprise Administrator

SKILLS MEASURED FOR EXAM 70-640: WINDOWS SERVER 2008 ACTIVE DIRECTORY, CONFIGURATION

Configuring Domain Name System (DNS) for Active Directory (16 Percent)

Configure zones. May include but is not limited to Dynamic DNS (DDNS), Non-dynamic DNS (NDDNS), Secure Dynamic DNS (SDDNS), Time to Live (TTL), GlobalNames, primary zones, secondary zones, Active Directory Integrated zones, Stub zones, SOA, zone scavenging, forward lookup, and reverse lookup.

Configure DNS server settings. May include but is not limited to forwarding, root hints, configuring zone delegation, round robin servers, disabling recursion, debug logging, and server scavenging.

B

Configure zone transfers and replication. May include but is not limited to configuring replication scope (forestDNSzone and domainDNSzone), incremental zone transfers, using DNS Notify, secure zone transfers, configuring name servers, and application directory partitions.

Configuring the Active Directory Infrastructure (25 Percent)

Configure a forest or a domain. May include but is not limited to removing a domain, performing an unattended installation, using the Active Directory Migration tool (ADMT) v3 (pruning and grafting), raising forest and domain functional levels, understanding interoperability issues with previous versions of Active Directory, understanding the alternate user principal name (UPN) suffix, using forestprep, and using domainprep.

Configure trusts. May include but is not limited to forest trusts, selective authentication versus forest-wide authentication, transitive trusts, external trusts, shortcut trusts, and SID filtering.

Configure sites. May include but is not limited to creating Active Directory subnets, configuring site links, configuring site link costing, and configuring a site's infrastructure.

Configure Active Directory replication. May include but is not limited to using a Distributed File System, one-way replication, using bridgehead servers, replication scheduling, configuring replication protocols, and forcing inter-site replication.

Configure the global catalog. May include but is not limited to Universal Group Membership Caching (UGMC), using a partial attribute set, promoting to global catalog.

Configure operations masters. May include but is not limited to seizing and transferring, backup operations master, operations master placement, using Schema Master, extending the schema, and using the time service.

Configuring Additional Active Directory Server Roles (9 Percent)

Configure Active Directory Lightweight Directory Service (AD LDS). May include but is not limited to migration to AD LDS, configuring data within AD LDS, configuring an authentication server, using Server Core, and using Windows Server 2008 Hyper-V.

Configure Active Directory Rights Management Service (AD RMS). May include but is not limited to certificate request and installation, self-enrollments, delegation, Active Directory Metadirectory Services (AD MDS), and Windows Server virtualization.

Configure the read-only domain controller (RODC). May include but is not limited to unidirectional replication, administrator role separation, using read-only DNSs, using BitLocker, credential caching, password replication, using syskey, and Windows Server virtualization.

Configure Active Directory Federation Services (AD FS). May include but is not limited to installing the AD FS server role, exchanging certificates with AD FS agents, configuring trust policies, configuring user and group claim mapping, and Windows Server virtualization.

Creating and Maintaining Active Directory Objects (24 Percent)

Automate creation of Active Directory accounts. May include but is not limited to bulk import, configuring the UPN, creating computer, user, and group accounts (scripts, import, migration), using template accounts, creating contacts, and using distribution lists.

Maintain Active Directory accounts. May include but is not limited to configuring group membership, account resets, delegation, AGDLP/AGGUDLP, deny domain local group, local versus domain, Protected Admin, disabling accounts versus deleting accounts, deprovisioning, contacts, creating organizational units (OUs), and delegation of control.

Create and apply Group Policy objects (GPOs). May include but is not limited to using Enforce, OU hierarchy, block inheritance, enabling user objects, Group Policy processing priority, using WMI, Group Policy filtering, and Group Policy loopback.

Configure GPO templates. May include but is not limited to user rights, using the ADMX Central Store, using administrative templates, using security templates, using restricted groups, understanding the security options, using starter GPOs, and understanding the shell access policies.

Configure software deployment GPOs. May include but is not limited to publishing to users, assigning software to users, assigning GPOs to computers, and software removal.

Configure account policies. May include but is not limited to domain password policy, account lockout policy, and fine-grain password policies.

Configure audit policy by using GPOs. May include but is not limited to auditing logon events, auditing account logon events, auditing policy change, auditing access privilege use, auditing directory service access, and auditing object access.

Maintaining the Active Directory Environment (13 Percent)

Configure backup and recovery. May include but is not limited to using the Windows Server Backup feature, creating backup files and system state data to media, backing up and restoring by using removable media, performing an authoritative or non-authoritative Active Directory restore, linked value replication, Directory Services Recovery Mode (DSRM) (reset admin password), backing up and restoring GPOs.

Perform offline maintenance. May include but is not limited to offline defragmentation and compaction, using Restartable Active Directory, and Active Directory database storage allocation.

Monitor Active Directory. May include but is not limited to Network Monitor, Task Manager, Event Viewer, ReplMon, RepAdmin, Windows System Resource Manager, Reliability and Performance Monitor, Server Performance Advisor, and RSoP.

Configuring Active Directory Certificate Services (13 Percent)

Install Active Directory Certificate Services. May include but is not limited to standalone versus enterprise, CA hierarchies (root versus subordinate), certificate requests, and certificate practice statement.

Configure CA server settings. May include but is not limited to key archival, certificate database backup and restore, and assigning administration roles.

Manage certificate templates. May include but is not limited to certificate template types, securing template permissions, managing different certificate template versions, and using key recovery agent.

B

Manage enrollments. May include but is not limited to network device enrollment service (NDES), auto-enrollment, web enrollment, Smart Card enrollment, and creating enrollment agents.

Manage certificate revocations. May include but is not limited to configuring Online Responders, using a Certificate Revocation List (CRL), using a CRL Distribution Point (CDP), and using Authority Information Access (AIA).

Skills Measured for Exam 70-642: Windows Server 2008 Active Directory, Configuration

Configuring IP Addressing and Services (24 Percent)

Configure IPv4 and IPv6 addressing. May include but is not limited to configuring IP options, subnetting, supernetting, and using alternative configurations.

Configure Dynamic Host Configuration Protocol (DHCP). May include but is not limited to DHCP options, creating new options, PXE boot, using default user profiles, DHCP relay agents, exclusions, authorizing server in Active Directory, using scopes, using server core, and using Windows Server Hyper-V.

Configure routing. May include but is not limited to static routing, persistent routing, using the Routing Internet Protocol (RIP), and using Open Shortest Path First (OSPF).

Configure IPsec. May include but is not limited to creating IPsec policy, using IPsec Authentication Header (AH), and using IPsec Encapsulating Security Payload (ESP).

Configuring Name Resolution (27 Percent)

Configure a Domain Name System (DNS) server. May include but is not limited to conditional forwarding, using external forwarders, using root hints, using cache-only servers, using Server Core, WINS and DNS integration, and Windows Server virtualization.

Configure DNS zones. May include but is not limited to using DNS Refresh no-refresh, configuring intervals, using the DNS listserv address (NSLOOKUP), using primary/secondary zones, Active Directory integration, using Dynamic Domain Name System (DDNS), using GlobalNames, and using SOA refresh.

Configure DNS records. May include but is not limited to using record types, hosts, pointers, MX, SRV, NS, using dynamic updates, and using Time to Live (TTL).

Configure DNS replication. May include but is not limited to using DNS secondary zones, using DNS stub zones, using the DNS scavenging interval, and using the replication scope.

Configure name resolution for client computers. May include but is not limited to DNS and WINS integration, configuring the HOSTS file, using LMHOSTS, configuring node type, using Link-Local Multicast Name Resolution (LLMNR), broadcasting, using the resolver cache, using the DNS Server list, understanding Suffix Search order, and managing client settings by using group policy.

Configuring Network Access (22 Percent)

Configure remote access. May include but is not limited to configuring dial-up, using the Remote Access Policy, using Network Address Translation (NAT), using Internet Connection Sharing (ICS), using VPN, using Routing and Remote Access Services (RRAS), using inbound/outbound filters, configuring Remote Authentication Dial-In User Service (RADIUS) server, configuring RADIUS proxy, using remote access protocols, and using Connection Manager.

Configure Network Access Protection (NAP). May include but is not limited to network layer protection, DHCP enforcement, VPN enforcement, configuring NAP health policies, IPsec enforcement, 802.1x enforcement, and flexible host isolation.

Configure network authentication. May include but is not limited to LAN authentication by using NTLMv2 and Kerberos, WLAN authentication by using 802.1x, RAS authentication by using MS-CHAP, using MS-CHAP v2, and using EAP.

Configure wireless access. May include but is not limited to using the Set Service Identifier (SSID), using Wired Equivalent Privacy (WEP), using Wi-Fi Protected Access (WPA), using Wi-Fi Protected Access 2 (WPA2), understanding ad hoc versus infrastructure mode, and using Group Policy for wireless connections.

Configure firewall settings. May include but is not limited to incoming and outgoing traffic filtering, Active Directory account integration, identifying ports and protocols, Microsoft Windows firewall versus Windows firewall with advanced security, configuring firewalls by using Group Policy, and configuring the isolation policy.

Configuring File and Print Services (13 Percent)

Configure a file server. May include but is not limited to file share publishing, using offline files, setting share permissions, setting NTFS permissions, and using the encrypting file system (EFS).

Configure Distributed File System (DFS). May include but is not limited to using the DFS namespace, using DFS configuration and application, creating and configuring targets, and DFS replication.

Configure shadow copy services. May include but is not limited to recovering previous versions, setting the schedule, and setting storage locations.

Configure backup and restore. May include but is not limited to configuring backup types and backup schedules, managing backups remotely, and restoring data.

Manage disk quotas. May include but is not limited to managing quota by volume or quota by user, using quota entries, and using quota templates.

Configure and monitor print services. May include but is not limited to configuring printer share, publishing printers to Active Directory, setting the printer permissions, deploying printer connections, installing printer drivers, exporting and importing print queues and printer settings, adding counters to Reliability and Performance Monitor to monitor print servers, print pooling, and setting print priorities.

B

Monitoring and Managing a Network Infrastructure (14 Percent)

Configure Windows Server Update Services (WSUS) server settings. May include but is not limited to updating type selection, using client settings, using the Group Policy object (GPO), client targeting, software updates, testing and approval, and configuring disconnected networks.

Capture performance data. May include but is not limited to Data Collector Sets, Performance Monitor, Reliability Monitor, and monitoring the System Stability Index.

Monitor event logs. May include but is not limited to custom views, application and services logs, subscriptions, and using the DNS log.

Gather network data. May include but is not limited to using Simple Network Management Protocol (SNMP), using the Baseline Security Analyzer, and using Network Monitor.

Skills Measured for Exam 70-646: Windows Server 2008, Server Administrator

Planning for Server Deployment (19 Percent)

Plan server installations and upgrades. May include but is not limited to Windows Server 2008 edition selection, rollback planning, and BitLocker implementation requirements.

Plan for automated server deployment. May include but is not limited to standard server images and automation and scheduling of server deployments.

Plan infrastructure services server roles. May include but is not limited to address assignment, name resolution, network access control, and using directory services, application services, and certificate services.

Plan application servers and services. May include but is not limited to virtualization server planning, and testing server availability, resilience, and accessibility.

Plan file and print server roles. May include but is not limited to accessing permissions, storage quotas, replication, indexing, file storage policy, print server availability, and printer publishing.

Planning for Server Management (23 Percent)

Plan server management strategies. May include but is not limited to remote administration, remote desktop, server management technologies, Server Manager and ServerManagerCMD, and delegation policies and procedures.

Plan for delegated administration. May include but is not limited to delegating authority, delegating Active Directory objects, and application management.

Plan and implement group policy strategy. May include but is not limited to GPO management, GPO backup and recovery, group policy troubleshooting, and group policy planning.

Monitoring and Maintaining Servers (20 Percent)

Implement patch management strategy. May include but is not limited to operating system patch level maintenance, Windows Server Update Services (WSUS), and application patch level maintenance.

Monitor servers for performance evaluation and optimization. May include but is not limited to server and service monitoring, optimization, event management, and trending and baseline analysis.

Monitor and maintain security and policies. May include but is not limited to remote access, monitoring and maintaining NPAS, network access, server security, firewall rules and policies, authentication and authorization, data security, and auditing.

Planning Application and Data Provisioning (19 Percent)

Provision applications. May include but is not limited to presentation virtualization, terminal server infrastructure, resource allocation, application virtualization alternatives, application deployment, and using System Center Configuration Manager.

Provision data. May include but is not limited to using shared resources and offline data access.

Planning for Business Continuity and High Availability (19 Percent)

Plan storage. May include but is not limited to storage solutions and storage management.

Plan high availability. May include but is not limited to service redundancy and service availability.

Plan for backup and recovery. May include but is not limited to data recovery strategy, server recovery strategy, directory service recovery strategy, and object level recovery.

Skills Measured for Exam 70-620: Windows Vista, Configuring

Installing and upgrading Windows Vista:

- Identify hardware requirements.
- Perform a clean installation.
- Upgrade to Windows Vista from previous versions of Windows.
- Upgrade from one edition of Windows Vista to another.
- Troubleshoot Windows Vista installation issues.
- Install and configure Windows Vista drivers.

Configuring and troubleshooting post-installation system settings:

- Troubleshoot post-installation configuration issues.
- Configure and troubleshoot Windows Aero.
- Configure and troubleshoot parental controls.
- Configure Microsoft Internet Explorer.

Configuring Windows security features:

- Configure and troubleshoot User Account Control.
- Configure Windows Defender.

B

- Configure Dynamic Security for Microsoft Internet Explorer 7.
- Configure security settings in Windows firewall.

Configuring network connectivity:

- Configure networking by using the Network and Sharing Center.
- Troubleshoot connectivity issues.
- Configure remote access.

Configuring applications included with Windows Vista:

- Configure and troubleshoot media applications.
- Configure Windows Mail.
- Configure Windows Meeting Space.
- Configure Windows Calendar.
- Configure Windows Fax and Scan.
- Configure Windows Sidebar.

Maintaining and optimizing systems that run Windows Vista:

- Troubleshoot performance issues.
- Troubleshoot reliability issues by using built-in diagnostic tools.
- Configure Windows Update.
- Configure data protection.

Configuring and troubleshooting mobile computing:

- Configure mobile display settings.
- Configure mobile devices.
- Configure Tablet PC software.
- Configure power options.

SKILLS MEASURED FOR EXAM 70-624 MCTS: DEPLOYING AND MAINTAINING WINDOWS VISTA CLIENT AND 2007 MICROSOFT OFFICE SYSTEM DESKTOPS

Deploying the 2007 Microsoft Office System:

- Configure Microsoft Office settings and components
- Install the 2007 Microsoft Office system
- Migrate from earlier versions of Microsoft Office

Configuring Windows Vista automated installation settings:

- Configure Windows Vista automated installation settings
- Manage Windows Vista catalogs
- Add device drivers to Windows Vista installations
- Manage Windows components
- Configure and manipulate Windows Imaging Format (WIM) images

Deploying Windows Vista:

- Deploy Windows Vista by using LTI
- Deploy Windows Vista by using ZTI
- Customize the Windows Preinstallation Environment (PE)
- Troubleshoot Windows Vista

Using Business Desktop Deployment (BDD) Workbench:

- Install BDD
- Configure a distribution point in BDD 2007 Workbench
- Create a reference computer image
- Manage XML files in BDD Workbench
- Automate installation of the 2007 Microsoft Office system
- Customize and maintain Windows PE by using BDD Workbench

Using Application Compatibility Toolkit:

- Install and configure Application Compatibility Toolkit (ACT) 5
- Deploy ACT 5 agents
- Report application compatibility
- Fix compatibility issues

Managing user-state migration:

- Upgrade user state from Windows XP to Windows Vista
- Automate user state migration
- Manage Vista deployments by using SMS 2003
- Determine OSD prerequisites
- Install the Microsoft Systems Management (SMS) 2003 Operating System Deployment (OSD) Feature Pack
- Configure SMS 2003 OSD
- Troubleshoot user-state migration
- Plan user-state migration

SKILLS MEASURED FOR EXAM 70-647: WINDOWS SERVER 2008, ENTERPRISE ADMINISTRATOR

Planning Network and Application Services (23 Percent)

Plan for name resolution and IP addressing. May include but is not limited to internal and external naming strategy, naming resolution support for legacy clients, naming resolution for directory services, IP addressing scheme, and TCP/IP version coexistence.

Design for network access. May include but is not limited to network access policies, remote access strategy, perimeter networks, and server and domain isolation.

B

Plan for application delivery. May include but is not limited to application virtualization, presentation virtualization, using locally installed software, and using web-based applications.

Plan for Terminal Services. May include but is not limited to planning for Terminal Services licensing and Terminal Services infrastructure.

Designing Core Identity and Access Management Components (25 Percent)

Design Active Directory forests and domains. May include but is not limited to forest structure, forest and domain functional levels, intra-organizational authorization and authentication, and schema modifications.

Design the Active Directory physical topology. May include but is not limited to placement of servers, site and replication topology, and printer location policies.

Design the Active Directory administrative model. May include but is not limited to delegation, group strategy, compliance auditing, group administration, and organizational structure.

Design the enterprise-level group policy strategy. May include but is not limited to group policy hierarchy and scope filtering, control device installation, and authentication and authorization.

Designing Support Identity and Access Management Components (29 Percent)

Plan for domain or forest migration, upgrade, and restructuring. May include but is not limited to cross-forest authentication, backward compatibility, object migration, migration planning, implementation planning, and environment preparation.

Design the branch office deployment. May include but is not limited to designing the authentication strategy and server security issues.

Design and implement public key infrastructure. May include but is not limited to certificate services, PKI operations and maintenance, and certificate lifecycle management.

Plan for interoperability. May include but is not limited to inter-organizational authorization and authentication, application authentication interoperability, and cross-platform interoperability.

Designing for Business Continuity and Data Availability (23 Percent)

Plan for business continuity. May include but is not limited to service availability and directory service recovery.

Design for software updates and compliance management. May include but is not limited to patch management and patch management compliance, Microsoft Update and Windows Update, security baselines, and system health models.

Design the operating system virtualization strategy. May include but is not limited to server consolidation, application compatibility, virtualization management, and designing the placement of servers.

Design for data management and data access. May include but is not limited to data security, data accessibility and redundancy, and data collaboration.

C

INSTALLATION INSTRUCTIONS FOR CERTBLASTER

The CertBlaster practice software is on the CD at the end of this book. It allows you to:

- Assess your preparedness for the exam
- Familiarize yourself with the exam environment and format
- Familiarize yourself with the MCTS question types and formats
- Generate your very own customized Personal Study Plan

Copy the CertBlaster setup file (called c_640_setup.exe) from the CD to your desktop. Then follow the steps here to install the program:

1. Double click the set-up icon shown here.

2. Enter the installation password, **c_640**, into the text box shown here.

C

You will not see your actual password because the application shows only asterisks, so what you will see is shown here.

3. Next you will be in the Installation wizard. From this point on, you just follow the prompts to install the software.

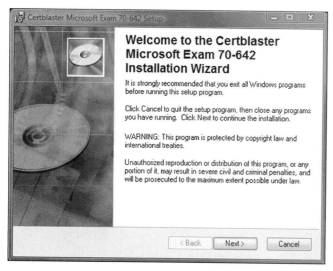

the fun way
to learn programming

Let's face it. C++, Java, and Perl can be a little intimidating. But now they don't have to be. The *for the absolute beginner*™ series gives you a fun, non-intimidating introduction to the world of programming. Each book in this series teaches a specific programming language using simple game programming as a teaching aid. All titles include source code on the companion CD-ROM or Web site.

C++ Programming for the Absolute Beginner
By Mark Lee
1-59863-875-0 | $29.99 | 464 pages

Microsoft WSH and VBScript Programming for the Absolute Beginner, Third Edition
By Jerry Ford, Jr.
1-59863-803-3 | $34.99 | 480 pages

C Programming for the Absolute Beginner, Second Edition
By Michael Vine
1-59863-480-1 | $29.99 | 336 pages

Microsoft Excel VBA Programming for the Absolute Beginner, Third Edition
By Duane Birnbaum and Michael Vine
1-59863-394-5 | $29.99 | 400 pages

Microsoft Access VBA Programming for the Absolute Beginner, Third Edition
By Michael Vine
1-59863-393-7 | $29.99 | 384 pages

Microsoft Windows Powershell Programming for the Absolute Beginner
By Jerry Lee Ford Jr.
1-59863-354-6 | $29.99 | 376 pages

Microsoft Visual Basic 2008 Express Programming for the Absolute Beginner
By Jerry Lee Ford, Jr.
1-59863-900-5 | $29.99 | 432 pages

Ajax Programming for the Absolute Beginner
By Jerry Ford, Jr.
1-59863-564-6 | $29.99 | 320 pages

Java Programming for the Absolute Beginner, Second Edition
By John Flynt
1-59863-275-2 | $29.99 | 480 pages

COURSE TECHNOLOGY
CENGAGE Learning
Professional • Technical • Reference

Call **1.800.648.7450** to order
Order online at **www.courseptr.com**

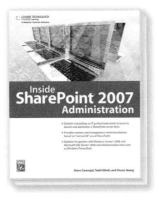
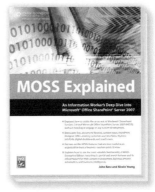

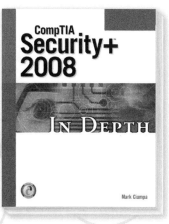

License Agreement/Notice of Limited Warranty

By opening the sealed disc container in this book, you agree to the following terms and conditions. If, upon reading the following license agreement and notice of limited warranty, you cannot agree to the terms and conditions set forth, return the unused book with unopened disc to the place where you purchased it for a refund.

License:
The enclosed software is copyrighted by the copyright holder(s) indicated on the software disc. You are licensed to copy the software onto a single computer for use by a single user and to a backup disc. You may not reproduce, make copies, or distribute copies or rent or lease the software in whole or in part, except with written permission of the copyright holder(s). You may transfer the enclosed disc only together with this license, and only if you destroy all other copies of the software and the transferee agrees to the terms of the license. You may not decompile, reverse assemble, or reverse engineer the software.

Notice of Limited Warranty:
The enclosed disc is warranted by Course Technology to be free of physical defects in materials and workmanship for a period of sixty (60) days from end user's purchase of the book/disc combination. During the sixty-day term of the limited warranty, Course Technology will provide a replacement disc upon the return of a defective disc.

Limited Liability:
THE SOLE REMEDY FOR BREACH OF THIS LIMITED WARRANTY SHALL CONSIST ENTIRELY OF REPLACEMENT OF THE DEFECTIVE DISC. IN NO EVENT SHALL COURSE TECHNOLOGY OR THE AUTHOR BE LIABLE FOR ANY OTHER DAMAGES, INCLUDING LOSS OR CORRUPTION OF DATA, CHANGES IN THE FUNCTIONAL CHARACTERISTICS OF THE HARDWARE OR OPERATING SYSTEM, DELETERIOUS INTERACTION WITH OTHER SOFTWARE, OR ANY OTHER SPECIAL, INCIDENTAL, OR CONSEQUENTIAL DAMAGES THAT MAY ARISE, EVEN IF COURSE TECHNOLOGY AND/OR THE AUTHOR HAS PREVIOUSLY BEEN NOTIFIED THAT THE POSSIBILITY OF SUCH DAMAGES EXISTS.

Disclaimer of Warranties:
COURSE TECHNOLOGY AND THE AUTHOR SPECIFICALLY DISCLAIM ANY AND ALL OTHER WARRANTIES, EITHER EXPRESS OR IMPLIED, INCLUDING WARRANTIES OF MERCHANTABILITY, SUITABILITY TO A PARTICULAR TASK OR PURPOSE, OR FREEDOM FROM ERRORS. SOME STATES DO NOT ALLOW FOR EXCLUSION OF IMPLIED WARRANTIES OR LIMITATION OF INCIDENTAL OR CONSEQUENTIAL DAMAGES, SO THESE LIMITATIONS MIGHT NOT APPLY TO YOU.

Other:
This Agreement is governed by the laws of the State of Massachusetts without regard to choice of law principles. The United Convention of Contracts for the International Sale of Goods is specifically disclaimed. This Agreement constitutes the entire agreement between you and Course Technology regarding use of the software.